The origins of ecological economics

In recent years, an increasing awareness of resource and environmental issues has created a demand for ecological economics, and a growing interest in the work of Nicholas Georgescu-Roegen. This book connects Georgescu-Roegen's earlier work on consumer choice theory and critique of the Leontief dynamic model with his later ambitious attempt to create a theoretical alternative to neoclassical economics, 'bioeconomics'.

The book includes detailed examinations of the following subjects:

- Reformulating the consumer choice theory for environmental valuation.
- Investigation on a Leontief dynamic model with two delays.
- Measure of information and its relationship with entropy in physics.
- Relations among energy analysis, Sraffa's analysis and Georgescu-Roegen's production model.
- The viability of solar technology.
- Economic and thermodynamic analysis of land since the Industrial Revolution.
- Development, environmental degradation and North–South trade issues.
- Robert Rosen's modelling relation and the biophysical approach to sustainability issues.

This work may serve as a source-book for research into solid theoretical bases and applications related to sustainability issues. It will prove essential reading for ecological economists, but will also be of interest to ecologists, economists and social theorists in general.

Kozo Mayumi graduated from the Graduate School of Engineering, at the Department of Applied Mathematics and Physics of Kyoto University. Between 1984 and 1988 he studied under Professor Georgescu-Roegen. Mayumi is now a full professor at the University of Tokushima. His research interests include energy analysis, ecological economics and complex hierarchy theory. In 1999 he edited *Bioeconomics and Sustainability: Essays in Honor of Nicholas Georgescu-Roegen*, and he is currently an editorial board member of *Ecological Economics* and *Population and Environment*.

Routledge Research in Environmental Economics

1 **The Origins of Ecological Economics**
The Bioeconomics of Georgescu-Roegen
Kozo Mayumi

The Origins of Ecological Economics

The bioeconomics of Georgescu-Roegen

Kozo Mayumi

Routledge
Taylor & Francis Group
LONDON AND NEW YORK

First published 2001
by Routledge
2 Park Square, Milton Park, Abingdon, Oxon OX14 4RN

Simultaneously published in the USA and Canada
by Routledge
52 Vanderbilt Avenue, New York, NY 10017

Routledge is an imprint of the Taylor & Francis Group, an informa business

First issued in paperback in 2012

Typeset in 10/12 pt Times by Newgen Imaging Systems (P) Ltd.,
Chennai, India

British Library Cataloguing in Publication Data
A catalogue record for this book is available
from the British Library

Library of Congress Cataloging-in-Publication Data

Mayumi, Kozo, 1954–
The origins of ecological economics : the bioeconomics of Georgescu-Roegen / Kozo Mayumi.
p. cm.
Includes bibliographical references and index.
1. Georgescu-Roegen, Nicholas. 2. Economists–United States. 3. Environmental economics. 4. Human ecology. I. Title.

HB119.G43 M39 2001
333.7–dc21

00-054740

ISBN13: 978-0-415-23523-5 (HBK)
ISBN13: 978-0-415-63811-1 (PBK)

Contents

List of Figures vii
List of Tables viii
Preface ix
Acknowledgements x

1 Introduction 1

2 Foundations of consumer choice theory for environmental valuation in view of Georgescu-Roegen's contribution 7

3 Conditions for balanced sustained growth of the open Leontief dynamic model and investigation on a Leontief dynamic model with two delays 21

4 Information, pseudo-measures and entropy: an elaboration on Georgescu-Roegen's critique 32

5 A critical appraisal of two entropy theoretical approaches to resources and environmental problems: Georgescu-Roegen and Tsuchida 45

6 Embodied energy analysis, Sraffa's analysis, Georgescu-Roegen's flow–fund model and viability of solar technology 65

7 Land: Achilles' Heel of ecology and economy 79

8 Environment and North–South trade: another view 97

9 Modelling relation, hierarchical systems and bioeconomic approach to sustainability issues 108

Appendix A: Integral curves around a saturation point 126
Appendix B: Conditions for balanced sustained growth of the open dynamic Leontief model 130
Appendix C: A Leontief dynamic model with two delays 139

Notes 142
Bibliography 145
Index 156

Figures

2.1 Integral curves around the saturation point 10
2.2 Probabilistic binary choice scheme 16
2.3 Hesitation regions and intransitivity 17
3.1 Domain of balanced sustained growth 24
3.2 Open dynamic Leontief model: (a) balanced sustained growth case and (b) imbalanced case 25
3.3 Numerical result for a dynamic Leontief model with two delays 29
3.4 Numerical result for a dynamic Leontief model with two delays for case (c) in Fig. 3.3 30
4.1 Tsuchida's apparatus 40
5.1 The nested-hierarchical structure of an open steady-state system of the second category 51
5.2 Diffusion of matter 55
5.3 The mixing entropy 62
5.4 The relationship between energy density and the amounts of material requirement 63
6.1 Comparison of solar energy for cases in Tables 6.2 and 6.3 76
6.2 Comparison of solar energy: prices for cases in Tables 6.3 and 6.4 77
6.3 Comparison of collectors: prices for cases in Tables 6.2 and 6.3 78
9.1 Modelling relation 111
9.2 Theoretical simile 112
9.3 Parallel allocation of exosomatic energy and human time 117
9.4 The double autocatalytic loop: (i) human time; (ii) exosomatic energy 123
A.1 Integral curves of Georgescu-Roegen's solution 127

Tables

5.1 The economic process according to the energetic dogma 60
6.1 The aggregated economic process 70
6.2 Flow–fund matrix of a viable solar technology 72
6.3 Flow–fund matrix of solar collectors produced by solar energy 73
6.4 Flow–fund matrix of the present mixed solar technology 73

Preface

This book by Kozo Mayumi deals most ably with crucial analytical and policy issues in ecological economics. A new perspective is presented in this book on the relations between the 'young' and 'mature' Georgescu-Roegen, i.e. the relations between his work on consumption theory and on the entropy law and the economic process. A profound analysis disposes of the notion of negentropy being equivalent to information. Also, Georgescu-Roegen's discussion of feasible and viable technologies is scrutinized and formalised in the context of an evaluation of solar technologies. In another chapter, an intriguing discussion of Clausius' notion of disgregation of matter leads to revaluation of Georgescu-Roegen's aphorism against energeticist dogmas: 'matter, matters too'. Some historical chapters deal with the land constraint in the era of fossil fuels, which is still not only relevant for agricultural production but increasingly also as a carbon sink. There is a chapter on some technical issues in Leontief's dynamic systems, and a new discussion is introduced on the relations between the Sraffian system and Georgescu-Roegen's flow–fund models (here I would emphasize the distributional aspects, i.e. whether the profit rate does not only depend on the 'class struggle', as in Sraffa, but also on the outcome of ecological distribution conflicts).

Kozo Mayumi was a student of Georgescu-Roegen in the 1980s. He has also been influenced by the Japanese entropy school, particularly by Tsuchida, and in this book he explains clearly the role of the water cycle in disposing of an enormous amount of solar energy input. Moving beyond Georgescu-Roegen, he also deals with reflexive systems or anticipatory systems, where the future affects the present, which is a way of introducing uncertainty and complexity.

To a large extent, the book is then a continuation, critique and expansion of Georgescu-Roegen's work. Is Kozo Mayumi an economist, a physicist, or a systems theorist? The reader might well wonder. What Georgescu-Roegen (1906–94) called 'bioeconomics' has come to be called 'ecological economics'. This is a growing transdisciplinary field and Kozo Mayumi is indeed one of its most competent representatives internationally.

Joan Martinez-Alier,
Universitat Autònoma de Barcelona

Acknowledgements

This monograph results from research that started in 1984 during my graduate study at Vanderbilt University in Nashville. As a thousand words will not suffice to describe my respect and thanks to the great scholar, I can express my acknowledgements to my teacher, Prof. Nicholas Georgescu-Roegen, only in a most abstract way: Georgescu-Roegen never stopped revising his economic theory. Georgescu-Roegen's theory is a critique from within the conceptual edifice of economics which he himself helped build. It was a privilege to be guided by Georgescu-Roegen, the finest scholar I have ever been privileged to meet.

Prof. Joan Martinez-Alier of Universitat Autònoma de Barcelona kindly agreed to write a foreword to this monograph. Prof. Martinez-Alier has invited me to Barcelona to take part in several stimulating workshops on integrated environmental assessment.

It has been my pleasure to work with Dr. Mario Giampietro of Istituto Nazionale di Ricerca per gli Alimenti e la Nutrizione and Prof. John Gowdy of Rensselaer Polytechnic Institute. Chapters 8 and 9 are a result in part from joint work with Dr. Giampietro. I must acknowledge Dr. Giampietro's seminal role in developing methodological tools using hierarchy theory in Chapter 9. Chapter 2 is a result in part from joint work with Prof. Gowdy. I would like to express my debt to these two great friends and my thanks to them for allowing reproduction of our joint work in this monograph.

I would like to express sincere thanks to Mr. Don Sturge of the University of Tokushima for his tremendous help in improving the language in this monograph.

I would like to express my sincere thanks to Prof. Hasegawa of Nanzan University, my former supervisor at the Department of Applied Mathematics and Physics of Kyoto University, for continuous moral support and encouragement.

I am deeply grateful to Mr. Isaka of Nihon Keizai Shimbun, my best friend. He introduced me to Georgescu-Roegen's bioeconomic paradigm.

Dr. Yegor Budnikov of the Cardiological Scientific Center of Russian Academy of Medical Sciences in Moscow and Dr. Lev Balykov, a former Ph.D. student at the University of Tokushima deserve my thanks for their translation of the Russian text written by Čebotarev and Meĭman (1949). In particular, Dr. Budnikov translated Chapters IV–VII of the Russian text into English. Without their help, Chapter 3 would never have been completed. Dr. Dongliang Huang of Kyoto University gave great help with the numerical analysis of the Leontief dynamic model. Dr. Miroru Sasaki of the University of Tokushima drew many computer aided figures for this monograph.

I would like to emphasize that all responsibility for the way in which I have taken advice and criticism into consideration remains with me.

I would like to thank James Whiting, Simon Whitmore, Annabel Watson, Fiona Allan at Routledge for their help at various stages of writing this monograph. I would also like to thank Aneeta Madhavan and Ganesh Bhatt at Newgen Imaging Systems. Special thanks are due to Ganesh Bhatt for an excellent job of editorial and other production-related issues.

I gratefully acknowledge financial support for my research since 1993 provided by Asahi Glass Foundation, The Foundation for Earth Environment, Japan Society for the Promotion of Science, The Ministry of Education in Japan, Showa Shell Sekiyu Foundation for Environmental Research, and Zengin Foundation for Studies on Economics and Finance.

This monograph contains some revised versions of previously published papers. Permission to reproduce the materials published in the following papers was granted by Edward Elgar, Elsevier Science, Guilford Publications, *Methodus*, Nagard Publisher and Routledge.

1. Mayumi, K. (1991) 'Temporary emancipation from land: from the industrial revolution to the present time', *Ecological Economics* **4**: 35–56.
2. Mayumi, K. (1993) 'The exosomatic mode of human evolution, and a clarification of Nicholas Georgescu-Roegen's thoughts on entropy, the economic process, dialectics and evolution', *Methodus: Bulletin of the International Network for Economic Method* 5, **1**: 88–92.
3. Mayumi, K. (1993) 'Georgescu-Roegen's fourth law of thermodynamics and the flow–fund model', in J. C. Dragan, E. K. Seifert and M. C. Demetrescu (eds) *Entropy and Bioeconomics*, Milano: Nagard Publisher, 399–413.
4. Mayumi, K. (1993) 'Georgescu-Roegen's 'fourth law of thermodynamics', the modern energetic dogma, and ecological salvation', in L. Bonati, U. Cosentino, M. Lasagni, G. Moro, D. Pitea and A. Schiraldi (eds) *Trends in Ecological Physical Chemistry*, Amsterdam: Elsevier, 351–64.
5. Mayumi, K. (1994) 'Farming versus manufacturing', *Capitalism, Nature, Socialism* 5, **1**: 115–20.
6. Mayumi, K. (1995) 'Nicholas Georgescu-Roegen (1906–1994): an admirable epistemologist', *Structural Change and Economic Dynamics* 6, **3**: 261–5.
7. Mayumi, K. (1997) 'Viability of solar technology and the flow–fund model', in J. C. Dragan, M. C. Demetrescu and E. K. Seifert (eds) *Implications and Applications of Bioeconomics*, Milano: Nagard Publisher, 255–64.
8. Giampietro, M. and Mayumi, K. (1997) 'A dynamic model of socioeconomic systems based on hierarchy theory and its application to sustainability', *Structural Change and Economic Dynamics* **8**: 453–69.

9. Giampietro, M. and Mayumi, K. (1998) 'Another view of development, ecological degradation and North–South trade', *Review of Social Economy* **56**: 20–36.
10. Mayumi, K., Giampietro, M. and Gowdy, J. M. (1998) 'Georgescu-Roegen/Daly versus Solow/Stiglitz revisited', *Ecological Economics* **27**: 115–17.
11. Mayumi, K. (1999) 'Embodied energy analysis, Sraffa's analysis, Georgescu-Roegen's flow-fund model and viability of solar technology', in K. Mayumi and J. M. Gowdy (eds) *Bioeconomics and Sustainability: Essays in Honor of Nicholas Georgescu-Roegen*, Cheltenham: Edward Elgar, 173–93.

1 Introduction

Nicholas Georgescu-Roegen (1906–94) was one of the first economists to investigate rigorously the interplay between economic activity and natural environment in the light of thermodynamics. His achievements made him a perennial candidate for the Nobel prize in economics and the father of a new and rapidly growing school of economic thought, *ecological economics*. According to Georgescu-Roegen, nature consists only of what can be perceived; beyond, there are only hypothesized abstractions. His ideas about the relation between nature and human perception of nature led to a particular epistemology concerned mainly with valid analytical representations of relations among facts. For Georgescu-Roegen, any worthwhile economic theory must be a logically ordered description of how reality functions.

The pinnacle of Georgescu-Roegen's theoretical development may well be his ambitious attempt to reformulate economic process as 'bioeconomics', a new style of dialectical economic thought. His bioeconomics is not a new branch of economics. Rather, bioeconomics is a new discipline that combines elements of evolutionary biology, conventional economics and biophysical analysis (Miernyk 1999). Bioeconomics continuously highlights the biological origin of economic process and the human problems associated with a limited stock of accessible resources that are unevenly located and unequally appropriated. Important aspects of Georgescu-Roegen's approach to the economic process (Georgescu-Roegen 1977*c*) can be summarized as follows:

1 Humans have transgressed biological evolution developing into a new mode of evolution in which exosomatic organs are manufactured instead of being inherited somatically. Exosomatic production evolved into an economic process. Institutions of the market, money, credit, enterprises of all sorts and an internal logic inherent in these institutions emerged in response to the progressive evolution of the exosomatic nature of humankind. The human mode of existence is not dominated by biology or economics. People became completely dependent on exosomatic organs and the production of those organs, justifying Georgescu-Roegen's claim that scarcity of mineral resources *as well as* energy shortage sets a limit on the survival of the human species on this planet. Georgescu-Roegen's profound concern for ecological salvation culminates in his proposal for the 'Fourth Law of Thermodynamics'.

2 Qualitative change, a central theme of life sciences such as biology and economics, eludes arithmomorphic schematization rooted in mechanistic epistemology of neoclassical economics. Because of the emergence of novelty in the economic process, Georgescu-Roegen insists that reality can be grasped only when analysis is combined with dialectics (Mayumi 1993*a*). J. A. Schumpeter was a sympathetic mentor for Georgescu-Roegen who shares the view that the most important economic changes are qualitative, not quantitative. Schumpeter's vision of the economic process, the process of innovation in particular which anticipated biologist Richard Goldschmidt's idea of the hopeful monster (Goldschmidt 1933), is now rediscovered by the proponents of punctuated equilibrium theory in evolutionary biology (Gould and Eldredge 1977).

Recent concern for sustainability issues attracted attention to the comprehensive theory of economy, society and environment developed by Georgescu-Roegen during the later phase of his career after 1960. However, Georgescu-Roegen's original and path-breaking contributions have still not received deserved attention from mainstream economists. Perusing Georgescu-Roegen's early work, particularly on consumer choice theory and the Leontief dynamic model, reveals many innovative aspects that have never been incorporated into standard economic theory (Mayumi and Gowdy 1999). These innovative aspects may give essential clues to investigating deep theoretical and policy implications for sustainability issues. Close examination of the entire spectrum of Georgescu- Roegen's work and new theoretical developments based on his work are now necessary.

This book consists of this introduction and eight chapters. A brief explanation of each chapter follows.

Chapter 2 discusses consumer choice theory for environmental valuation in view of Georgescu-Roegen's contributions. Georgescu-Roegen is widely regarded as the father of mathematical economics by his seminal contributions to neoclassical consumer choice theory. Yet, it is not as widely recognized that most of his contributions to consumer choice theory are critiques from within, drastic revisions of the conceptual edifice which he himself helped build. This chapter (i) examines Georgescu-Roegen's basic ideas of consumer choice theory and identifies areas that need further theoretical development; and (ii) throws new light on the relevance of Georgescu-Roegen's utility theory to sustainability issues, especially regarding monetary evaluation of natural resources and environmental services.

In addition, this chapter discusses axioms of consumer choice within the neoclassical framework of methodological individualism. Then, the discussion broadens to include the social and environmental context of economic behaviour. In the spirit of 'consilience' proposed by E. O. Wilson (1998), this chapter argues that the basic assumptions of any particular science should be consistent with the basic body of knowledge understood by other sciences. Axioms of consumer choice theory when applied to environmental assessments are shown to be so unrealistic that policy recommendations based on them may not be reliable. The following topics are discussed: (i) postulates of consumer choice, (ii) non-satiation,

(iii) principle of complementarity, (iv) lexicographic preferences and psychological threshold, (v) invariance of preferences and hierarchy of wants, (vi) marginal utility of money, (vii) probabilistic binary choice scheme and (viii) methodological individualism.

Chapter 3 investigates conditions for a balanced sustained growth of the open Leontief dynamic model and a Leontief dynamic model with two delays.

This chapter discusses Georgescu-Roegen's critique of the dynamic economic model, particularly the open Leontief dynamic model. It is shown that severe conditions must be imposed on initial net product flows and planned consumption flows for achieving balanced sustained growth in a model with two productive processes.

A Leontief dynamic model with two delays is introduced to answer Georgescu-Roegen's critique concerning the inadequacy of dynamic models without delay and the quasi-explosive nature of dynamic models usually adopted by economists. There is consideration of a Leontief system consisting of two productive processes P_1 and P_2 producing commodities C_1 and C_2. Explicit introduction of two types of delays τ_1 and τ_2 (τ_i is the time interval before the additional flow of P_i becomes available) produces a linear differential model with two delays. The dynamic behaviour of this model is examined closely to show that, contrary to intuition, small delays can greatly influence the behaviour of the model. The system stability is shown to be closely related to the internal economic structure (saving process and building and priming new processes). The peculiar aspect of this model is that, even with linearity assumptions, chaotic behaviour might appear with delays. Recent developments in delay differential mathematics are used to investigate the behaviour of the system with different lag time structures.

Chapter 4 concerns a critical evaluation of the measure of information and its relationship with entropy in physics elaborating on Georgescu-Roegen's critique.

The chapter introduces C. E. Shannon's measure of information touching upon a historical development of the concept of information in communication engineering. Three points are emphasized: (i) the concept of information and the capacity of a communication channel should have been treated as separate concepts; (ii) it is accidental that Shannon reaches the function $H = -\sum p_i \log_2 p_i$, where $\sum p_i = 1$, through two different routes, an axiomatic treatment of information and a method of typical sequences; (iii) Shannon misidentifies a source of vernacular language with an ergodic stochastic Markov chain.

Further, this chapter analyses N. Wiener's measure of information or uncertainty on a stochastic process. The main results are: (i) any measure of uncertainty, one of which is H, is a pseudo-measure and not an ordinal variable; (ii) the amount of Wiener's information for all continuous distributions becomes infinite; and (iii) the expected amount of Wiener's information for any absolutely continuous distribution depends only on the ordinal measure adopted.

It questions the alleged equivalence between negative entropy and information, suggested implicitly or explicitly by L. Szilard, E. T. Jaynes and L. Brillouin. Georgescu-Roegen's critique of the measure of information and of the alleged equivalence is briefly related to his interest in epistemology.

Chapter 5 makes a critical appraisal of two entropy theoretical approaches to resources and environmental problems investigated by Georgescu-Roegen and Tsuchida.

In the light of Schrödinger's pioneering contribution to the analysis of living things, this chapter discusses a necessary condition for living things to continue life in terms of entropy disposal. The mechanism of how the earth system disposes thermal entropy increases toward outer space is also explained in terms of the nested-hierarchical structure of the open steady-state system of the second category as proposed by Tsuchida.

Georgescu-Roegen's Fourth Law of Thermodynamics is reviewed critically. It is shown that (i) Georgescu-Roegen's formulation is not compatible with the framework of thermodynamics; (ii) 'material entropy' is not the same as the entropy in physics, depending on factors such as heterogeneity of matter, available technology, multidimensional value system of humans and overall availability of resources.

Complementary aspects of the theories of Georgescu-Roegen and Tsuchida are discussed. Georgescu-Roegen's theory emphasizes that the earth is a closed system with respect to matter, while Tsuchida's water cycle theory stresses that the earth is an open system with respect to energy. The implication of these two theories for the steady state of the earth is also discussed.

Chapter 6 discusses embodied energy analysis, Sraffa's analysis, Georgescu-Roegen's flow–fund model and the viability of solar technology.

The first part of this chapter is prompted by recent interest in ecological economics literature in linkages between embodied energy analysis and Sraffa's analysis and includes (i) a comparison of the theoretical basis of embodied energy analysis from the point of view of Sraffa, one not examined by Georgescu-Roegen; (ii) a critical examination of embodied energy analysis in terms of Georgescu-Roegen's flow–fund model; and (iii) a comparison of Sraffa's analysis and Georgescu-Roegen's flow–fund model.

The second part of this chapter is prompted by the fact that, despite the probable exhaustion of oil in the near future, no effective and drastic shift in energy resources has been implemented. An abundant use of coal is more destructive to the environment after energy transformation, and nuclear energy may be much more destructive due to problems associated with long-term nuclear waste management. It remains to be seen whether or not it is possible for solar technology to replace fossil and fissile fuels completely. Solar energy technology might remain a parasite to fossil and fissile fuels.

This second part concerns three types of aggregated reproducible flow–fund models based on solar technology. Here, flows are elements that enter but do not come out of the process, or elements that come out of the process without having entered. Funds are elements that enter and leave the process unchanged. They are agents that perform the transformation of input flows into output flows. This analytical framework was introduced by Georgescu-Roegen, but the schematization has not received adequate attention. This chapter shows that Georgescu-Roegen's flow–fund model is indispensable in analysing the viability of solar technology.

The successful substitution of land-based resources by fossil fuels and mineral resources has supported the material structure of economic process ever since the Industrial Revolution, and the land constraint has eased since then. However, it is dangerous to claim that people have become perfectly emancipated from the land constraint. Chapter 7 suggests that people can attain only temporary emancipation from the land constraint and also provides economic and thermodynamic analysis of land, mainly since the Industrial Revolution.

Chapter 7 considers the tremendous rate of matter and energy degradation, which causes rapid depletion of natural resources and destruction of the environment, particularly land. There is reconsideration of Liebig and Marx, who both had prophetic visions concerning modern agriculture and its possible effect on the future economy. It also addresses a thermodynamic analysis of temporary emancipation from land during the Industrial Revolution in England. Substitution of coal for wood, especially in the iron industry, and growth of the cotton industry is featured. It is shown that temporary emancipation from the land constraint in the United States is due to the vast amount of fertile land and intensive consumption of natural resources, especially oil. However, this chapter shows that even in the United States the food safety margin will eventually fall, thanks to the law of diminishing returns. Finally, in order to appreciate land constraint properly, the essential differences and similarities between farming and manufacturing processes are discussed.

Chapter 8 discusses another view of development, environmental degradation and North–South trade issues.

Based on Georgescu-Roegen's bioeconomic paradigm, this chapter reconsiders the neoclassical economic paradigm, which endorses continuous global economic growth through stimulated trade. It suggests that, in view of sustainability, it is necessary to acknowledge (i) the importance of preserving the identity and integrity of economic systems in different regions of the world by enhancing, as much as possible, self-sufficiency and equity assessed at the national and regional levels; and (ii) the importance of including respect for biospheric equilibria as one criterion for regulating world economic activity, particularly trade. The differences and similarities of past and present patterns of ecological degradation are examined. Two types of efficiencies assess the technological changes and the drive toward unsustainability. We discuss an entropy-based theory of North–South trade issues and three points for the promotion of sustainability. Finally, the true origin of current ecological crisis is shown to lie in a deep change in the perception of the relation between humans and nature that affects the mode of technological development of modern society.

Chapter 9 discusses Robert Rosen's modelling relation, hierarchical system perspectives and the biophysical approach of sustainability issues using the ideas of hierarchical system theory.

The current path of socioeconomic development is generating a new type of challenge for science – issue-driven research for sustainability rather than curiosity-driven research. Sustainability issues imply not only a new role for science in relation to human progress, but also a search for a more integrated approach for describing the complex interplay between human activity and the environment. In fact, for monitoring the sustainability of human progress, scientific analyses should be able to model various parallel effects induced by a particular change. These induced effects could be analysed only on different space–time scales and in relation to various legitimate and contrasting perceptions of reality.

Many attempts to apply traditional scientific analyses to sustainability issues are driven by the strong demand of society for numerical assessments. Decision makers require numerical assessments as crucial inputs for traditional procedures of decision support such as cost–benefit analysis. However, before considering any numerical assessment seriously, there must be a theoretical discussion about the use and abuse of numerical assessments based on the modelling relation for sustainability issues. In other words, before adopting any numerical assessment as input in any decision-making process, there must be answers to questions concerning the theoretical assumptions and procedural steps which have been followed by the scientist to generate this assessment. There must also be answers to questions concerning the implications of the chain of choices made by the scientists to establish the validity and applicability of the resulting numerical assessment.

Using Rosen's (1985, 1991) modelling relation as a starting point, Chapter 9 argues that traditional scientific activity cannot guide sustainability issues. Some objective lessons are extracted from Rosen's arguments for scientists working on these issues. A methodological tool based on hierarchy theory is presented, which establishes a relation between the description of socioeconomic systems on one particular level (the focal level) with descriptions of the corresponding higher and lower hierarchical levels.

2 Foundations of consumer choice theory for environmental valuation in view of Georgescu-Roegen's contribution

1 Introduction

Until relatively recently, the assumptions of neoclassical utility theory were hotly debated by economists (see, e.g. Alchian 1953; Armstrong 1958; Samuelson 1952). However, with the ascendance of the neoclassical synthesis in the decades following World War II, most economists took the basic axioms of consumer choice as given and placed the question of 'tastes' outside the realm of economic analysis.[1] Preferences were taken to be given and constant and were assumed to be adequately revealed in market choices. Armed with these axioms, economists turned their attention to refining applications within the neoclassical paradigm. Several almost contemporary microeconomic textbooks do not even consider it necessary to justify the axioms of consumer choice. In recent years, however, attention has returned to some of the earlier controversies in utility theory because of the questions about environmental valuation, especially regarding the techniques based on neoclassical axioms of consumer choice such as the contingent valuation method (CVM). I believe that many issues relevant to the environmental valuation debates can be put into proper perspective by drawing on Georgescu-Roegen's contributions to utility theory.

The neoclassical theory of consumer choice describes the process by which an autonomous rational consumer allocates income at the margin among an array of consumer goods. As any scientific model does, neoclassical utility theory describes part of reality in the simplest way possible to explain the phenomena under consideration. The choice theory draws an 'analytical boundary' (Georgescu-Roegen 1971) around an individual consumer, ignoring the social and ecological contexts, to examine how an individual makes choices in a well-defined market. It is widely recognized that the axioms of consumer choice theory are quite restrictive, but its defenders argue that this simplification still captures the basic features of decision-making and is necessary in any analytical representation of complex reality.

Section 2 presents a set of axioms used in consumer choice theory. Section 3 discusses implications of the following five aspects in the set of axioms for environmental valuation: (i) non-satiation, (ii) the principle of complementarity, (iii) lexicographic preferences, (iv) invariance and hierarchical nature of wants, (v) the marginal utility of money and the Walrasian system. Section 4 introduces a new scheme based on probabilistic binary choice to illuminate profound issues concerning environmental valuation. Section 5 examines the methodological individualism and its problematic issues for environmental valuation.

2 The axioms of consumer choice

The economic valuation of environmental features is based on the well-known set of axioms which constitute the neoclassical theory of consumer behaviour. The description of the consumer as Homo oeconomicus (*HO*) is based on various versions (Frisch 1926; Georgescu-Roegen 1954*b*; Jehle 1991; Mas-Colell *et al.* 1995) of the following set of axioms:[2]

1 *HO* is faced with alternative combinations of various quantity-measurable commodities that involve neither risk nor uncertainty. Every point $C = (x_1, x_2, \ldots, x_n)$ in the commodity space is an alternative.
2 Given two commodity bundle alternatives C^1 and C^2, *HO* will either prefer one to the other, or regard the two alternatives as indifferent. Indifference is a symmetric relation, but preference is not. We write $C^1 P C^2$ for preference and $C^1 I C^2$ for indifference.
3 The preferences of *HO* do not change over time.
4 There is no saturation. This is sometimes called the axiom of monotonicity. Given any C^1, C^2 is preferred to C^1 if C^2 is obtained by adding to C^1 more of at least one commodity.
5 The relation of non-preference $\bar{P}$ (the negation of P) is transitive. That is, if $C^1 \bar{P} C^2$ and $C^2 \bar{P} C^3$, then $C^1 \bar{P} C^3$ ($C^1 \bar{P} C^2$ means either $C^2 P C^1$ or $C^1 I C^2$).
6 If $C^1 \bar{P} C^2$ and $C^1 \bar{P} C^3$, then $C^1 \bar{P} [aC^2 + (1-a)C^3]$, where $0 \leq a \leq 1$. It means that C^1 is not preferred to a mix of C^2 and C^3, no matter what the composition of the combination.

Although Axiom 2 allows for a region of indifference, it is not strong enough to guarantee that an indifference region actually exists. Consequently, Axiom 7, the indifference postulate, is necessary to construct a complete ordinal measure of utility (Georgescu-Roegen 1936).

7 A set (C^α) is called *a preferential set* if α takes all the values of an interval of real numbers and if $C^\beta P C^\gamma$ whenever $\beta > \gamma$. If the preferential set (C^α) contains C^β and C^γ, and if $C^\beta P C$ and $C P C^\gamma$, then the preferential set contains a combination indifferent to C.

3 The axioms of consumer choice and environmental valuation

3.1 Non-satiation

Many environmental services must be present within a narrow range in order to support human life. The effect of changes in environmental services cannot be delineated into continuous marginal quantities. Individual preferences have some grounding in biophysical reality. They are not independent of the biological and social worlds surrounding the decision-maker. Attempts to place an economic value on nature's services may just be meaningless because of the lack of biophysical context of the valuation (Gowdy 1997; Toman 1998).

Axiom 4 is sometimes referred to as non-satiation or monotonicity. This axiom is relevant to environmental valuation because, without the assumption of non-satiation, CVM loses operational meaning as a practical tool of monetary evaluation of environmental services. This postulate has been criticized by ecological economists because many, if not most, of the environmental services provided by ecosystems (water, food, oxygen, etc.) have a saturation region. For example, the composition of gases in the atmosphere must fall within a certain range to support human life. If there is too little oxygen, people will die of asphyxiation; too much oxygen will cause the earth's organic material to burn uncontrollably. Other atmospheric gases must also be present in fairly fixed amounts. The level of nitrogen, for example, is critical for the regulation of breathing in animals. As is well-known by now, small changes in the level of CO_2 in the earth's atmosphere can have a dramatic effect on its temperature.

It should also be pointed out here that the notion that human wants are infinite is also inconsistent with the evidence from a number of human societies. The craving for material goods as a dominant feature of human societies evidently began with the agricultural revolution (Sahlins 1972). Indeed, in some societies the morbid craving for wealth is considered to be a serious disease (Sahlins 1996). As Georgescu-Roegen states, '[a] life of material austerity and self-negation still represents the greatest happiness for him who has chosen to be a monk' (Georgescu-Roegen 1971: 323).

A weaker version of the non-satiation or monotonicity is local non-satiation (Jehle 1991; Mas-Colell *et al.* 1995). The local non-satiation axiom rules out the possibility of having an area in which all points are indifferent. However, as the above examples show, the local non-satiation axiom cannot apply to some environmental goods. In addition to this difficulty, a particular metric space must be introduced in order to define the notion of 'vicinity'. To proceed independently of a particular metric space, a more rigorous definition is needed. So, a saturation point S is a point such that the direction to S is a preferred direction from any non-saturation point. For the sake of simplicity, assume that there is only one such point (in general, the set of saturation points is a convex set, but the conclusion is not affected). If this assumption is adopted, integral curves have spiral forms around a saturation point even for the case with two commodities (see Appendix A). Figure 2.1 shows such curves around a saturation point. Given some amount of the first commodity, there are many values of the amount of the second commodity which result in the same utility index. Hence, it is impossible to build a unique index of utility even with the weaker version of non-satiation.

3.2 The Principle of Complementarity

Axiom 6 is referred to by Georgescu-Roegen (1954*a*) as the Principle of Complementarity. This axiom is slightly weaker than the axiom of convexity usually

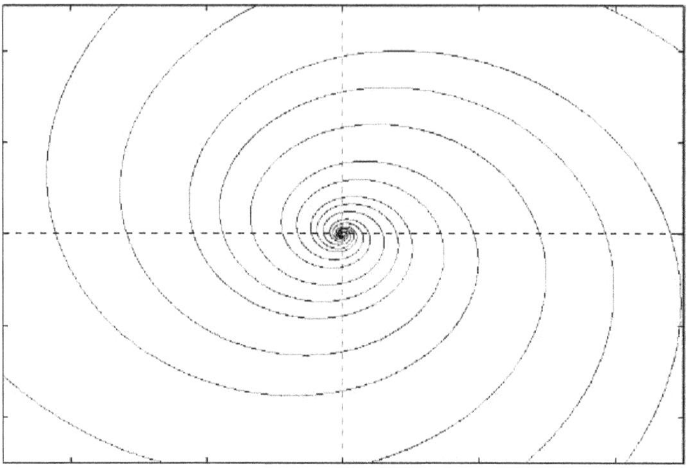

Figure 2.1 Integral curves around the saturation point.

adopted in advanced texts (Jehle 1991; Mas-Colell *et al.* 1995). In the two-commodity case, the convexity axiom is equivalent to the principle of decreasing marginal rate of substitution, one of the theoretical lynchpins of utility theory. In general, indifference maps convex to the origin imply a decreasing marginal rate of substitution between any two commodities. Axiom 6 has no meaning if commodities are only ordinally measurable. For example, 'half' of a commodity would not be defined uniquely without some notion of cardinality. Neoclassical texts usually argue that any scale is as good as another, i.e. only ordinal rankings of commodity bundles are necessary. However, the following example shows that this argument is not universally valid. The utility function $U = \sqrt{xy}$ exhibits a decreasing marginal rate of substitution. Adopting a new scale by the monotonic transformation: $x = \mathrm{e}^{-1/u}$ for $0 \le x \le \mathrm{e}^{-1}$, and $x = \mathrm{e}^{u^2-2}$ for $\mathrm{e}^{-1} \le x$ and using the same transformation for y into v, a new utility function $U = \mathrm{e}^{(u^2+v^2-4)/2}$ $(u, v \ge 1)$ is obtained. Transforming this new utility function monotonically produces another whose indifference function is $u^2 + v^2 =$ constant. The principle of decreasing marginal rate of substitution does not hold for this new utility function. This example shows that, without Axiom 6, it is impossible to determine what an appropriate scale of monotonic transformation in the commodity space is for obtaining a utility index. This points to an inconsistency in the claim that ordinal utility is sufficient to construct a consistent theory of consumer choice. The axiomatic system needed for utility theory includes an axiom which is inconsistent with the ordinality claim.

What is the relevance of Axiom 6 to environmental valuation? Axiom 6 suggests that any economic law describing the structure of consumer choice depends on the special type of measure used for commodities. But, how can people determine one specific measure when they evaluate various environmental services in a CVM scheme? What is the relation between commodity scale and the monetary metric used in CVM? Thus, even ordinal measurability does not fit in the simplest picture of a utility function.

3.3 Lexicographic preferences

Ordinalists like Hicks and Allen (1934) commonly believe that Axioms 1–6 are sufficient to build a utility function (or an ophelimity index) which is an ordinal measure of the preference of *HO*. However, suppose we remove Axiom 7 (the indifference postulate) and retain all the others. It can then be demonstrated that, without Axiom 7, there is a case in which it is impossible to obtain an ordinal measure of utility. In fact, this axiom is necessary to preclude a lexicographic ordering of preferences. Lexicographic preferences mean that, even if alternatives can be compared, this does not imply that an ordinal measure can be obtained.

Lexicographic preferences imply that consumers are not necessarily willing to substitute one object of utility for another. Everyday observations, as well as empirical tests, show that this ordering is ubiquitous: bread cannot save someone dying of thirst; life in a luxurious palace cannot substitute for food (Georgescu-Roegen 1954*b*). Lexicographic ordering implies that it is impossible to represent a variety of wants in terms of one linear, dimension-preserving utility index. Mathematically, lexicographic ordering is not a linear continuous series. A linear continuous series satisfies the following three postulates: (i) the Dedekind postulate, (ii) the density postulate and (iii) the linearity postulate. It has long been known that lexicographic ordering does not satisfy the linearity postulate (Huntington 1917). This fact prevents us from establishing an ordinal measure.

Lexicographic preference is more than a theoretical curiosity. Such preferences are pervasive in CVM surveys. Spash and Hanley (1995) argue that valuation methods which elicit bids for biodiversity preservation fail as measures of welfare changes due to the prevalence of lexicographic preferences. They find that a significant number of respondents refuse to make trade-offs between biodiversity and market goods. Stevens *et al.* (1991) also find evidence for lexicographic preferences in a study estimating the value of wildlife in New England. Forty-four per cent of respondents agree with the statement 'preservation of wildlife should not be determined by how much money can be spent'. Sixty-seven per cent agree with the statement '[a]s much wildlife as possible should be preserved no matter what the cost' (Stevens *et al.* 1991: 398–9).

As Arrow (1997) points out, lexicographic preferences need not be inconsistent with neoclassical utility theory if marginal valuation is possible. For example, people may place an infinite value on their own lives, but they may accept an increased risk of death for a price. The neoclassical explanation of lexicographic preferences would be that high risks do not have a monetary equivalent (Arrow 1997). Another explanation is that, in cases where people are willing to risk their lives, the risk is perceived to be so small that it is assumed to be zero. The problem of lexicographic ordering revolves around the appropriateness of marginal valuation.

3.4 Invariance and hierarchy of wants

Axiom 3 states that consumer preferences may be assumed to be constant over the relevant time period of analysis. Psychologists have found, however, that individual preference for a particular item may vary considerably, depending on the context. Many of the criticisms of CVM have centred on the ephemeral nature of consumer tastes as expressed in survey responses. Diamond and Hausman (1994), for example, criticize CVM because the responses to CVM questions depend upon the sequence in which the questions are asked. They also criticize CVM because it captures a variety of 'non-market' consumer reactions including 'warm glow' effects, 'protest bids' and 'embedding'. The 'warm glow' criticism is that, in CVM surveys, individuals may be expressing support for good causes in general rather than for the specific item being evaluated. In protest bids, individuals may be expressing a reaction to a recent specific environmental event such as an oil spill rather than focusing on the specific item under consideration. These criticisms of specific CVM studies can just as easily be used to criticize consumer choice theory in general. As marketing and advertising experts know, warm glow and many other feelings are part of almost all consumer choices. Preferences are not invariant with respect to the social and environmental context.

Hanemann (1994), in a defence of CVM, points out that traditional consumer choice theory assumes a 'top-down' or 'stored-rule' decision-making process. This 'filing cabinet' conception of the mind still holds sway in economics but has been abandoned by those studying how the human mind actually works (see Bettman 1988; Martin and Tesser 1992). Psychologists now see cognition as a constructive process depending on context and history. How choices are actually constructed depends on time, place and immediate past experiences (Hanemann 1994: 28). It has been shown that consumer choices, including those made in 'real' markets, are made using a 'bottom-up' decision process (Olshavsky and Granbois 1979). Consumer choices are not based on a file cabinet of rational and consistent behavioural memories but are based on rules invoked on-the-spot for each situation. This is as true of market decisions involving monetary transactions as it is of survey responses. The problem is not that CVM responses are not real, but rather that humans may not act according to the assumptions of utility theory.

The seven axioms of consumer choice are inconsistent with a hierarchical ordering of human wants or the evolution of preferences over time. According to Georgescu-Roegen, the existence of a hierarchy of wants is necessary to explain the Principle of Decreasing Marginal Utility. Different levels of needs have different degrees of importance to us. However, it should be noted that what can generally be described as the hierarchy of human wants involves several other principles. The satisfaction of every want 'lower' in the scale creates a desire of 'higher' character. That is, the satisfaction of a lower want permits the higher want to manifest itself. In a way, the satisfaction of lower wants enhances the perception of wants higher in the hierarchy. Georgescu-Roegen (1954*b*) terms this the Principle of Subordination of Wants. Due to the fact that the hierarchy of wants is open-ended, as soon as humans manage to get close to the satiation of a new want, there is always another want higher on the ladder. This is the Principle of the Growth of Wants, which is tantamount to the absence of absolute saturation of human desire to want more, but not in terms of the physical quantity discussed in Section 3.1. Of course, this principle has an evolutionary character as well as being culturally specific.

Economic valuation assumes the existence of a common essence of all wants, a unique want into which all wants can be merged into a monodimensional definition of utility. Arguments for the plausibility of the existence of a common denominator (in terms of utility or ultimately in terms of money) have never seriously been made, perhaps because in real-world markets everything is reduced to a common monetary denominator. In fact, a close examination shows that theories of choice were only axiomatic moulds of utility theories and retained all the consequences of the belief in the reducibility of all wants into money. This is against the commonsense view, which is based upon a multidimensional value system. That is, according to Georgescu-Roegen's view, it would represent the Principle of the Irreducibility of Wants (1954*b*). Martinez-Alier *et al.* (1998) argue that the assumption of commensurability of wants principally separates the neoclassical from the ecological economics (see the discussion by Arrow (1997) and Radin (1996)). As discussed in Section 3.3, lexicographic choice is one example reflected in the hierarchical nature of human choice.

3.5 CVM, the marginal utility of money and the Walrasian system

The basic ideas behind CVM may be traced back to the Dupuit–Marshall principle, which holds that the money which a person is willing to pay for satisfaction, rather than doing without satisfaction, is the economic measure of that person's satisfaction. In practical terms, utility can be measured by money. In the Dupuit–Marshall scheme or the CVM scheme, utility of money that an individual has to pay for each additional 'util' must always increase because money is drawn away from increasingly important uses.

CVM must assume, as Marshall does, that the marginal utility of money is quasi-constant. However, this hypothesis deserves analysis. Marshall's aim is to analyse the economic reality of his own time and space, but according to Georgescu-Roegen (1968), the assumption of quasi-constancy of the marginal utility of money is compatible with a society consisting of 'middle-class individuals', a society typical of developed countries, where a substantial part of personal income is spent on numerous mere conveniences. Most mere conveniences are connected with marginal expenditures in relation to total income. So, variation in income causes one of these mere convenience items to disappear from the budget or to appear as a new entry in the list of expenditure. In such conditions, it is reasonable to assume that the utility of money among convenience items can be considered to be the same because individuals find it difficult to decide whether to buy one convenience item or another. However, it is questionable whether or not CVM can evaluate environmental services in developing countries, because in such countries only a minimal part of the consumer budget is spent on mere conveniences.

The mathematical solution of the Walrasian system investigated by Arrow and Debreu (1954) may not be suitable for the economic situation facing developing countries (Georgescu-Roegen 1960). However, assessing trade-offs between economic growth and ecological constraint in developing countries is certainly crucial in the debate on sustainability issues. Arrow and Debreu (1954: 270) assume that 'every individual could consume out of his initial stock in some feasible way and still have a positive amount of each commodity available for trading in the market'. However, they confess that this 'assumption is clearly unrealistic' (Arrow and Debreu 1954: 270). Arrow and Debreu have to make such an assumption because it is necessary for each individual to possess at least one commodity commanding positive price at equilibrium. Such an assumption sets aside the sustainability issues from the beginning! People in developing countries may be so poor that, for example, 'deforestation and the depletion of fuelwood supplies, . . . forces poor households to divert dung for use as fuel rather than for fertilizer and present value of the dung as fuel is higher than its value as a soil nutrient' (Barbier and Markandya 1990), resulting in a much worse ecosystem condition. In developed countries, the situation is entirely different, so Costanza *et al.* (1997) assume that 'wealthy nations [could] value their coasts 100 times as much as poorer ones, making the latter's contribution relatively tiny [in monetary terms]' (Pimm 1997).

Neoclassical economists came up with the Walrasian system with sufficient initial endowments as the theoretical scaffold. However, according to Georgescu-Roegen (1982), the doctrine of neoclassical economics was moulded on an economic reality of abundance after the Industrial Revolution and, in this framework, what is scarce is demand for each kind of product. So, utility is regarded as the source of value and incorporated into the consumption theory, including contingent evaluation of ecological services. For neoclassical economists, anything like ecological services included, or eventually to be included, in the utility function could theoretically be analysed by economics tools including CVM. Neoclassical economists could imagine limitless substitution among items in utility function, justifying monetary evaluation.

4 Probabilistic binary choice and environmental valuation

As a step toward overcoming some of the difficulties raised regarding consumer choice theory, in this section an extension of the neoclassical utility axioms is proposed in order to include a region of hesitation in which choices cannot be categorized as more preferred, less preferred or indifferent. We adopt the assumptions of a 'psychological threshold' (leading to a region of hesitation) proposed by Georgescu-Roegen. Axioms 2, 3 and 7 above exclude such a region of hesitation by making *HO* a perfect choosing instrument. However, hesitation is a common feature of choices made under conditions of uncertainty, as shown regularly in CVM surveys. Uncertainty as to the characteristics of the commodity and as to the consequences of choices are prevalent in the case of environmental services. Such services are characterized by what Vatn and Bromley (1994) call 'functional transparency'. That is, people do not know the effect of altering an ecosystem until after the alteration is made.

Designing an experiment to test the validity of Axiom 7 (the indifference postulate) directly seems impossible because there are no means for testing assertions involving the continuum between more preferred and less preferred. In a sense, the questions involved in the indifference postulate cannot be settled solely in terms of observable facts. This confronts people with the more difficult question as to whether or not indifference may be defined in such a way as to avoid all references to introspection and base the definition only on direct observation. As shown below, if Axioms 2, 3 and 7 are modified to incorporate the hesitation region, *HO* cannot make choices without considerable doubt. If the presence of this type of region is accepted, the choice between C^1 and C^2 may not always show a consistent preference ordering.

Following Georgescu-Roegen's scheme (1936, 1958: 159–60), a New Homo oeconomicus (*NHO*) is introduced:

1. Given two points, $A(a_1, a_2, \ldots, a_n)$ and $B(b_1, b_2, \ldots, b_n)$, in the commodity space, $w(A, B) + w(B, A) = 1$, where $w(A, B)$ is the probability that A be chosen.
2. If $A \geq B$, then $w(A, B) = 1$. $A \geq B$ means iff $a_i \geq b_i$, $i = 1, \ldots, n$ and $a_j > b_j$ for at least one j.
3. The probability $w(X, A)$ is a continuous function of X, except for $X = A$, where $w(X, A)$ can take any value in the closed interval [0, 1].
4. If $A \leq B$, then $w(A, C) \leq w(B, C)$, the equality sign holding only if $w(A, C) = 1$ or $w(B, C) = 0$.
5. Pseudo-transitivity: If $w(A, B) = w(B, C) = p \geq \frac{1}{2}$, then $w(A, C) \geq p$.
6. General principle of persisting non-preference direction: If $C = \lambda A + (1 - \lambda)B$, with $0 < \lambda < 1$, then $w(A, B) \leq w(C, B)$.

From this set of axioms, a simple model with two parameters p and d can be constructed. Here the parameter p is taken as probability $w(X, A)$, given the point A. The point (d, d) is taken as the reference point A. One possible model is the following one-parameter family of differential equations satisfying the classical conditions of indifference directions (convexity) and $(\partial/\partial p)(-\mathrm{d}x_2/\mathrm{d}x_1) > 0$:

$$p x_1^{p-1} x_2^{1-p}\, \mathrm{d}x_1 + (1 - p) x_1^p x_2^{-p}\, \mathrm{d}x_2 = 0. \tag{2.1}$$

This equation can be solved to obtain a two-parameter family of integral curves (equation (2.3) below). Assuming that $x_1^p x_2^{1-p} < (x_1^*)^p (x_2^*)^{1-p}$ for $(x_1, x_2) < (x_1^*, x_2^*)$, the other values of $w(X, A)$ can be defined according to the following rules:

(a) $w(X, A) = p$, if either $x_1^p x_2^{1-p} = d$, or $x_1^{1-p} x_2^p = d$, and $x_1^{1/2} x_2^{1/2} > d$ when $\frac{1}{2} < p < 1$;

(b) $w(X, A) = p$, if either $x_1^p x_2^{1-p} = d$, or $x_1^{1-p} x_2^p = d$, and $x_1^{1/2} x_2^{1/2} < d$ when $0 < p < \frac{1}{2}$;

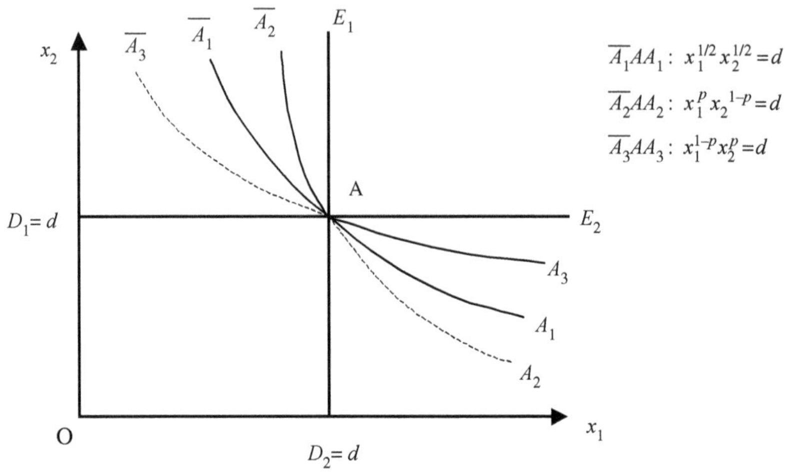

Figure 2.2 Probabilistic binary choice scheme.

(c) $w(X, A) = 1$, if $x_1 \geq d$, $x_2 \geq d$ and $x_1^{1/2}x_2^{1/2} > d$;
(d) $w(X, A) = 0$, if $x_1 \leq d$, $x_2 \leq d$ and $x_1^{1/2}x_2^{1/2} < d$.

It is relatively easy to show that this model satisfies the set of axioms for *NHO*.

In Fig. 2.2, the three curves, $\bar{A}_1AA_1$, $\bar{A}_2AA_2$ and $\bar{A}_3AA_3$, represent the following three equations in turn:

$$x_1^{1/2}x_2^{1/2} = d, \tag{2.2}$$

$$x_1^p x_2^{1-p} = d, \tag{2.3}$$

$$x_1^{1-p}x_2^p = d. \tag{2.4}$$

The curve $\bar{A}_1AA_1$ in Fig. 2.2 represents the locus with $w(X, A) = \frac{1}{2}$, where X and A are perfectly indifferent. This smooth differentiable curve $\bar{A}_1AA_1$ is similar to the one obtained in the neoclassical utility theory. On the other hand, the curve $\bar{A}_2AA_3$ represents the locus with $w(X, A) = p$, where $\frac{1}{2} < p < 1$. However, the curve $\bar{A}_2AA_3$ is not differentiable, but is still convex toward the origin. The case in which $0 < p < \frac{1}{2}$ can be depicted in a similar way. It should be noted that the case for which either $w(X, A) = 1$ or $w(X, A) = 0$ is represented by the areas E_1AE_2 or D_1AD_2O. The limiting lines relative to A ($x_1 = d$ and $x_2 = d$) can be obtained if p approaches either 0 or 1 in equation (2.3). The areas E_1AD_1 and E_2AD_2 may be termed as *hesitation regions* relative to the point A in which $w(X, A)$ is neither 0 nor 1: for all price lines within this angle, *NHO* can only attach some probability

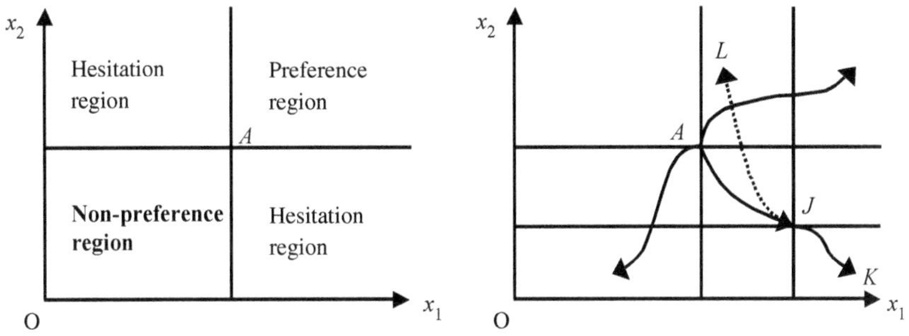

Figure 2.3 Hesitation regions and intransitivity.

of selecting a direction from the initial position A. In Georgescu-Roegen's words: people 'should also be aware of the possibility of interpreting as "indifferent states" those which people cannot order without a great deal of hesitation or without some inconsistency. Such cases are the symptoms of imperfections in the mechanism of choice caused by a psychological threshold which is absent' (Georgescu-Roegen 1954*b*: 522) in *HO*. This is not indifference but rather an inability to choose, as in the case of Buridan's ass, which starves to death between two identical piles of hay.

Three different regions of the *NHO* model are shown in Fig. 2.3. If any path moving toward a preferred ($w(X, A) = 1$) or non-preferred ($w(X, A) = 0$) direction is taken, the choices in these two regions are consistent, i.e. transitive. However, in the hesitation region, the choice is not transitive in general. This situation is shown in Fig. 2.3, where the path from A to J and from J to L is possible, but L is preferred to A. The lack of transitivity with respect to hesitation is obvious because in this case there is a range of probability ($0 < p < 1$) between any two commodities. This type of hesitation emerges whenever a new situation is given to a consumer. So, in a sense, the state of mind described by indifference in neoclassical economics is rather strange. I share the view of Georgescu-Roegen that the states of indifferent mind must be those in which people cannot order without a great deal of hesitation or without some inconsistency. The behaviour described by *NHO* shows exactly these sorts of indifferent states with great hesitation rather than the states of mind willing to trade and are described by *HO*. The notion of hesitation region discussed in this section can be regarded as a consequence of people's inability to visualize an imaginary situation exactly as they feel it after many experiences of the situation.

The basic issue discussed in this section, the consumer's inability to choose among alternatives in many situations, has plagued CVM researchers since the inception of that survey method. Consumers frequently are unable to choose among alternatives because of incongruity (Martinez-Alier *et al.* 1998), difficulties in conceptualizing discounted streams of cost and benefit (see the discussions in Hausman 1993), and 'functional transparency' (Vatn and Bromley 1994). These problems are usually swept under the rug by invoking the argument relating to revealed preferences. That is, when people spend actual money in actual markets, it must be assumed that they are acting 'rationally', in contrast to the 'irrational' responses given in hypothetical surveys. There is no reason to believe, however, that people somehow suddenly become strictly rational, calculating economic persons as soon as they enter the marketplace. Rather than to invoke restrictive *ad hoc* explanations as a matter of pure faith, I believe that seeking a more realistic foundation for consumer choice theory is a more fruitful approach.

5 Economic man and methodological individualism

Much of the criticism of neoclassical economics concerns the notion that humans are rational calculating individuals. According to neoclassical economists, *HO* lies at the heart of consumer choice theory. In connection with the rationale of *HO*, Arrow (1997: 760) recalls a skit performed by graduate students at the University of Chicago in the late 1940s. The leading character, Rational Economic Man, stands with a slide rule prepared to answer all questions. He is asked 'How much would you charge to kill your grandmother?' and, after some calculations, he looks up and asks, 'Do I have to dispose of the remains?' The fact that this skit is taken by the audience to be satire shows that the graduate students are aware of the limits of the rationality assumption in a set of axioms of consumer choice theory. Still, economists consider the individual to be a sort of mechanical calculator of pleasure and pain who exists at the centre of the universe.

So, for such economists, social welfare is merely the sum of the welfare of each rational and independent individual, though even natural scientists overtly recognized long ago: 'the whole is never equal simply to the sum of its various parts' (Max Planck cited in Georgescu-Roegen 1971: 328).

The notion of individual self-interest is elevated to a moral position in standard theory in which each individual knows what is best for that individual and any attempt to circumvent individual choice by any form of collective action is met with charges of totalitarianism. As Randall (1988: 217) puts it, 'mainstream economic approach is doggedly nonjudgmental about people's preferences: what the individual wants is presumed to be good for that individual'. Georgescu-Roegen is eloquent in discussing the point that what is good for an individual with a finite lifespan, acting at a particular point in time, may not be best for society as a whole.

> It is utterly inept to transpose to the entire human species, even to a nation, the laws of conduct of a single individual. It is understandable that an individual should be impatient (or myopic), i.e. to prefer an apple now over an apple tomorrow. The individual is mortal. But the human species or a nation has no reason to be myopic. They must act as if they were immortal, because with the immediate horizon they are so. The present turning point in mankind's evolution calls for the individual to understand that he is part of a quasi immortal body and hence must get rid of his myopia.
>
> (Georgescu-Roegen 1976: xix)

In standard utility theory, only individual perceptions count. There is no social, biological or physical reality outside the individual, only the subjective feelings of unconnected utility maximizers. Economists who focus on methodological individualism typical in consumer choice theory systematically ignore the hierarchical nature of social and ecological systems when they aggregate preferences and utility within social systems. In nested hierarchical systems, it is useless to deduce characteristics of higher-level elements by only considering characteristics of lower-level elements. In the literature of hierarchy theory, the problem of such extrapolation is known as 'scaling' (see e.g. Allen and Starr 1982). Scaling implies that crossing a hierarchical level of organization requires a consideration of 'emergent' behaviour and such behaviour cannot be deduced by using only information gathered at the lower level.

Limitations of methodological individualism due to the hierarchical nature of social systems are clear in the example of three individuals A, B and C. A prefers Chinese food rather than fast food or Japanese food. B prefers fast food rather than Japanese food or Chinese food. C prefers Japanese food rather than Chinese food or fast food.

If the three people decide to eat out together, they are supposed to choose a restaurant which serves only one kind of food. Economists who ignore the hierarchical nature of social systems believe that the information gathered about their individual preferences about a restaurant helps predict where they will end up eating on any particular night.

Clearly, such an inference cannot be made without a lot of additional information. For example, because of the existence of crossed constraints, probably, the group will end up eating in a 'generic restaurant' compatible with the 'aggregate' constraints. The group behaviour can escape certain restrictions imposed on a particular group by each member of that group: using the landscape fitness analysis metaphor – the larger the group, the easier it settles on lower peaks on the fitness landscape (Kauffman 1993). Using the commonsense approach of choosing a generic restaurant implies a hypothesis that the aggregate preference curve of the group is actually something that cannot be defined 'once and for all'. To check the validity of such a hypothesis, it is useful to consider possible alternative situations in which the three individuals decide to eat out together for dinner:

Situation 1. In this situation, no special attribute affects the aggregation of preferences. The set of individual constraints will operate without weighting factors. In this case, the same set of attributes that lead to the preference of Chinese food, fast food or Japanese food no longer operate. There is another crucial attribute, that of spending the night with others rather than eating alone. However, this new attribute opens the door to a myriad of unexpected complications.

Situation 2. In this situation, dinner is planned on a day which is the birthday of one of the three people. In this case, the group can decide to please the person celebrating by going to that person's favourite restaurant.

Situation 3. In this situation, some social hierarchy operates among the three. For example, one of the three is a VIP to be considered 'special' by the other two.

Situation 4. In this situation, some special event such as the winning of a lottery or a job promotion affects the usual preference structure of one or more persons. The special event provided by a person could remove constraints among the group members that usually operate and, therefore, the overall preference structure might change dramatically.

In all four situations, the curve of preference of the group is the result of social processes emerging from the complex web of effects determined by large-scale processes and small-scale details.

6 Conclusion

Following the triumph of neoclassical theory after World War II, the utility theory has been relegated to a secondary field of inquiry. Criticisms of the basic axioms of consumer choice are more or less limited to those outside the mainstream of the economics profession. Economists are, for the most part, satisfied with Stigler and Becker's position (1977) that tastes are not a matter of dispute and with Friedman's argument (1953) that the realism of the assumptions of economic theory is not a matter of concern as long as the theory could be used to make accurate predictions. With the weakening of economic orthodoxy following the energy price shocks of the 1970s and the global financial instability in the 1980s and 1990s, some of the basic tenets of economic theory have come under attack. Within the field of environmental economics, major crises such as global climate change and the worldwide loss of biodiversity have called into question the theoretical foundations of the basic tools of economic analysis used in environmental policy. A number of environmental policy failures have led to new approaches. For example, the failure of fisheries policies based on economic models has triggered a number of studies of common property (as opposed to open access) management systems. Daniel Bromley (1989), Susan Hanna (1997), Elinor Ostrom (1990) and many others argue for the reformulation of institutions for democratic collective action as a means to manage environmental resources. In the past, a number of methodological breakthroughs in economics have been the direct result of policy failures, a notable example being Keynes' *General Theory*. It is my hope that some of the current controversies surrounding environmental valuation will convince economists of the importance of reconciling economic theory with basic knowledge in other sciences (Wilson 1998). It is my belief that some of the fundamental assumptions of neoclassical utility theory, non-satiation, the indifference postulate, the commensurability of wants and, indeed, methodological individualism itself are not only unrealistic but also have had unforeseen and unfortunate consequences for environmental and social policy. It is hoped that a reformulation of consumer choice theory to allow for phenomena consistently found in consumer surveys can lead to more effective environmental policies.

3 Conditions for balanced sustained growth of the open Leontief dynamic model and investigation on a Leontief dynamic model with two delays

1 Introduction

About forty years ago, in *Econometrica* there was a hot debate between W. Leontief and J. D. Sargan concerning the stability of the Leontief dynamic model and the need of introduction of delays into the model (Sargan 1958, 1961; Leontief 1961*a*,*b*). There have been several investigations on the introduction of delays into other economic models rather than the dynamic Leontief model in economic science (e.g. Frisch and Holme 1935; Kalecki 1935; El-Hodiri *et al.* 1972). However, perhaps because of mathematical and technical difficulty necessary to tackle these two issues, no progress in investigations on the issues of delay in the Leontief dynamic model had ever been achieved since then. Georgescu-Roegen describes the situation as follows:

> The analytical advantages of the lag systems over the purely dynamic ones have been repeatedly stressed in the literature, . . . But the fact that their solutions do not possess the analytical simplicity of the purely dynamic systems has made their study less profitable and has deterred their use in concrete applications.
>
> (Georgescu-Roegen 1971: 274f.)

The objectives of this chapter are: (i) establishing balanced sustained growth conditions of the open dynamic Leontief model and (ii) investigating a Leontief dynamic model with two delays. We consider a model with two productive processes; however, extension to the general case with many productive processes could be done without much difficulty. Mathematical details appear in Appendices B and C. We adopt the standard notation for the Leontief system, without otherwise mentioning.

2 Conditions for balanced sustained growth of the open dynamic Leontief model

We consider a system consisting of two productive processes P_1 and P_2, each process P_i producing commodity C_i ($i = 1$ or 2). The unit-scale processes are

$$P_1^0(a_{11} = 1, -a_{21}; B_{11}, B_{21}), \qquad P_2^0(-a_{12}, a_{22} = 1; B_{12}, B_{22}). \tag{3.1}$$

Here, P_i^0 describes the process capable of producing one unit of C_i per unit time ($i = 1$ or 2). So, a_{ik} is a flow rate, and B_{ik} is a fund that is an agent for production. Given the scale of P_i, x_i ($i = 1$ or 2), in relation to the corresponding unit-scale process, the flow rate of net product (y_1, y_2) is determined by the well-known relationships

$$a_{11}x_1 - a_{12}x_2 = y_1, \qquad -a_{21}x_1 + a_{22}x_2 = y_2, \tag{3.2}$$

where the following condition must be satisfied:

$$D = a_{11}a_{22} - a_{12}a_{21} > 0. \tag{3.3}$$

Increases in the flow rates of (y_1, y_2),

$$\Delta y_1 \geq 0, \quad \Delta y_2 \geq 0, \quad \Delta y_1 + \Delta y_2 > 0, \tag{3.4}$$

require the increases Δx_1 and Δx_2 in the scales of P_1 and P_2, satisfying the following two relations:

$$a_{11}\Delta x_1 - a_{12}\Delta x_2 = \Delta y_1, \qquad -a_{21}\Delta x_1 + a_{22}\Delta x_2 = \Delta y_2. \tag{3.5}$$

These increases in Δx_1 and Δx_2 require, in turn, increases in the original funds $B_1 = x_1 B_{11} + x_2 B_{12}$ and $B_2 = x_1 B_{21} + x_2 B_{22}$ as follows:

$$\Delta B_1 = B_{11}\Delta x_1 + B_{12}\Delta x_2, \qquad \Delta B_2 = B_{21}\Delta x_1 + B_{22}\Delta x_2. \tag{3.6}$$

To accumulate commodities for these increases in funds, a part of the net products must be saved rather than being consumed during some time period Δt. So, during Δt, the flow rate of net product for consumption (z_1, z_2) must be dropped to

$$z_1 = y_1 - \frac{\Delta B_1}{\Delta t}, \qquad z_2 = y_2 - \frac{\Delta B_2}{\Delta t}. \tag{3.7}$$

Using (3.5) and (3.6), relation (3.7) can be transformed into

$$z_1 = y_1 - M_{11}\left(\frac{\Delta y_1}{\Delta t}\right) - M_{12}\left(\frac{\Delta y_2}{\Delta t}\right) \tag{3.8}$$

and

$$z_2 = y_2 - M_{21}\left(\frac{\Delta y_1}{\Delta t}\right) - M_{22}\left(\frac{\Delta y_2}{\Delta t}\right), \tag{3.9}$$

where

$$M_{11} = \frac{a_{22}B_{11} + a_{21}B_{12}}{D}, \tag{3.10}$$

$$M_{12} = \frac{a_{11}B_{12} + a_{12}B_{11}}{D}, \tag{3.11}$$

$$M_{21} = \frac{a_{22}B_{21} + a_{21}B_{22}}{D}, \tag{3.12}$$

$$M_{22} = \frac{a_{11}B_{22} + a_{12}B_{21}}{D} \tag{3.13}$$

and

$$M = \begin{bmatrix} M_{11} & M_{12} \\ M_{21} & M_{22} \end{bmatrix}. \tag{3.14}$$

As Δt approaches zero, relations (3.8) and (3.9) become

$$z_1(t) = y_1(t) - M_{11}\frac{\mathrm{d}y_1(t)}{\mathrm{d}t} - M_{12}\frac{\mathrm{d}y_2(t)}{\mathrm{d}t} \tag{3.15}$$

and

$$z_2(t) = y_2(t) - M_{21}\frac{\mathrm{d}y_1(t)}{\mathrm{d}t} - M_{22}\frac{\mathrm{d}y_2(t)}{\mathrm{d}t}. \tag{3.16}$$

Relations (3.15) and (3.16) represent the open dynamic Leontief model. The main application of (3.15) and (3.16) concerns the case of determining the flow rate of net products $(y_1(t), y_2(t))$, given planned net consumption $(z_1(t), z_2(t))$.

Turning to the question of what conditions are required for balanced sustained growth of the open dynamic Leontief model represented by relations (3.15) and (3.16), a balanced sustained growth means

$$\frac{\mathrm{d}y_1(t)}{\mathrm{d}t} > 0, \qquad \frac{\mathrm{d}y_2(t)}{\mathrm{d}t} > 0. \tag{3.17}$$

Georgescu-Roegen (1971: 273f.) investigates the condition of balanced sustained growth of a system involving only one commodity. In order to have a solution of sustained growth, $y_1(t) - z_1(t)$ and $y_2(t) - z_2(t)$ must be inside the domain indicated in Fig. 3.1 *for any t* provided that $B_{11}B_{22} - B_{12}B_{21} > 0$. Because the rank of the inverse matrix of M is two for the system represented by relations (3.15) and (3.16), there always exists a solution of (3.15) and (3.16) with balanced sustained growth under certain conditions. This existence result is obtained using elementary arguments on linear inequalities (Gale 1960: Chapter 2; Rockafellar 1970: Part IV). However, the construction of a balanced sustained growth solution for the open dynamic Leontief model is complicated (see Appendix B).

To have a balanced sustained growth solution, the following four conditions must be satisfied (ξ_2 is the smaller eigenvalue of matrix M^{-1}):

$$y_1(0) - z_1(0) - \int_0^t \frac{\mathrm{d}z_1(\tau)}{\mathrm{d}\tau}\mathrm{e}^{-\xi_2\tau}\,\mathrm{d}\tau > 0, \tag{3.18}$$

$$y_2(0) - z_2(0) - \int_0^t \frac{\mathrm{d}z_2(\tau)}{\mathrm{d}\tau}\mathrm{e}^{-\xi_2\tau}\,\mathrm{d}\tau > 0, \tag{3.19}$$

$$y_1(0) = qy_2(0), \tag{3.20}$$

$$z_1(t) = qz_2(t), \tag{3.21}$$

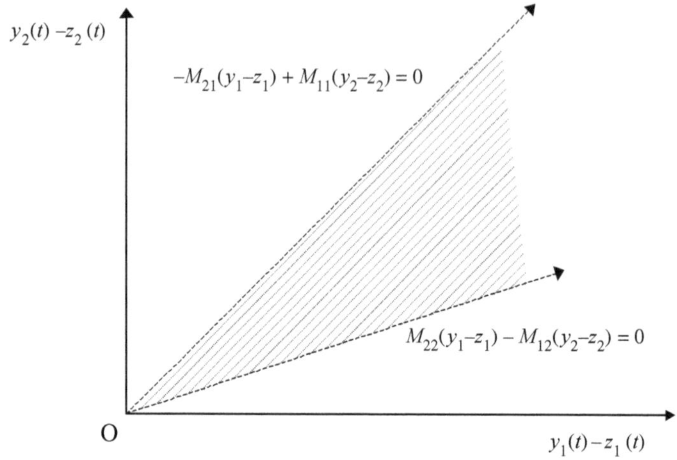

Figure 3.1 Domain of balanced sustained growth.

with

$$q = \frac{a - d - \sqrt{(a-d)^2 + 4bc}}{2c} > 0 \tag{3.22}$$

and

$$M^{-1} = \begin{bmatrix} a & b \\ c & d \end{bmatrix} = \frac{1}{\det(M)} \begin{bmatrix} M_{22} & -M_{12} \\ -M_{21} & M_{11} \end{bmatrix}. \tag{3.23}$$

Conditions (3.18) and (3.19) imply that the quantity of initial net product $y_i(0)$ in sector i must exceed the sum of initial net consumption $z_i(0)$ and the total increase in net consumption discounted by the smaller eigenvalue of matrix M^{-1} for any t.

As noticed by Georgescu-Roegen (1971: 273), 'the net product starts to increase the very moment the old level of consumption is decreased. This is the quasi explosive feature of the dynamic [Leontief] model'. While this quasi-explosive feature indicates an unrealistic aspect of the dynamic Leontief model, it is still possible to use the model as a planning tool for economic development. Given technological coefficients such as a_{ij} and B_{ij}, severe restrictions must be imposed on the initial values $(y_1(0), y_2(0))$ and the net product for consumption $(z_1(t), z_2(t))$.

Given a matrix M ($M_{11} = 1.3$; $M_{12} = 0.55$; $M_{21} = 0.5$; $M_{22} = 1.25$), Fig. 3.2 shows (a) the balanced sustained growth case and (b) the imbalanced case. Data on (a) are $y_1(0) = 3.08$, $y_2(0) = 2.8$, $z_1(t) = 2.2$ and $z_2(t) = 2$. Data on (b) are $y_1(0) = 3.1$, $y_2(0) = 2.8$, $z_1(t) = 2.2$ and $z_2(t) = 2$.

3 A dynamic Leontief model with two delays

We now consider the dynamic Leontief model with two delays. Admitting that an increase in the product flow requires creation of additional processes, it is

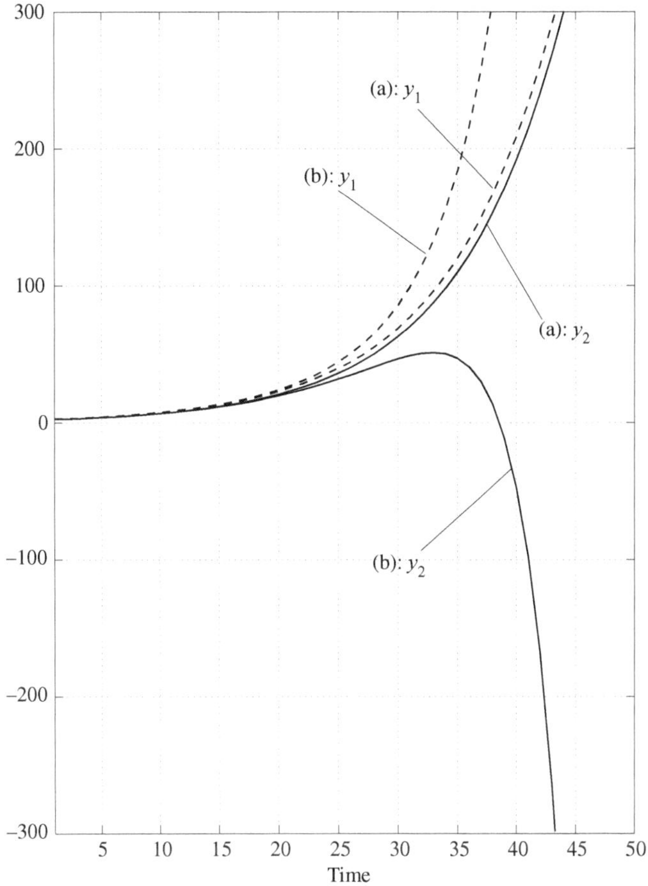

Figure 3.2 Open dynamic Leontief model: (a) balanced sustained growth case and (b) imbalanced case.

absolutely necessary to introduce two delays τ_1 and τ_2. τ_1 represents an additional time interval covering the time required for building and priming the new processes after the additional funds $B_{11}\Delta x_1$ and $B_{21}\Delta x_1$ have been accumulated during Δt. τ_2 represents an additional time interval covering the time required for building and priming the new processes after the additional funds $B_{12}\Delta x_2$ and $B_{22}\Delta x_2$ have been accumulated during Δt. So, instead of (3.6), the following relations must be used:

$$\Delta B_1 = B_{11}\Delta x_1(t - \Delta t - \tau_1) + B_{12}\Delta x_2(t - \Delta t - \tau_2) \tag{3.24}$$

and

$$\Delta B_2 = B_{21}\Delta x_1(t - \Delta t - \tau_1) + B_{22}\Delta x_2(t - \Delta t - \tau_2). \tag{3.25}$$

Combining the relations (3.7), (3.24) and (3.25) and taking the limit $\Delta t \to 0$ produces

$$z_1(t) = a_{11}x_1(t) - a_{12}x_2(t) - B_{11}\frac{\mathrm{d}x_1(t-\tau_1)}{\mathrm{d}t} - B_{12}\frac{\mathrm{d}x_2(t-\tau_2)}{\mathrm{d}t} \tag{3.26}$$

and

$$z_2(t) = -a_{21}x_1(t) + a_{22}x_2(t) - B_{21}\frac{\mathrm{d}x_1(t-\tau_1)}{\mathrm{d}t} - B_{22}\frac{\mathrm{d}x_2(t-\tau_2)}{\mathrm{d}t}. \tag{3.27}$$

The Laplace transforms of (3.26) and (3.27) are

$$\begin{bmatrix} a_{11} - B_{11}s\mathrm{e}^{-\tau_1 s} & -a_{12} - B_{12}s\mathrm{e}^{-\tau_2 s} \\ -a_{21} - B_{21}s\mathrm{e}^{-\tau_1 s} & a_{22} - B_{22}s\mathrm{e}^{-\tau_2 s} \end{bmatrix}\begin{bmatrix} X_1(s) \\ X_2(s) \end{bmatrix} = \begin{bmatrix} Z_1(s) + B_{11}P_1(s) + B_{12}P_2(s) \\ Z_2(s) + B_{21}P_1(s) + B_{22}P_2(s) \end{bmatrix}, \tag{3.28}$$

where

$$P_1(s) = -x_1(-\tau_1) + s\mathrm{e}^{-\tau_1 s}\int_{-\tau_1}^{0} x_1(\xi)\mathrm{e}^{-\xi s}\,\mathrm{d}\xi \tag{3.29}$$

and

$$P_2(s) = -x_2(-\tau_2) + s\mathrm{e}^{-\tau_2 s}\int_{-\tau_2}^{0} x_2(\xi)\mathrm{e}^{-\xi s}\,\mathrm{d}\xi. \tag{3.30}$$

In relation (3.28), $X_i(s)$ is the Laplace transform of $x_i(t)$ and $Z_i(s)$ that of $z_i(t)$.

To have the inverse Laplace transforms of $X_1(s)$ and $X_2(t)$ requires the following proposition (see Appendix C).

Proposition 1 *In order for* $f(s) = -\beta s\mathrm{e}^{-\tau_1 s} - \gamma s\mathrm{e}^{-\tau_2 s} = 0$ *to have no zeros over the half-plane* $\mathrm{Re}(s) > 0$*, if* $\tau_1 > \tau_2$*, then* $\gamma > \beta$*, or if* $\tau_1 < \tau_2$*, then* $\gamma < \beta$*, where*

$$\beta = a_{12}B_{21} + a_{22}B_{11} \tag{3.31}$$

and

$$\gamma = a_{11}B_{22} + a_{21}B_{12}. \tag{3.32}$$

In Appendix C it is shown that, due to the introduction of unavoidable delays, the Hawkins–Simon condition (1949) does not hold for the dynamic Leontief model with delay. So, the following conditions must be satisfied:

$$\alpha = a_{11}a_{22} - a_{12}a_{21} = 0 \tag{3.33}$$

and

$$\delta = B_{11}B_{22} - B_{12}B_{21} = 0. \tag{3.34}$$

The final form of the Laplace transforms of the model is as follows:

$$\begin{bmatrix} X_1(s) \\ X_2(s) \end{bmatrix} = \frac{1}{f(s)} \begin{bmatrix} a_{22} - B_{22}se^{-\tau_2 s} & a_{12} + B_{12}se^{-\tau_2 s} \\ a_{21} + B_{21}se^{-\tau_1 s} & a_{11} - B_{11}se^{-\tau_1 s} \end{bmatrix} \times \begin{bmatrix} Z_1(s) + B_{11}P_1(s) + B_{12}P_2(s) \\ Z_2(s) + B_{21}P_1(s) + B_{22}P_2(s) \end{bmatrix}, \tag{3.35}$$

where

$$f(s) = -\beta se^{-\tau_1 s} - \gamma se^{-\tau_2 s}. \tag{3.36}$$

Using relations (3.28) and (3.34), β and γ can be rewritten as

$$\beta = (a_{11}B_{21} + a_{21}B_{11})t_1 \tag{3.37}$$

and

$$\gamma = (a_{11}B_{21} + a_{21}B_{11})t_2, \tag{3.38}$$

where

$$\frac{a_{12}}{a_{11}} = \frac{a_{22}}{a_{21}} = t_1 \tag{3.39}$$

and

$$\frac{B_{12}}{B_{11}} = \frac{B_{22}}{B_{21}} = t_2. \tag{3.40}$$

Relations (3.37) and (3.38) suggest that the condition of Proposition 1 can be represented in terms of t_1 and t_2 instead of using β and γ as follows: in order for $f(s) = -\beta se^{-\tau_1 s} - \gamma se^{-\tau_2 s} = 0$ to have no zeros over the half-plane $\mathrm{Re}(s) > 0$, if $\tau_1 > \tau_2$, then $t_2 > t_1$, or if $\tau_1 < \tau_2$, then $t_2 < t_1$.

To summarize, the following are the conditions for $f(s) = \alpha - \beta se^{-\tau_1 s} - \gamma se^{-\tau_2 s} + \delta s^2 e^{-(\tau_1+\tau_2)s} = 0$ to have no zeros over the half-plane $\mathrm{Re}(s) > 0$:

Case (a): If $\tau_1 = \tau_2$, then $\alpha = a_{11}a_{22} - a_{12}a_{21} = 0$ and $\delta = B_{11}B_{22} - B_{12}B_{21} = 0$.

Case (b): If $\tau_1 < \tau_2$, then $t_2 < t_1$, $\alpha = a_{11}a_{22} - a_{12}a_{21} = 0$ and $\delta = B_{11}B_{22} - B_{12}B_{21} = 0$.

Case (c): If $\tau_1 > \tau_2$, then $t_2 > t_1$, $\alpha = a_{11}a_{22} - a_{12}a_{21} = 0$ and $\delta = B_{11}B_{22} - B_{12}B_{21} = 0$.

Suppose $\tau_1 > \tau_2$. $t_1 < t_2$ implies that if the two fund elements B_{12} and B_{22} in P_2 are larger than the two fund elements B_{11} and B_{22} in P_1 in comparison to the relative size of the flow elements in P_1 and P_2, then the behaviour of the dynamic Leontief model with delay is not affected by τ_1 that is larger than τ_2.

It should be noted that the following condition is satisfied for the dynamic Leontief model with two delays:

$$\begin{vmatrix} a_{11} + B_{11} & -a_{12} + B_{12} \\ -a_{21} + B_{21} & a_{22} + B_{22} \end{vmatrix} = \beta + \gamma > 0. \tag{3.41}$$

This is a kind of extension of the Hawkins–Simon condition in the case of the dynamic Leontief model with delays. However, because of the existence of delays, it is necessary to have an additional condition on the relative sizes of β and γ depending on the relative sizes of τ_1 and τ_2 given in the three cases above.

Figure 3.3 shows three cases: (a) $\tau_1 = \tau_2$, (b) $\tau_1 < \tau_2$, (c) $\tau_1 > \tau_2$. Cases (b) and (c) show that the smaller delay determines the overall behaviour of $x_1(t)$ and $x_2(t)$. For example, the size of τ_2, the smaller delay, is 100 units in Case (c) of Fig. 3.3 and 10 units in Fig. 3.4.

The following data are used in Fig. 3.3(a)–(c):

(a) $a_{11} = 1, a_{12} = 2, a_{21} = 2, a_{22} = 4; B_{11} = 0.1, B_{12} = 0.2, B_{21} = 0.2, B_{22} = 0.4; \tau_1 = 0.1, \tau_2 = 0.1; x_1(-\tau_1) = \sin(-\tau_1) + 4, x_2(-\tau_2) = \sin(-\tau_2) + 5; z_1(t) = \sin(5t) + 1, z_2(t) = \sin(5t) + 2.$

(b) $a_{11} = 1, a_{12} = 2, a_{21} = 2, a_{22} = 4; B_{11} = 0.3, B_{12} = 0.1, B_{21} = 0.3, B_{22} = 0.1; \tau_1 = 0.1; \tau_2 = 0.2, x_1(-\tau_1) = \sin(-\tau_1) + 4, x_2(-\tau_2) = \sin(-\tau_2) + 5; z_1(t) = \sin(5t) + 1, z_2(t) = \sin(5t) + 2.$

(c) $a_{11} = 1, a_{12} = 2, a_{21} = 2, a_{22} = 4; B_{11} = 0.1, B_{12} = 0.3, B_{21} = 0.1, B_{22} = 0.3; \tau_1 = 0.2, \tau_2 = 0.1; x_1(-\tau_1) = \sin(-\tau_1) + 4, x_2(-\tau_2) = \sin(-\tau_2) + 5; z_1(t) = \sin(5t) + 1, z_2(t) = \sin(5t) + 2.$

The discontinuity of $x_1(t)$ and $x_2(t)$ that appeared in the early stages disappears as time passes (Fig. 3.4). The negative values of $x_1(t)$ and $x_2(t)$ in Figs 3.3 and 3.4 must be regarded as relative because a part of production flows is always consumed to repair fund elements in the present dynamic Leontief model with delay.

4 Conclusion

The introduction of delays into the dynamic Leontief model in the last section was aimed at removing unrealistic features of the open dynamic Leontief model. As shown in Fig. 3.4, the quasi-explosive feature of the open dynamic Leontief model has partially been eliminated. However, dynamic models treated here still belong to a class of systems called reactive models (Rosen 1985). The behaviour of reactive models depends only on present and past states. Many biological systems and social systems have a peculiar character that cannot be represented by reactive models. These systems violate the mechanism of reactive systems and are called 'anticipatory systems' whose behaviour depends on future states or future inputs as well (Rosen 1985). An anticipatory behaviour is one in which a change of states

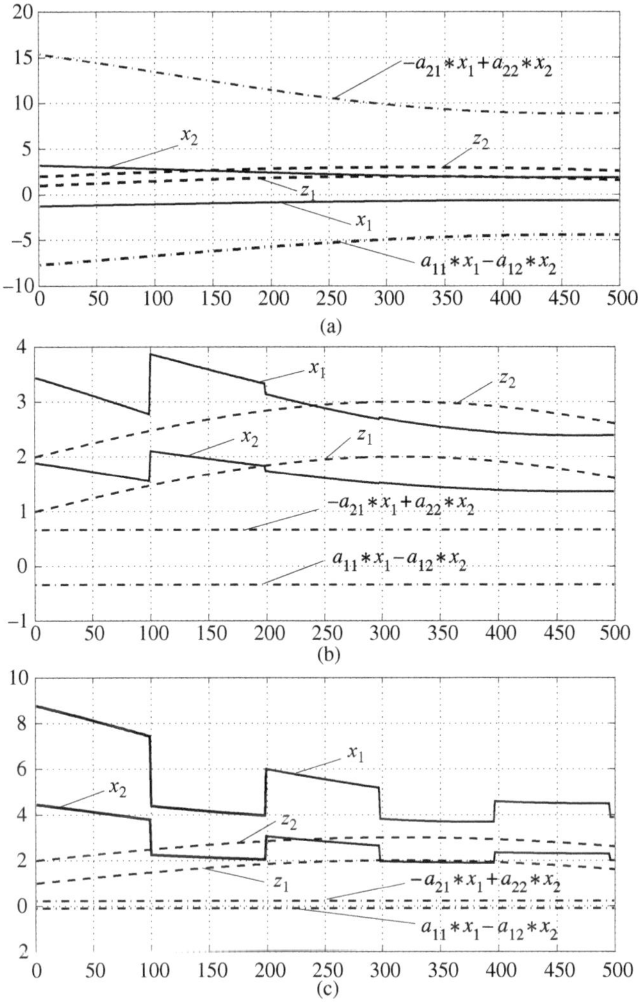

Figure 3.3 Numerical result for a dynamic Leontief model with two delays.

in the present occurs as a function of some predicted future states, and that the agent through which the prediction is made must be a model in the broadest sense. We will use concepts from anticipatory systems theory. Anticipatory behaviour is especially important when we deal with the issue of sustainability. Rosen writes

> a negatively phototropic organism changes state in the present in accord with a prediction about the future, made on the basis of a model which associates darkness (a neutral characteristic in itself) with some quality which favors survival.
>
> (Rosen 1985: 7)

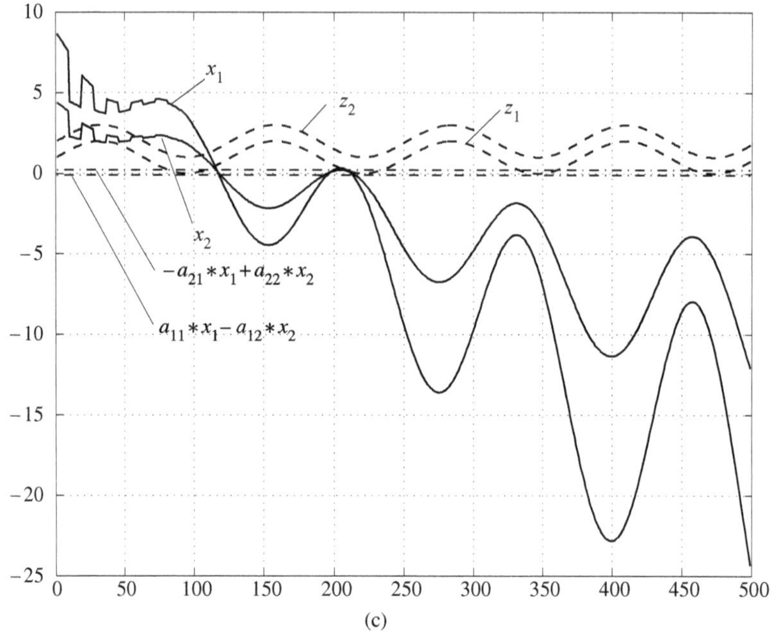

Figure 3.4 Numerical result for a dynamic Leontief model with two delays for case (c) in Fig. 3.3.

Unfortunately, the process of anticipatory behaviour within a system and possible future effects of this process on each component of that system cannot be represented by an arithmomorphic model such as reactive models. The reason is simple: anticipatory processes are deeply associated with the process of evolution in which qualitative change and its dialectical feature escape any attempt to represent the qualitative change in terms of a mathematical model.

According to Georgescu-Roegen, economic life transgresses not only the inorganic but also the organic domain. Because of the intrinsic nature of humans as economic agents, social evolution displays a strong interplay between the institutional aspects and the exosomatic mode by which human wants are satisfied through the incessant transformation of low-entropy resources into high-entropy waste. Economic prediction is not available under perfect uncertainty, either. According to Georgescu-Roegen, evolutionary change cannot adequately be represented by dynamic models used by economists. He has two basic objections to the use of dynamic economic models: (i) Dynamic models allow for the production of commodities but not for the reproduction of the production process itself. The production of production processes is inherent to human exosomatic evolution. This omission is responsible for the quasi-explosive feature typical of dynamic models. (ii) Dynamic models have difficulty in throwing any light on the problem of how growth comes about within the economic process. Truly endogenous aspects of economic life cannot adequately be simulated by dynamic models.

The previous model is dependent on the past state of the system. However, a truly astonishing aspect of humans as economic agents is that they may envision future states of a system in which they live. Strictly speaking, an anticipatory system is one in which the present change of state depends on future envisioned circumstances, rather than merely on the present or past. This type of system has heretofore been excluded from system theory. This is natural because it violates the causal foundation on which all theoretical science must rest. In a sense, it is forbidden to allow the present change of state to depend upon future states. This is another reason why arguments from final causes have been excluded from science. In the Aristotelian parlance, a final cause is one which involves a purpose or goal. As in the case of organisms, we desperately need internal predictive models of the economic processes and their environment to deal with sustainability issues.

4 Information, pseudo-measures and entropy: an elaboration on Georgescu-Roegen's critique

1 Introduction

When new concepts are introduced in science, they are usually identified by new names. However, the new concepts are sometimes labelled either by using words taken from common vocabulary or by adopting a name which is already used in other fields. The term 'information' is an example of the first case, and the use of the term 'entropy' in information science and cybernetics is an example of the second case.

Information is a highly ambiguous term. Thus, this name turns out to be a continuous source of misunderstandings (Bar-Hillel 1955; Tillman and Russell 1965). As Georgescu-Roegen (1977*a*: 189) aptly remarks, 'the meaning of "information" shifts freely among that of "messages", "choice", "uncertainty", to be finally confused with that of "knowledge" in the academic sense of this term'. This aggravated situation has led none other than C. E. Shannon to lament that the concept of information originally set out in communication engineering has been 'ballooned to an importance beyond its actual accomplishments' and that 'the basic results of the subject are aimed in a very specific direction, a direction that is not necessarily relevant to such fields as psychology, economics, and other social sciences' (Shannon: 1956).

On the other hand, negative entropy in information science is mathematically similar to Ludwig Boltzmann's famous formula for statistical entropy. The purely algebraic relationship between the two concepts has led many scholars to claim that negative entropy and information are essentially identical (e.g. Lewis 1930; Brillouin 1951*b*; Tribus and McIrvine 1971; Ayres 1994). It is beyond doubt that some connections and similarities between entropy and information exist: 'no information [in the broadest sense] can be obtained, transmitted, or received without the expenditure of some free energy' and 'like free energy (negentropy), information is subject to degradation' (Georgescu-Roegen 1971: 405). However, these connections and similarities cannot justify, by themselves, the alleged equivalence between the two concepts (Mayumi 1993*b*).

The aim of this chapter is twofold: (1) to clarify some of the issues related to the concept of information based on Georgescu-Roegen's critique of the measure of information; (2) to examine the claim of the alleged equivalence between negative entropy and information elaborating on Georgescu-Roegen's analysis (1971: Appendix B, 1977*a*, 1990).

Section 2 introduces Shannon's concept of information and discusses related issues, together with a historical development of the concept of information in communication engineering. Section 3 evaluates critically N. Wiener's concept of information and uncertainty. Any measure of uncertainty is shown to be not an ordinal variable but a pseudo-measure in the sense that two pseudo-measures of the same variable can yield entirely different rankings. It is also shown that the expected amount of information for a continuous distribution cannot be obtained by passage to the limit from that for a discrete distribution as in mathematical analysis. Section 4 shows that the alleged equivalence between negative entropy and information is physically baseless through close examination of the works of L. Szilard, E. T. Jaynes and L. Brillouin. Section 5 treats Georgescu-Roegen's epistemological position (1976, 1992) connected with his critique of the measure of information and of the alleged equivalence between negative entropy and information.

2 Shannon's concept of information: a case of misnomer

Shannon's concept of information has its roots in a classical paper by H. Nyquist (1924). Nyquist uses the term 'intelligence', instead of 'information', in the sense of military intelligence during wartime. Nyquist considers two fundamental factors – signal shaping and choice of codes – for improving the speed of transmission of signal elements by telegraph. Nyquist then derives a formula for the speed of transmission of intelligence. His approach makes perfect sense from one of the objectives of communication engineering, i.e. transmitting signal elements as speedily as possible.

However, Georgescu-Roegen (1977*a*) correctly indicates that, from the beginning, a serious and regrettable imbroglio was introduced into communication engineering by Nyquist and R. V. L. Hartley (1928). This was continued later by Shannon (Shannon and Weaver 1964), followed by many writers. These authors, Shannon in particular, regard two different concepts – the number of messages to be transmitted and the capacity of a communication channel – as equivalent and call them as information.

In order to explain the issue more clearly, let us consider a channel capable of transmitting n distinct signal elements and assume that there are M distinct messages. If M messages are represented by the codified n^N sequences of signal elements of the same duration, the number of signal elements in each message, N, must be chosen to satisfy the following inequality:

$$n^{N-1} < M \leq n^N. \tag{4.1}$$

In this inequality, there are two distinct concepts: one is the totality of messages M and the other the number of different sequences of signal elements (with given length N) n^N. The latter is a measure of the capacity of the corresponding channel. Shannon as well as other communication engineers should have treated these concepts as distinct ones. Capacity is a characteristic of a communication channel adopted and varies with technological progress. On the other hand, the totality of messages to be transmitted is independent of the type of communication systems used. In my view, a more appropriate choice of a name could have been *capacity of channel transmission*, instead of information.

From an engineering viewpoint, it is perfectly reasonable to regard the capacity of a communication channel with s identical channels, for example, to be s times the capacity of one channel of the same type. Thus, the following definition on the capacity of channel transmission using the logarithmic function makes perfect sense:

$$\text{Capacity of channel transmission} = \log_2 n^N = N \log_2 n \;\; \text{(bits)}. \tag{4.2}$$

The capacity of channel transmission per signal element independently of the length of a message is:

$$\text{Capacity of channel transmission per signal} = \log_2 n. \tag{4.3}$$

Because of the confusion of the totality of messages with the capacity of a channel, it might be said that $\log_2 n$ measures the amount of information per signal element. However, this interpretation should not have been adopted. Hartley and Shannon define information without careful discrimination between the two concepts. Hartley writes:

> What we have done then is to take as our practical measure of information the logarithm of the possible number of symbol sequences [$\log_2 n^N$].
>
> (Hartley 1928: 540)

Shannon regards $\log_2 M$ as a measure of information in one place:

> If the number of messages in the set is finite then this number or any monotonic function of this number [$\log_2 M$] can be regarded as a measure of the information.
>
> (Shannon and Weaver 1964: 32)

However, elsewhere Shannon defines H as a measure of information, even though H is actually the capacity of channel transmission per signal for a stochastic case to be shown later:

> Quantities of the form $H = -\sum p_i \log_2 p_i$ play a central role in information theory as measures of information.
>
> (Shannon and Weaver 1964: 50)

Let us consider a source which produces n independent signal elements with probability p_i ($i = 1, 2, \ldots, n$). The number of different sequences of signal elements with a given length N, which supplies again a measure of the capacity of the corresponding channel in a stochastic case, is given by the combinatorial formula

$$W = \frac{N!}{N_1!N_2!\cdots N_n!}, \tag{4.4}$$

where

$$N_i = Np_i, \quad \sum_{i=1}^{n} p_i = 1. \tag{4.5}$$

Using Stirling's asymptotic formula, equation (4.3) becomes

$$\begin{aligned}\text{Capacity of channel transmission per signal} &= \lim_{N\to\infty} \frac{\log_2 W}{N} \\ &= H \ \text{(bits)},\end{aligned} \tag{4.6}$$

for a stochastic case. Shannon interprets H not as a coefficient related to the number of some special categories of signals but as a measure of 'information, choice, and uncertainty' (Shannon and Weaver 1964: 50).

There is another issue that can hardly be overemphasized: Shannon reaches the function H not through the procedure above but through two different routes. One is an axiomatic treatment based on three formal conditions. The other is based on the idea of typical sequences. Let us examine here only the second route. Shannon calls any message in which signal elements appear with their expected relative frequencies as typical (Shannon and Weaver 1964: 54). The probability of this particular message is roughly

$$p \doteq p_1^{p_1 N} p_2^{p_2 N} \ldots p_n^{p_n N}. \tag{4.7}$$

From this equation, Shannon arrives at the function H:

$$-\frac{\log_2 p}{N} \doteq H = -\sum p_i \log_2 p_i. \tag{4.8}$$

According to Shannon's definition, H is the information per signal (which is a wrong interpretation in the present author's view). However, a close examination shows that the information per signal in any typical sequence becomes zero as $N \to \infty$, because it can be shown by using Stirling's asymptotic formula that

$$\lim_{N\to\infty} \frac{\log_2(Wp)}{N} = 0. \tag{4.9}$$

Let us turn to the final issue in this section. Even though Shannon himself admits that 'there is still considerable sampling error in these figures due to identifying the observed sample frequencies with the prediction probabilities' (1951: 64), he nevertheless has tried to identify a source of vernacular language with an ergodic stochastic Markov chain (1951 and 1964). The appearance of each character in any language is subject to some kind of 'mechanism' inherent in the language and not independent of the roots of the language, its syntax and so many other factors. Naturally, those factors cannot be treated in the framework of a stochastic chain. The frequency of each character thus can never be identified with a random mechanism conceived by Shannon. On this issue, Georgescu-Roegen's right verdict is:

> We must note however that this position, by now traditional in the so-called statistical interpretation of many phenomena, glosses over the fundamental difference between statistical probability and the ergodic limit in a non-stochastic sequence, such as the sequence of the decimal digits of $\frac{1}{7}$, for example.
>
> (Georgescu-Roegen 1977*a*: 193)

3 Wiener's concept of information and related issues

In contrast to the concept of information investigated by Nyquist, Hartley and Shannon, Wiener's information concept is *ab initio* related to the knowledge that *a certain stochastic event has occurred.* Wiener defines the measure of information (information$_w$ for short, following Georgescu-Roegen's notation) as $-\log_2 p_A$, knowing that some event A with probability p_A has occurred (1961: 61). Wiener's excellent idea recalls G. L. S. Shackle's idea of a measure of surprise in the face of uncertainty (1955). Because the smaller is the *ex ante* degree of belief in a stochastic event, the greater is *ex post* surprise at the knowledge that the event has actually occurred, any positive decreasing function with respect to p_A can be regarded as a measure of information$_w$:

$$\text{Amount of information}_w = F(p_A). \tag{4.10}$$

If probability distribution of a stochastic event is introduced into Wiener's original framework, the expected amount of information$_w$ is

$$\text{Expected amount of information}_w = \sum_{i=1}^{n} p_i F(p_i). \tag{4.11}$$

The function H is a member of this general form. The general form can also be regarded as a measure of uncertainty. However, if one wants to regard the general form $\sum_{i=1}^{n} p_i F(p_i)$ *only* as a measure of uncertainty, what conditions should be imposed on the form? Any measure of uncertainty should have the property that it attains the maximum value when all the outcomes of a stochastic distribution are equally probable and reaches the minimum value when one outcome is absolutely certain. Georgescu-Roegen (1971) derives a necessary and sufficient condition for the general form to have the property that the function $pF(p)$ be a concave function over [0,1]. Besides the function H, there are many instances of the general form of uncertainty, one being Octav Onicescu's informational energy (Georgescu-Roegen 1977*a*: 203):

$$\text{Informational energy} = G = 1 - \sum_{i=1}^{n} p_i^2. \tag{4.12}$$

The general measure of uncertainty represented by $\sum_{i=1}^{n} p_i F(p_i)$ is called pseudo-measure by Georgescu-Roegen (1971). The pseudo-measures are not ordinal variables because they do not necessarily stand in the same ordinal relationship with each other if the variable basis changes. As Georgescu-Roegen (1971: 389) mentions, 'because of the dialectical nature of the pseudo measures, there is no way of eliminating the cases in which two pseudo measures of the same variable yield entirely different rankings'. By taking the total differential of H and G, for instance, it can easily be shown that for $n > 2$, there are cases in which $\mathrm{d}H$ and $\mathrm{d}G$ do not necessarily have the same sign for some combination of $\mathrm{d}p_i$'s. Georgescu-Roegen (1964) establishes an interesting result related to the issue of measurability: the Archimedean Axiom is not a sufficient condition for an ordinal set to be ordinally measurable. In plain terms, the Archimedean property is in essence tantamount to the example presented by Georgescu-Roegen: if the water in a reservoir is to be measured with the aid of a pail, people must be able to empty the reservoir by removing a finite number of pails of water (1964: 239).

Up to this point, there has been consideration only of the cases of discrete distributions. However, Wiener defined a measure of information for continuous distributions (information$_{\mathrm{wc}}$ for short) based on the analogy of discrete distributions, $\sum_{i=1}^{n} p_i F(p_i)$, without considering serious and problematic issues (1961: 61),

$$\text{The expected amount of information}_{\mathrm{wc}} = \int_{-\infty}^{\infty} f(x) \log_2 f(x)\, \mathrm{d}x, \tag{4.13}$$

where

$$\int_{-\infty}^{\infty} f(x)\, \mathrm{d}x = 1. \tag{4.14}$$

First of all, because the probability that a stochastic variable X, for example, is equal to any value x in a given domain is zero,

$$\text{Information}_{\mathrm{w}} = F[\mathrm{Prob}(X = x)] = F(0). \tag{4.15}$$

According to Wiener's idea of defining information, $F(0)$ should be infinite: people never imagined this event to occur but it actually occurred. In fact, Wiener's function, $-\log_2 x$, becomes infinite as $x \to 0$.

Second, it is possible to think that $\mathrm{Prob}(X = x_1)$ is greater than $\mathrm{Prob}(X = x_2)$ if $f(x_1) > f(x_2)$. Hence, it seems 'reasonable' to replace the definition of information$_{\mathrm{w}}$ by

$$\text{Information}_{\mathrm{wc}} \text{ of } (X = x) = F[f(x)]. \tag{4.16}$$

Wiener's definition on his information for continuous distribution is based on the idea that, by a passage to limit, the formula for the information for continuous cases, $\lim_{n\to\infty}\sum_{i=1}^{n} p_i F(p_i)$ is equivalent to $\int_{-\infty}^{\infty} f(x)F[f(x)]\,\mathrm{d}x$. Wiener should not have adopted his definition for the continuous case.

In order to see this, following Georgescu-Roegen (1971: 397), let us assume that $h(p) = pF(p)$ is strictly concave and that $h(0) = 0$. Under these assumptions,

$$h(x) \geq \frac{y-x}{y}h(0) + \frac{x}{y}h(y) > \frac{x}{y}h(y), \tag{4.17}$$

where

$$0 < x < y. \tag{4.18}$$

Hence, the following relation holds for any x, $0 < x < y$:

$$F(x) > F(y). \tag{4.19}$$

Let us assume further that

$$\int_{-\infty}^{t} f(u)\,\mathrm{d}u, \tag{4.20}$$

where $f(u)$ is a probability density, is absolutely continuous. Then there exist n intervals $-\infty < x_1 < \cdots < x_{n-1} < +\infty$ such that the probability over each of these intervals is $1/n$. For this way of dividing the stochastic field,

$$\Phi_F(\vec{p}) = \sum_{i=1}^{n} p_i F(p_i) = F(1/n). \tag{4.21}$$

From (4.19), $F(1/n)$ has a limit, finite or infinite, for $n \to \infty$:

$$\lim_{n\to\infty} \Phi_F(n) = \lim_{p\to 0} F(p). \tag{4.22}$$

Thus '*the expected amount of information for an absolutely continuous distribution depends only of the ordinal measure adopted – more exactly, on the* $\lim F(p)$ *for* $p \to 0$ *– and not on the distribution itself*' (Georgescu-Roegen 1971: 398).

For $F(p) = -\log p$,

$$\lim_{n\to\infty} \Phi_F(n) = +\infty. \tag{4.23}$$

Hence, it is proved that Boltzmann's H function cannot be extended to a continuous distribution and that Wiener's definition on information given by (4.13) is not acceptable. It is also proved that Wiener's concept of information has nothing to do with entropy in physics. Boltzmann makes a similar mistake when he introduces his H-function, by using the Stirling formula (1964: 55–62).

4 The alleged equivalence between information and negative entropy

There can be no doubt about the fact that to receive, store and transmit information in general requires some available energy. Just like energy, information of any kind is subject to degradation during the process of transmission, for example, in the sense that the meaning of messages might sometimes change because of errors of recording. Thus, there exist some connections and similarities between information and negative entropy. However, some scholars have gone beyond this: 'it is now established to the satisfaction of virtually all physicists that information is the reduction of uncertainty and that uncertainty and entropy are essentially identical (not mere analogs)' (Ayres 1994: 36).

There are three principal researchers regarded as responsible for the alleged equivalence between information and negative entropy: Szilard (1964, originally published in Germany in 1929), Jaynes (1957) and Brillouin (1950, 1951*a*,*b*, 1953, 1962). Let us examine their works closely in sequence.

Szilard (1929) considers several inanimate devices which can achieve the same essential result as would be achieved by the intervention of intelligent beings like Maxwell's demon. In order to examine his idea, let us introduce briefly one of these devices. At a given time, a piston is inserted into a cylinder. Then a given molecule is caught in the upper or lower part of the cylinder. The molecule bounces many times against the piston and, in the process, does a certain amount of work on the piston (the work corresponding to the isothermal expansion of an ideal gas). The piston moves up or down until reaching the top or bottom of the cylinder, depending on whether the molecule is caught in the lower or upper half of the cylinder divided by the piston. After the piston has reached the top or the bottom of the cylinder, it is removed. This procedure can be repeated as many times as desired. In Szilard's device, the human intervention (ignoring biological phenomena) consists only in the coupling of a coordinate x (determining the altitude of the molecule) with another coordinate y (the value of which is either 1 or -1, determining the position of the lever by which an upward or downward motion is imparted to the piston). Szilard derives some conditions on the magnitudes of entropies produced by the measurements if the law of entropy is not to be violated, e.g.

$$\mathrm{e}^{\,S_1/k} + \mathrm{e}^{-S_2/k} \leq 1, \tag{4.24}$$

where entropy S_1 is produced when, during the measurement, y assumes the value 1 and entropy S_2, when y assumes the value -1, and k is the Boltzmann–Planck constant. Szilard showed that, as long as the entropies S_1 and S_2 satisfy the inequality (4.24), the expected decrease of entropy caused by the later utilization of the measurement is fully compensated; thus, the second law of thermodynamics is not violated.

However, A. Tsuchida devises a similar mental apparatus in order to show that Szilard's apparatus, as well as Tsuchida's, is not compatible with the framework of statistical thermodynamics (Tsuchida 1992). Let us explain Tsuchida's apparatus

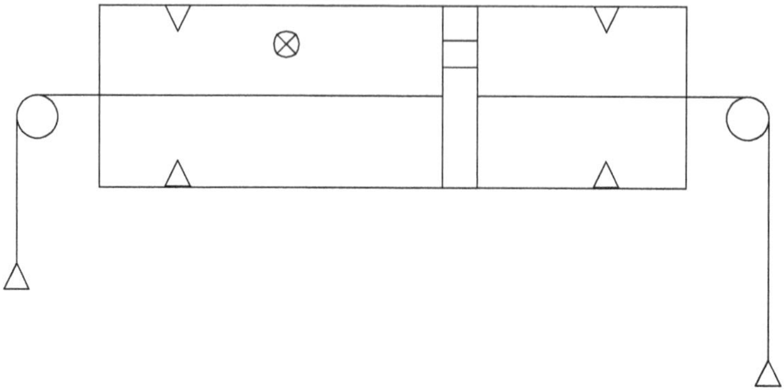

Figure 4.1 Tsuchida's apparatus.

(Fig. 4.1). A molecule is inside a container and two weights are tied with a piston with a small hole. There are four catches fixed on the container so that the piston stays inside a pre-assigned area of the container. Suppose that the molecule is on the left hand of the piston; a molecule bounces against the piston many times and the piston moves to the right until it touches two of the catches. As time passes, the molecule could pass into the right hand of the piston, and then the piston begins to move to the opposite direction. This procedure can continue indefinitely. It is important to take care of the adjustment of the size of the hole on the piston: the mean stay time of the molecule on the right or left of the piston should be sufficiently long compared with the duration in which the molecule bounces against the piston. Thus, it is possible to obtain a perpetual motion of the second kind without any measurements or information!

Then what is wrong with Szilard's idea? The concept of irreversibility (or entropy) is the cornerstone in classical thermodynamics. However, in quantum mechanical systems there is a *principle of detailed balancing*: 'in equilibrium the number of processes which destroy a situation A and produce a situation B will be equal to the number of processes which produce A and destroy B' (Haar 1954). According to this principle, all phenomena should be reversible. In order to derive irreversibility, statistical thermodynamics is constructed on this principle and the other 'compromising' principle: statistical thermodynamics approaches should be applied to physical systems with 'many' molecules (at least of the order of Avogadro number).[1] In Szilard's model, the principle of detailed balancing implies that a molecule can move between the left and right part of the container with an equal probability. However, the model, unfortunately, violates the other principles of statistical mechanics. The concept of entropy, for example, must not apply to a system with few molecules, which is the case in Szilard's model. Thus, Szilard's model is, from the outset, incompatible with the framework of statistical thermodynamics.

Jaynes proposes a scheme of maximum-entropy inference (1957). For the sake of brevity, the simplest formulation of Jaynes' idea is considered. Jaynes' concern is how to find a probability assignment with no bias based on the expectation value of a given function. One must find a probability assignment to maximize (4.25) subject to constraints (4.26) and (4.27):

$$H(p_1 \ldots p_n) = -\sum_{l=1}^{n} p_l \ln p_l. \tag{4.25}$$

$$\overline{f(x)} = \sum_{l=1}^{n} p_l f(x_l). \tag{4.26}$$

$$\sum_{l=1}^{n} p_l = 1. \tag{4.27}$$

Jaynes calls H the entropy or uncertainty. Lagrange multipliers λ and μ can be introduced in the usual way:

$$p_l = e^{-\lambda - \mu f(x_l)}, \tag{4.28}$$

$$\overline{f(x)} = -\frac{\partial}{\partial \mu} \ln Z(\mu), \tag{4.29}$$

$$\lambda = \ln Z(\mu), \tag{4.30}$$

where

$$Z(\mu) = \sum_{l=1}^{n} e^{-\mu f(x_l)}. \tag{4.31}$$

However, Jaynes' formulation is essentially identical to a problem in statistical thermodynamics: 'to determine the distribution of an assembly of N identical systems over the possible states in which this assembly can find itself, given that the energy of the assembly is a constant E (Schrödinger 1957: 1). Let a_l be the number of systems out of N belonging to the state l whose eigenvalue of energy is ϵ_l. Mathematically, the problem is one of maximization of (4.32) subject to (4.33) and (4.34):

$$\ln P = \ln \left[\frac{N!}{a_1! a_2! \cdots a_l! \cdots} \right], \tag{4.32}$$

$$\sum_{l} a_l = N, \tag{4.33}$$

$$\sum_{l} \epsilon_l a_l = E. \tag{4.34}$$

The quantities a_l/N and E in Schrödinger's formulation correspond, respectively, to p_l and $\overline{f(x)}$ in Jaynes'.

It is true that Jaynes' formulation is mathematically identical to Schrödinger's, which is based on Gibbs' idea. However, from a physical point of view, Schrödinger's formulation differs from that of Jaynes' in two important ways.

First, the interaction between the possible states is so weak that the energy of interaction can be disregarded. Thus, it is safe to speak of an energy of each of the individual states and that the sum of their energies is equal to E. As Schrödinger aptly remarks, the 'distinguished role of the energy is, therefore, simply that it is a constant of the motion' (Schrödinger 1957).

Second, a much more important point is related to one of the two fundamental principles in statistical thermodynamics. Because N is enormously large, the total number of distributions is very nearly exhausted by the sum of those P's whose number sets a_l do not deviate appreciably from the set which gives P its maximum value subject to the two constraints. This assumption is rigorously correct for $N \to \infty$, which corresponds physically to an 'infinite' heat-bath. Even though the 'enormity' of the number N is dialectical, the use of Shannon's measure of uncertainty cannot be justified because the number of elements usually considered in communication systems is too small.

There is another point to be noticed. Even though Jaynes considers the function $-\sum p_l^2$ as one of other candidates for uncertainty measure, he does not seem to realize that the measure of uncertainty is not an ordinal variable and that there are several other measures for uncertainty represented, for example, by $\sum p_i F(p_i)$, where $pF(p)$ is a concave function over [0, 1].

To be fair to Jaynes, however, it must be noticed that he himself admits the following: the 'mere fact that the same mathematical expression $-\sum p_i \log p_i$ occurs both in statistical mechanics and in information theory does not in itself establish any connection between these fields' (Jaynes 1957: 621). Jaynes' contribution should be regarded as a construction of a new type of statistical inference rather than a proof of the equivalence between information and negative entropy.

Now let us turn to Brillouin's position. Brillouin proposes several measures of information (see e.g. Brillouin 1950). However, he claims the equivalence only between negative entropy and *bound information.* Let us introduce Brillouin's definition on bound information (1951*b*, 1953, 1962). Consider a physical system with initially P_0 different states, all of them having equal *a priori* probabilities. With the information (or some constraints upon the system), the number of possible states is reduced to P_1. Then the bound information is obtained:

$$\text{Bound information} = K \ln \frac{P_0}{P_1} = \text{decrease in entropy}, \qquad (4.35)$$

where K is a constant.

There are several points to show how dubious the equivalence between bound information and negative entropy (Brillouin calls it negentropy) is.

First, Brillouin uses the concept of 'complexions', a term introduced by Max Planck (1959: 122). According to Brillouin, a 'quantized physical system is able to take *a number of discrete microscopic structures*, which Planck calls the distinct "complexions" of the system' (Brillouin 1953: 1152, italics added). To use the concept of 'complexions', a physical system with a very large number of molecules must be considered in the framework of statistical thermodynamics. In this case, the constant K is equal to k, the Boltzmann–Planck constant. Then, Brillouin defines as bound information what, in physics, is entropy with a negative sign. It seems that his definition of bound information is truly superfluous.

Second, there is an issue concerning dimension (Mayumi 1993*b*). It is impossible to place the physical dimension of entropy on a purely mathematical number, viz. bits. What Brillouin does is that he just equates information with negentropy (which is impossible because of the difference in the dimensions of the two concepts), and *then* tries to measure these quantities with the same units. To wit:

> Another unit system will be introduced when we compare 'information' with thermodynamical 'entropy' and *decide to measure both quantities with the same units*. . . . , we may go step further, and *decide to choose our units in such a way that both entropy and information will be dimensionless and represent pure numbers*.
>
> (Brillouin 1962: 3, italics added)

Third, Brillouin 'devises' a demon with an electric torch by which the demon can see molecules in a system. Brillouin states that the torch 'pours negative entropy into the system. From this negative entropy the demon obtains "information"' (Brillouin 1951*a*: 334). The present author does not understand how the torch could possibly pour negative entropy into the system, even if one accepts that the torch is the source of single photons. Hence, Brillouin's statement does not make sense physically. Maxwell's original idea about his demon is how to create a difference of temperature from equilibrium. In the same paper, however, Brillouin assumes the conclusion – a difference of temperature to be obtained – which he should actually have proved. To wit:

> We may *assume* that, a certain time, the demon has been able to obtain a difference of temperature.
>
> (Brillouin 1951*a*: 335, italics added)

Fourth, Brillouin tries to calculate the lower limit of energy required for reading ammeters (1951*a*, 1953). Brillouin refers to G. Ising's work (1926) as a starting point for this limit, stating that an additional energy $4kT$ is required for reading ammeters. However, a perusal of Ising's work shows that the coefficient 4 in Ising's paper has an entirely different meaning. Ising tries to estimate the least deviation of an instrument (denoted by $(\overline{\delta x})_{\mathrm{min}}$, the overbar means the root-mean-square value of δx) like a galvanometer caused by change in a physical quantity (current intensity, for instance). Ising concludes that the least deviation discernible with confidence, as being really caused by the change in the physical quantity and not a mere Brownian fluctuation, is about $4\delta x$, where δx is in 'absolute' units (cm, radian, etc.). According to Smoluchowsky (quoted by Ising), the following relation between the mean kinetic energy ϵ and the deviation δx holds:

$$\tfrac{1}{2}A\overline{\delta x^2} = \epsilon, \tag{4.36}$$

where A is a directional force. Thus, it is now clear that the coefficient 4 has nothing to do with the lower limit of the required energy.

Brillouin 'proves' that the lower limit is $k \ln 2$, considering a harmonic oscillator of frequency ν with quantized energy levels $E_n = nh\nu$. The reason behind this result is simple. Brillouin intentionally defines a vacuous concept, i.e. a median quantum number m. The probability that all the energy levels are equal to or greater than $E_m = mh\nu$ is $\frac{1}{2}$. To accept a 50 per cent of error produces his result. Why does Brillouin desperately want the value $k \ln 2$? From inequality (4.24) of Szilard's model, the mean value of the quantity of entropy produced by a measurement is exactly $k \ln 2$ even though, as already shown, the model violates one of the two fundamental principles of statistical physics.

Having followed three principal scholars' works, regarded as responsible for the alleged equivalence between information and negative entropy, it is now clear that this alleged equivalence is physically baseless.

5 Conclusion

Information theory has truly developed as one of the youngest branches of applied probability (McMillan 1953; Khinchin 1957; Rényi 1970). The theory has applications in many fields. However, as Shannon warns, 'the establishing of such applications [of information theory to other fields] is not a trivial matter of translating words to a new domain, but rather the slow tedious process of hypothesis and experimental verifications' (Shannon 1956: 3).

Despite Shannon's caveat against the bandwagon of information theory (Shannon 1956) and Georgescu-Roegen's critique of the prevailing epistemological temper among scholars, 'a pseudoscientific outgrowth of pure symbolism and empty verbalism' seems to be 'a dominant article of scientific faith' (Georgescu-Roegen 1977*a*), thus leading finally to the alleged equivalence between information and negative entropy. Georgescu-Roegen is one of the brightest minds who tackles sincerely the epistemological basis of information theory, and its relation to entropy in physics. Georgescu-Roegen's epistemological attitude is influenced particularly by Karl Pearson and Joseph A. Schumpeter (Mayumi 1995). For Georgescu-Roegen, a theory of any kind should be a logically ordered description of a reality's mode of functioning. He has always been concerned with the problem of valid analytical representation of the relations among facts. One of the examples in which Georgescu-Roegen shows his keen interest in epistemology is a paper, dedicated to P. C. Mahalanobis, related to the discussion of measures of information in the present chapter (Georgescu-Roegen 1964). He constructs an axiomatic basis for cardinal measurability based on the idea that any kind of measure *must* reflect some physical properties or possible actual operations. His epistemological taste obliges him, in my view, to examine the meaning of information and its possible relationship with physical entropy. The present chapter is an attempt to reinforce his arguments concerning these issues.

5 A critical appraisal of two entropy theoretical approaches to resources and environmental problems: Georgescu-Roegen and Tsuchida

1 Introduction

The material structure of economic processes may be represented in terms of the relation between low-entropy inputs (inputs of valuable resources) and high-entropy outputs (final outputs of valueless waste). This representation clearly shows that, in terms of entropy degradation, resources and environmental limitations are different sides of the same coin.

Attention has continuously shifted from one energy and environmental problem to another, from the energy crisis of the 1970s to environmental constraints, especially the greenhouse effect and the destructive influence of chloro-fluoro-carbon on the ozone layers, in the 1990s. As the authors of *The Limits to Growth* (Meadows *et al.* 1972) explain, resources and environmental limitations are deeply connected with each other: evading the problem of resource constraints creates an environmental trap, but managing only the environmental limitations creates a resource problem.

The concept of entropy is indispensable for appreciating resource and environmental constraints which occur generation after generation. The ineffectiveness of market mechanisms in the allocation of resources over generations is proved ingeniously by Georgescu-Roegen (1975). He also states:

> To suggest further that man can construct at a cost a new environment tailored to his desires is to ignore completely that cost consists in essence of low entropy, not of money, and is subject to the limitations imposed by the natural laws.
>
> (Georgescu-Roegen 1975: 359)

Inputs of low-entropy resources into the economic process and outputs of high-entropy waste from it are two unavoidable flows of economic activities as long as people remain as bioeconomic beings. The tremendous rate of entropy increase may well be the most troublesome characteristics of modern technological systems with respect to the resource and environmental constraints (Mayumi 1990, 1991; see also Chapter 7 of this monograph). The true question facing bioeconomic beings consists in *the choice of the suitable rate of increase in entropy in the long term.*

The main purpose of this chapter is to evaluate two entropy theoretical approaches (Georgescu-Roegen and Tsuchida) to resources and environmental problems. Georgescu-Roegen's flow–fund model is used to show the impossibility of complete recycling.

Section 2 briefly reviews the Schrödinger theory of living things. A necessary condition for living things to continue life is investigated. Section 3 considers how the earth disposes of thermal entropy increases into outer space in terms of the nested-hierarchical structure of an open steady-state system of the second category. Even though Georgescu-Roegen's 'Fourth Law of Thermodynamics' cannot be accepted as a law of physics, Section 4 deals with that law and its implication for resource and environmental constraints. The view that complete recycling is possible with a sufficient amount of energy is shown to be questioned using a flow–fund model. The rationale for the impossibility of complete recycling is also presented. Section 5 explains the complementary nature of Georgescu-Roegen's theory and Tsuchida's water cycle theory. Georgescu-Roegen's theory emphasizes that the earth is closed with respect to matter, whereas, the water cycle theory stresses that the earth is open with respect to energy.

2 Schrödinger's theory

Since entropy flows with heat or matter, a system can be classified according to whether or not there is entropy flow due to exchange of heat or matter with the environment. If there is no entropy flow due to exchange of heat or matter with the environment, the system is considered to be closed. Otherwise, the system is open.[1] This definition allows a similar theoretical treatment for both a heat engine and a living system (Tsuchida 1985).

In a closed system as defined above, the entropy S_0 in the initial state becomes S_{er} during the process of change, finally reaching the maximal value S_{f}. There exist the following inequalities among these three variables:

$$S_{\mathrm{f}} \geq S_{\mathrm{er}} \geq S_0 \tag{5.1}$$

or

$$\Delta S_{\mathrm{f}} \geq \Delta S_{\mathrm{er}} \geq 0, \tag{5.2}$$

where

$$\Delta S_{\mathrm{f}} = S_f - S_0 \tag{5.3}$$

and

$$\Delta S_{\mathrm{er}} = S_{\mathrm{er}} - S_0. \tag{5.4}$$

These inequalities delineate the second law of thermodynamics. In a closed system, there is a final state which has a maximal level of entropy. Then, what about living things?

It is L. Boltzmann who aptly points out:

> The general struggle for existence of animate beings is therefore not a struggle for raw materials – these, for organisms, are air, water and soil, all abundantly available – nor for energy which exists in plenty in any body in the form of heat (albeit unfortunately not transformable), but a *struggle for entropy*, which becomes available through the transition of energy from the hot sun to the cold earth. In order to exploit this transition as much as possible, plants spread their immense surface of leaves and force the sun's energy, before it falls to the earth's temperature, to perform in ways as yet unexplored certain chemical syntheses of which no one in our laboratories has so far the least idea. The products of this chemical kitchen constitute the object of struggle of the animal world (italics added).
>
> (Boltzmann 1974: 24)

Put simply, Boltzmann admits that, in his time, there were still questions concerning how life struggles for entropy and whether or not life needs a new law other than the second law.

In 1944, Schrödinger stated in his seminal book, *What is life?*: 'What is the characteristic feature of life? When is a piece of matter said to be alive?. . . How does the living organism avoid decay?' (Schrödinger 1967: 74–5). His answer is: ' "It [a living organism] feeds upon negative entropy", attracting, as it were, a stream of negative entropy upon itself, to compensate the entropy increase it produces by living and thus to maintain itself on a stationary and fairly low entropy level' (Schrödinger 1967: 78). What is negative entropy? Schrödinger explains negative entropy as entropy with the negative sign. However, entropy can never be negative, according to the third law of thermodynamics. At the time, Schrödinger did not consider an important factor that plays an essential role in maintaining a steady state.

In 1945, Schrödinger added a note to Chapter VI, concluding 'that we give off heat [thermal entropy] is not accidental, but essential. For this is precisely the manner in which we dispose of the surplus [thermal] entropy we continually produce in our physical life process' (Schrödinger 1967: 80). Schrödinger finally reaches the right conclusion that disposal of surplus thermal entropy is necessary for living things to continue life. Schrödinger's idea about disposal of surplus thermal entropy attracted physicists only when a physicist, M. Sugita, emphasized the importance of Schrödinger's theory on life. In 1952, Sugita explained this point in the following way:

> Schrödinger added a note to Chapter VI in which he revised his view of living thing's intake of negative entropy to a new one of its disposing of [thermal] entropy. . . Putting it in an extreme way, the place of intaking negative entropy is, so to speak, a lavatory. Precisely speaking, however, his idea is nothing but a mirror image of positive entropy disposal by a living thing concerning the

> total balance sheet of intake, excretion and thermal radiation. It is necessary to study entropy metabolism.
>
> (cited in Tsuchida 1985)

A living thing continues life by feeding upon energy and matter of low entropy and by disposing of waste matter and heat of high entropy. Entropy exchange with the environment as well as entropy production within a living thing is fundamental in the maintenance of steady state. This is what Boltzmann means by the struggle for entropy.

However, negentropy or free energy has been discussed more often than Schrödinger's idea of thermal entropy disposal and Sugita's entropy metabolism. There is a bias developed toward 'input'. Very few people recognize the importance of the process of discarding waste matter and heat. Only after pollution problems in the 1970s, the importance of entropy disposal has widely been recognized (Tsuchida 1985).

Schrödinger's view of disposal of thermal entropy by heat emission is a new idea in physics.

Both, the process of entropy production and the process of entropy flow, operate simultaneously in an open system. However, for the sake of simplicity, it is assumed that entropy flow with the environment occurs first, and entropy production follows. After a system receives entropy flow σ_0 at an initial state, entropy in this system changes due to entropy production within this system

$$\Delta S_{\mathrm{f}} \geq \Delta S_{\mathrm{er}} \geq \sigma_0, \tag{5.5}$$

where we regard σ_0 as positive if entropy flows into the system. Inequality (5.5) contains the second law for a closed system as a special case where $\sigma_0 = 0$. The relationship between ΔS_{er} and σ_0 in (5.5) shows that entropy production within the system is not less than entropy flow at the initial state. The relationship between $\Delta S_{\mathrm{total}}$ and ΔS_{er} shows that entropy production has a limit. At this juncture, introduction of what Tsuchida calls Schrödinger's inequality is necessary. A living system feeds upon energy and matter, and discards waste matter and heat. Dividing the whole process into n small processes, from (5.5), produces:

$$\Delta S_{\mathrm{total}} \geq \sum_{i=1}^{n} \Delta S_{\mathrm{er}(i)} \geq \sum_{i=1}^{n} \sigma_{i0}, \tag{5.6}$$

where $\Delta S_{\mathrm{total}}$ is the total change in entropy, $\Delta S_{\mathrm{er}(i)}$ is the change in entropy en route in the ith process, and σ_{i0} is entropy flow at the initial state of the ith process. The steady state is characterized by the condition that $\Delta S_{\mathrm{total}} = 0$, thus obtaining

$$0 \geq \sum_{i=1}^{n} \sigma_{i0}. \tag{5.7}$$

According to the definition of σ_{i0},

$$\sigma_{\mathrm{out}} \geq \sigma_{\mathrm{in}}, \tag{5.8}$$

where σ_{in} is the total sum of entropy flow into the system and σ_{out} is the total sum of entropy flow out of the system.

Inequality (5.8) shows that a necessary condition for a living thing to maintain a steady state is that the entropy flow out of the system must be greater than the entropy flow into the system.

This difference between the entropy inflow and outflow guarantees the steady state of a living system temporarily. Inequality (5.8) can apply to a heat engine. Ecosystems themselves, as well as the earth itself, must satisfy (5.8). The implications of (5.8) are very important. First, to maintain a system requires effective entropy disposal as well as low-entropy flow into the system. Second, there must be miscellaneous interconnections within living systems as a whole in order to discard entropy generated within those systems. One should turn attention to the output flow of waste matter and heat (Tsuchida 1985). A weak point of (5.8) is that it does not consider the magnitude of $d\sigma_{in}/dt$ and $d\sigma_{out}/dt$. The relevance of this point has been investigated by the present author (Mayumi 1990).

3 Properties of open systems and the nested-hierarchical structure of open steady-state systems of the second category

A system is said to be a steady state if the state variables do not evolve in time. If a system satisfies inequality (5.8) and maintains the steady state, it is said to be an open steady-state system.

However, an open steady-state system does not entirely encapsulate a living thing. One important feature is missing from the argument in the previous section. Following Tsuchida's argument, there are two categories of open steady-state systems (an analytical definition of the steady state of the second category is yet to be made). Heat flow, electric current and water flow are examples of systems belonging to the first category. These systems are not in equilibrium as a whole. Nevertheless, it is possible to study these systems as if they were at equilibrium (i.e. local equilibrium). The open steady-state system of the first category has been investigated extensively by the Prigogine school. If the steady state of a system occurs sufficiently close to an equilibrium state, it may be characterized by the principle of minimum entropy production: the entropy production has minimum value at steady state. However, this principle is subject to severe restrictions because it is valid in the range of linear thermodynamics of irreversible processes and because the phenomenological coefficients may be considered as constants satisfying the Onsager relations.[2]

Some physicists think that the principle of minimum entropy production can be applicable to the study of the entire domain of biology. They regard the 'preventing' power of a living thing from increasing entropy as the power to minimize entropy production within the living entity. However, a living thing is really a big entropy production 'factory'. At room temperature, glucose is very stable and is not oxidized easily but, in a living thing, glucose is oxidized very easily. It turns out that the idea of a steady-state system of the first category and the principle of minimum entropy production are not powerful tools for studies in biology.[3]

Another clue to studies of life concerns cycles in a living system. For life on earth, this means that we consider many cycles and that each 'cycle' could be the subject of a specific scholarly field. For example, the water cycle and convection current in the atmosphere are subjects for meteorology. The water cycle in the ocean is a subject for oceanography. Biocycles in the ecosystem are relevant for ecology. Scientists regard these various ongoing cycles as representing a 'good condition' and imbalances among cycles a 'bad condition' (Tsuchida 1985). We rewrite (5.8) as

$$\sigma_{\text{in}} + \sigma = \sigma_{\text{out}}, \tag{5.9}$$

where σ is the amount of entropy production within a system. After a complete cycle, it is necessary to dispose of the entropy σ generated within the system into a larger system that contains the original system as a part. Without the ability of entropy disposal, a living thing cannot maintain a steady state. Therefore, there must be harmonious connections among subsystems in order to dispose of entropy which ultimately belongs outside those subsystems.

The above argument implies an important corollary first mentioned by Tsuchida: 'a necessary condition for an open steady-state system [of the second category] to continue life is that this system must be contained within a larger open steady state system [of the second category]'.[4] In a closed system, entropy increases monotonously and reaches the maximum value allowed by that system, at which time all activities must stop.

Several points should be noted in connection with Tsuchida's theory. First, in Tsuchida's theory there is no analytical definition of cycle. Second, what Tsuchida calls an open steady-state system of the second category can be interpreted in an anthropomorphic way: an open steady-state system of the second category is a system which maintains steady state *consciously* by disposing of entropy outside the system. Third, the nested-hierarchical structure of an open steady-state system of the second category can be formulated as follows (see Fig. 5.1). Suppose that there are n open steady-state systems of the second category and that system i is contained in system $(i+1)$ $(i = 1, \ldots, n-1)$. Both, the process of entropy production and the process of entropy flow, operate simultaneously in a living system. However, for the sake of simplicity assume that entropy exchange with its environment occurs first, and entropy production follows. Also, assume that entropy flow for system i ($\sigma_{\text{in}(i)}$ or $\sigma_{\text{out}(i)}$) can be regarded as entropy production for system $(i+1)$ $(i = 1, \ldots, n-1)$. After system i $(i = 1, \ldots, n)$ receives net entropy flow $\sigma_{\text{in}(i)} - \sigma_{\text{out}(i)}$ at the initial state, entropy in system i changes due to entropy production within this system:

$$\Delta S_{\text{total}(i)} \geq \Delta S_{\text{er}(i)} \geq \sigma_{\text{in}(i)} - \sigma_{\text{out}(i)}, \tag{5.10}$$

where $\Delta S_{\text{total}(i)}$ is the total change in entropy within system i after the initial state, $\Delta S_{\text{er}(i)}$ is the change in entropy en route $(i = 1, \ldots, n)$. Since the steady state is

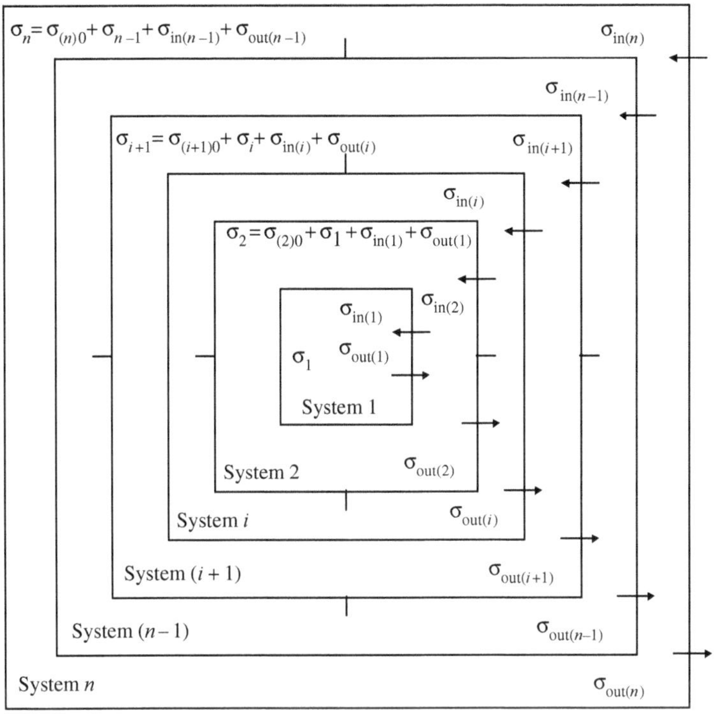

Figure 5.1 The nested-hierarchical structure of an open steady-state system of the second category.

characterized by the condition $\Delta S_{\text{total}(i)} = 0$, introducing the amount of entropy production σ_i within system i produces

$$\sigma_{\text{out}(i)} = \sigma_i + \sigma_{\text{in}(i)}. \tag{5.11}$$

Here, σ_{i+1} includes σ_i, $\sigma_{\text{in}(i)}$, $\sigma_{\text{out}(i)}$, and entropy production $\sigma_{(i+1)0}$ generated within system $(i + 1)$, but does not include entropy production in system i. Therefore,

$$\sigma_{i+1} = \sigma_{(i+1)0} + \sigma_i + \sigma_{\text{in}(i)} + \sigma_{\text{out}(i)}. \tag{5.12}$$

From (5.11) and (5.12),

$$\sigma_{\text{out}(i+1)} - \sigma_{\text{in}(i+1)} = \sigma_{(i+1)0} + \sigma_i + \sigma_{\text{in}(i)} + \sigma_{\text{out}(i)}, \tag{5.13}$$

$$\sigma_{\text{out}(1)} - \sigma_{\text{in}(1)} = \sigma_1, \tag{5.14}$$

where $i = 1, \ldots, n-1$. Equation (5.14) is the ordinary relationship characterizing a steady state for system i: the sum of entropy flow and entropy production is zero ($\sigma_1 + \sigma_{\text{in}(1)} - \sigma_{\text{out}(1)} = 0$). Equation (5.13) is characteristic of the nested-hierarchical structure of an open steady-state system of the second category. System $(i + 1)$

has to dispose of entropy production $\sigma_{(i+1)0}$ and entropy flow $\sigma_{\text{in}(i+1)} - \sigma_{\text{out}(i+1)}$. In addition, system $(i + 1)$ has to have an *ability* (again anthropomorphic!) to dispose of entropy production σ_i and entropy flow $\sigma_{\text{in}(i)} + \sigma_{\text{out}(i)}$ for system i. A nested-hierarchical structure of this kind is characteristic of a living thing in order to dispose of entropy effectively. Boltzmann calls this process of entropy disposal 'the struggle for entropy' and, more recently, Tsuchida calls it 'harmonious cycles'. Georgescu-Roegen calls it 'sorting'.

It is necessary to consider how the earth disposes of thermal entropy generated within its system and the essential role played by land in thermal entropy disposal.

Air convection and the water cycle constitute an atmospheric heat engine which guarantees the existence of life on earth by continually discarding entropy to outer space. Within this heat engine, water and air circulate between the surface area of the earth (15°C on average) and the air at high altitudes (−18°C). Roughly (Tsuchida and Murota 1985), the thermal entropy generated after various activities on the earth is discarded annually at a rate of 34.6 cal/deg cm^2.

The degree of coldness of the upper air (−18°C) is also important. This low temperature is created by the adiabatic expansion of the air. It is possible to dispose more of the thermal entropy of radiation of the same quantity of heat at a lower temperature than at a higher temperature. In addition, at about −18°C, the vapour pressure is sufficiently low and air is dried so that sunlight can pass easily through the atmosphere because of fine weather, except close to an ascending current.

Water cycles emerge due to the asymmetry of the atmosphere. This asymmetry is created by the fact that the molecular weight of water vapour is 18, while the average molecular weight of air is 29 (Tsuchida 1985). This difference in molecular weight creates an air pump, as it were, to lift water vapour up to the upper atmosphere against gravity. If the earth's primitive atmosphere had consisted mainly of methane, CH_4 (molecular weight is 16), instead of carbon dioxide, neither asymmetry nor life would have been possible.[5] Through the water cycles created by the earth's primitive atmosphere, living things on the earth can dispose of heat entropy and material entropy into solution.

A nested-hierarchical structural model of an open steady-state system of the second category can be used to illustrate how, in earth systems, entropy production is effectively disposed. To repeat: in order to maintain steady state, an open steady-state system of the second category must be contained in a larger open steady-state system of the second category.

Plants use sunlight to produce glucose. Entropy generated in a plant is discarded mainly by evaporation of water from leaves. Activities of animals are accompanied by the production of waste heat and matter. This heat entropy is disposed of ultimately by water cycles and air convection. When organic wastes, excreta and dead matter from the grazing food chain are decomposed, water plays a vital role in the disposal of thermal entropy generated during the process of decomposition. There are water cycles outside of the food chain. There is a heat radiation system outside of the water cycles. In this way, entropy produced at each stage in a given system of the earth is passed to a larger system which contains the original system.

Tsuchida writes:

> ... the earth is not a dead celestial body, but the one with numerous kinds of lively activities. Their presence is guaranteed by the surplus [thermal] entropy disposal through the atmospheric heat engine in the form of air and water cycles. As a result, one had been witnessing the [quasi-] steady earth in the sense that [thermal] entropy had not increased on it for several billion years, and that a year was similar to its preceding year and so on so forth, without succumbing to a nightmare of heat death.
>
> (Tsuchida and Murota 1985)

Soil and sea are contact points, so to speak, with the water cycle and the food chain. Soil is composed of inorganic minerals as well as humus. Humus ultimately transforms material entropy (detritus) into heat entropy. Without sufficient moisture in land, soil cannot dispose of entropy and no life in humus is possible – a typical situation in the desert.

For all living things, excreta and debris must be discarded on land, in surface water or in sea water. The resources people can utilize should be those which can be discarded on land and in water. There are problems with modern agriculture and manufacturing which we will discuss further in Chapter 7. Modern agriculture replaces most of the material cycles in nature by manufactured products such as chemical fertilizers and petroleum refined products. Such manufactured products are not compatible with the cycles of nature. In modern manufacturing, there is enormous entropy production and the time rate of entropy increase ($\mathrm{d}S/\mathrm{d}t$) is large, since both energy and matter are transformed on a large scale and at an accelerated rate. This tendency of energy and material transformation stresses the harmonious connections among cycles in nature and results in higher rates of entropy production, which the atmospheric heat engine of the earth cannot dispose of effectively. Water pollution by radioactive substances or by chemical detergents is just one example.

Modern era requires a drastic change of view on technology itself. If human society can be characterized as a living system, attempts must be made to recover various natural cycles already damaged or destroyed. Unless natural cycles can be recovered, the future will be ominous.

4 Georgescu-Roegen's theory on matter and the impossibility of complete recycling

4.1 Compatibility of Georgescu-Roegen's formulation with the thermodynamics framework

First, let us review the impossibility of the classical perpetual motions of the first and second kinds (Planck 1945) and raise some questions about Georgescu-Roegen's formulation of the 'Fourth Law'.

> The first kind: 'it is impossible to construct an engine which will work in a cycle and produce continuous work, or kinetic energy, from nothing'.

> The second kind: '*it is impossible to construct an engine which will work in a complete cycle, and produce no effect except the raising of a weight and the cooling of a heat reservoir*'.

Planck selects the formulation of the second kind because of its technical significance. Following these two classical perpetual motions, Georgescu-Roegen defines the perpetual motion of the 'third kind' as a closed thermodynamic system that can perform work at a constant rate *forever* or that can perform, *forever*, work between its subsystems. He then claims that perpetual motion of the 'third kind' is impossible.

The two classical formulations *implicitly accept* that it takes an infinite amount of time to achieve any finite movement. The theoretical trick is assuming a 'quasi-static process', an imaginary limiting process without friction. Thus, time (the term, forever or indefinitely) should not be introduced explicitly in the context of the theoretical framework of thermodynamics. Furthermore, the boundary between a system and its environment is ambiguous in Georgescu-Roegen's formulation, because his motion of the 'third kind' is *in* a closed system. It is not so clear whether or not work is done on another object in the closed system or on the environment. In thermodynamics, it should be clear whether or not a system can do work *on* its surroundings or whether or not the surroundings can do work *on* the system. If the theoretical framework of thermodynamics is followed strictly, it is relatively easy to reach the following conclusion: it is *possible* to construct a *closed* engine which will work in a complete cycle, and produce no effect except the raising of a weight, the cooling of a heat reservoir at a higher temperature, and the warming of a heat reservoir at a lower temperature. In short, this closed system is nothing but a Carnot engine. The Carnot engine with fluid is a closed system because heat can be exchanged during two isothermal processes (expansion and compression) through the base of the cylinder.

A meteorite which falls onto the earth consists of a rare form of dust. The amount of particles that escape the earth's gravitational field is also negligible. The amount of heat produced by consumption of fossil fuels is about 20,000 times less than the amount of solar radiation reaching the earth. Similarly, the amount of geothermal heat is about 6,000 times less than the amount of solar radiation. Therefore, heat produced by fossil fuels and geothermal heat might be ignored at the global level (Koide and Abiko 1985). Hence, if the economic process is set aside, the earth, our abode, can be regarded as a big (closed) Carnot engine powered by the temperature difference between the sun (a heat reservoir at a higher temperature) and the outer space (a heat reservoir at a lower temperature).

4.2 Entropy in physics revisited

A brief review of entropy is in order before we examine the physical logic of the equivalence between entropy of energy (heat) diffusion and that of matter diffusion. Consider the case of matter diffusion, as in classical thermodynamics (Fig. 5.2): 1 mol of an ideal gas is stored in a container (which has a volume of V_1) and then

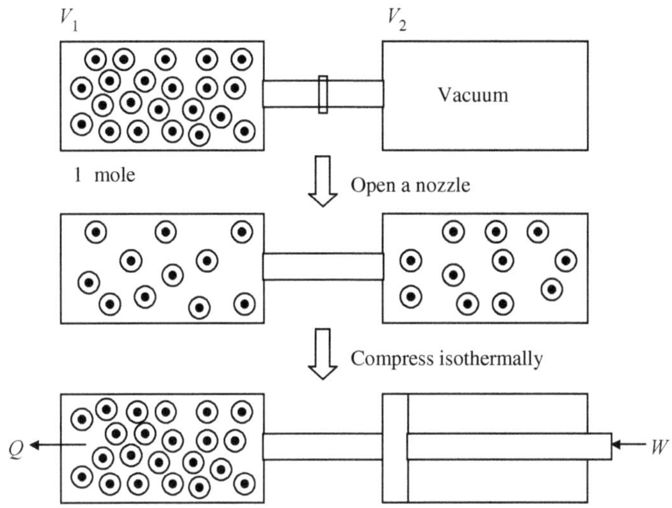

Figure 5.2 Diffusion of matter.

allowed to expand freely into another container (V_2) after opening a nozzle. To calculate the amount of entropy increase, compress the ideal gas in container 2 isothermally into container 1 by moving a piston. In this process of isothermal compression, the work W done on the system is

$$W = RT \ln \frac{V_1 + V_2}{V_1}. \tag{5.15}$$

Because the process involves isothermal compression and the gas is ideal, all the work W comes out of the system as heat Q, i.e.

$$Q = W. \tag{5.16}$$

The entropy of mechanical work is zero, so increase in entropy through the work done is also zero. The entropy flow as heat from the system S is given by

$$S = \frac{Q}{T} = R \ln \frac{V_1 + V_2}{V_1}, \tag{5.17}$$

where S corresponds to the entropy increase due to diffusion of matter. Hence, if 1 mol of an ideal gas expands to a volume N times as large as the initial volume, the increase in entropy is $R \ln N$.

Equations (5.15)–(5.17) show clearly that entropy of matter diffusion is a perfect substitute for entropy of energy diffusion in classical thermodynamics. A decrease in the entropy of matter is accomplished by the same amount of increase in the entropy of heat diffusion. Therefore, from a purely physical point of view, there is no essential difference between a closed system and an open system.

However, the procedure in Fig. 5.2 clearly shows the limitations of applying a purely thermodynamic consideration to ecological issues. For all those concerned with the future of our planet, Georgescu-Roegen's remarks are worth keeping in mind:

> . . . the Van't Hoff reaction box describes in an ideal way a procedure for unmixing gases . . . No similar device, however, has been thought up yet for mixing of liquids or solids (and from what we know now, none seems reliable).
>
> (Georgescu-Roegen 1982: 16)

The concept of entropy cannot be applied directly to 'phenomena of the macrolevel, that is, of the level of our direct senses'.

4.3 Entropy degradation of matter (the 'material entropy') in Georgescu-Roegen's formulation

As shown already, the concept of entropy is, in essence, tantamount to entropy of energy diffusion. Therefore, degradation of matter in bulk at the level of our direct senses cannot be treated in terms of entropy in thermodynamics. As Fermi states, thermodynamics 'is mainly concerned with the transformations of heat into mechanical work and the opposite transformations of mechanical work into heat' (Fermi 1956). The 'material entropy' proposed by Georgescu-Roegen deserves examination.

As several passages from Georgescu-Roegen's writing show his rationale:

> All over the material world there is rubbing by friction, cracking and splitting by changes in temperature or evaporation, there is clogging of pipes and membranes, there is metal fatigue and spontaneous combustion. Matter is thus continuously displaced, altered, and scattered to the four corners of the world. It thus becomes less and less available for our own purposes . . . In the economic process it is not mass as such that counts. What counts is matter in bulk (and, of course, energy).
>
> (Georgescu-Roegen 1979: 1034–5)

Physicists and engineers (e.g. Ozaki 1983; Takamatsu 1983; Tsuchida 1985) clearly state that the degradation of matter in bulk in our daily life does not give rise to increase in entropy treated in physics. Nevertheless, 'material entropy' will be critically important for our ecological salvation.

Georgescu-Roegen aptly remarks, 'to arrive at an entropy formula seems impossible at this stage'. Energy is a homogeneous quantity, and energy conversion from one form into another can easily be accomplished. On the other hand, matter is highly heterogeneous and every element has some unique physicochemical properties. This feature of matter explains why the practical procedures for unmixing liquids or solids differ from case to case and consist of many complicated steps.

There will probably never be a general blueprint for unmixing all liquids and solids without distinction.

Seemingly, the only possible way of reaching a quantitative measure of 'material entropy' is to calculate *indirectly* the amounts of matter and energy for returning to the initial state of matter in bulk in question, given the available technology. The proper initial state of matter in bulk is deeply related to our multidimensional value system: to what state should the degraded matter be transformed? Because the amounts of matter in bulk and energy required for recovering depend on the available technology, the required amounts contain some factors of uncertainties that make predictions practically impossible. Further, Georgescu-Roegen states, because matter in bulk and energy are not convertible into each other, without considering the overall availability of energy and mineral resources, it is impossible to judge which equivalent recovering technology, the one with more energy and less matter, or the one with less energy and more matter, is preferable ecologically. It is necessary to have a general quantitative flow matrix representing macro-global and micro-local economic systems in terms of Georgescu-Roegen's flow–fund model to tackle formidable issues concerning integrated technological assessment.

4.4 Clausius' disgregation revisited

It is none other than Clausius who tries to search for a quantitative measure of dissipation of matter, 'the disgregation', in 1862. This concept of the disgregation is practically forgotten and has recently been attributed only a historical significance. After formulating the inequality in 1854, Clausius tries to investigate the possibility of extending the equivalence of transformations (not restricted to cyclic processes), instead of introducing immediately the new state function, entropy (Yamamoto 1987). Clausius states:

> Accordingly, since, in my former paper, I wished to avoid everything that was hypothetical, I entirely excluded the interior work, which I was able to do by confining myself to the considerations of *cyclic processes* – that is to say, operations in which the modifications which the body undergoes are so arranged that the body finally returns to its original condition. In such operations the interior work . . . neutralizes itself, so that nothing but exterior work remains.
>
> (Clausius 1867: 216)

In the original formulation given by Clausius in 1862,

$$\mathrm{d}Q = \mathrm{d}H + A\,\mathrm{d}I + A\,\mathrm{d}W, \tag{5.18}$$

where $\mathrm{d}H$ (H is not enthalpy) is heat added to the quantity already present in a body (im Körper wirklich vorhandene Wärme [Wärmeinhalt]), $A\,\mathrm{d}I$ is heat expended in interior work (A is the thermal-equivalent of a unit of work), and $\mathrm{d}W$ is exterior work performed by heat during the change in the condition of the body.

Clausius adopts a new assumption: the maximum work, interior plus exterior, which *can* be done by heat during any change in the arrangement of a body is proportional to the absolute temperature at which this change occurs. Based on this assumption, (5.18) can be rewritten:

$$\mathrm{d}Q = \mathrm{d}H + T\,\mathrm{d}Z, \tag{5.19}$$

where $\mathrm{d}I + \mathrm{d}W = KT\,\mathrm{d}Z(K = 1/A)$.

Clausius states:

> Now the effect of heat always tends to loosen the connexion between the molecules, and so to increase their mean distances from one another. In order to be able to represent this mathematically, we will express the degree in which the molecules of a body are separated from each other, by introducing a new magnitude, which we will call the *disgregation* of the body [$\mathrm{d}Z$], and by help of which we can define the effect of heat as simply *tending to increase the disgregation.*
>
> (Clausius 1867: 220)

Clausius' aim is to extend the transformation between heat and exterior work into the transformation between heat and increase in volume under the above assumption and to allot the equivalence-value $\mathrm{d}Z$ to the transformations in which heat does not give rise to exterior work in actuality.

Under this new assumption, Clausius shows that H is a function of temperature alone. In fact, it can easily be shown that this assumption is equivalent to the following: H depends only on temperature and not on the arrangement of the constituent particles. In the case of an ideal gas,

$$\frac{\mathrm{d}H}{T} = \frac{C_V \mathrm{d}V}{T} \tag{5.20}$$

and

$$\mathrm{d}Z = \frac{R\,\mathrm{d}V}{V}. \tag{5.21}$$

The quantities in (5.20) and (5.21) correspond to the various terms in the well-known relation

$$S(T, V) = C_V \ln \frac{T}{T_0} + R \ln \frac{V}{V_0}. \tag{5.22}$$

Finally, Clausius obtains

$$\int \frac{\mathrm{d}Q}{T} = S - S_0, \tag{5.23}$$

$$S = Y + Z, \tag{5.24}$$

$$S_0 = Y_0 + Z_0, \tag{5.25}$$

and

$$\int \frac{\mathrm{d}H}{T} = Y - Y_0, \tag{5.26}$$

$$\int \mathrm{d}Z = Z - Z_0, \tag{5.27}$$

where Y is the transformation value of the body's heat, estimated from a given initial condition, and Z is the disgregation, which is the transformation value of the existing arrangement of the particles of the body. Physically, Y corresponds to the entropy of thermal diffusion and Z to the entropy of matter diffusion.

Klein, a science historian, claims that 'Clausius saw the disgregation as a concept more fundamental than the entropy, since entropy was to be interpreted physically with the help of disgregation' (Klein 1969: 140). Clausius anticipates Georgescu-Roegen's emphasis on matter in bulk:

> On what *operational* basis can the loss of matter availability be treated as being the same essence as the loss of energy availability? In other words, why should the sum of the two entropies [Entropy of Energy Diffusion and Entropy of Matter Mixing] have one and the same meaning regardless of its distribution among two terms?
>
> (Georgescu-Roegen 1977*b*: 301–2)

Planck seems to support Georgescu-Roegen's idea of material entropy:

> The real meaning of the second law has frequently been looked for in a 'dissipation of energy'. This view, proceeding, as it does, from the irreversible phenomena of conduction and radiation of heat, presents only one side of the question. There are irreversible processes in which the final and initial states show exactly the same form of energy, *e.g.*, the diffusion of two perfect gases, or further dilution of a dilute solution. Such processes are accompanied by no perceptible transference of heat, nor by external work, nor by any noticeable transformation of energy. They occur only for the reason that they lead to an appreciable increase of the entropy. In this case it would be more to the point to speak of a dissipation of matter than of a dissipation of energy.
>
> (Planck 1945: 103–4)

Air convection and the water cycle constitute, as it were, an atmospheric heat engine which guarantees the existence of life on earth by continually discarding *thermal* entropy to outer space (Tsuchida and Murota 1985). Because the earth is a closed system, waste materials tend to remain on the earth unless there is an effective mechanism to transform waste materials into thermal entropy. Furthermore, the economic process depends not only on biological organs but also, to a much greater extent, on exosomatic organs. Unfortunately, there are no truely effective devices for recycling waste materials that also maintain the structure of the economic process. Flows of dissipated matter in bulk increase with the size of the economic process and there is great difficulty in maintaining the large-scale material structures in modern industrial society. Georgescu-Roegen has legitimate ecological concern about the distribution of entropy among two terms; entropy of energy diffusion and entropy of matter mixing. His concern is a matter of vital importance for ecological salvation.

4.5 *Technological and economic rationale of Georgescu-Roegen's proposed law using flow–fund analysis*

The view that complete recycling is impossible is not accepted as a law of physics, but the technological and economic rationale of Georgescu-Roegen's 'Fourth Law' can be explained in terms of a flow–fund model. The flow–fund matrix of Table 5.1 can represent the economic process according to 'the energetic dogma' which claims that, with sufficient energy, complete recycling is possible. The assumption adopted here is that the energetic dogma does not claim that actual processes do not require any material scaffold at the macro-level. In the matrix of Table 5.1, all outflows are represented by positive coordinates and inflows by negative ones. For the purpose of the present argument, the whole reproducible economic process (one period is t) is reduced to several consolidated sectors and aggregated categories:

P_1: transforms energy *in situ* ES into controlled energy CE, ultimately resulting in a form of dissipated energy DE;
P_2: produces maintenance capital MK;
P_3: produces consumer goods C;
P_4: recycles *completely* the material wastes W of all processes into recycled matter RM;
P_5: maintains the population H;

Table 5.1 The economic process according to the energetic dogma

Elements	P_1	P_2	P_3	P_4	P_5
Flow coordinates					
CE	x_{11}	$-x_{12}$	$-x_{13}$	$-\sum_{i=1}^{\infty} x_{14}^{i}$	$-x_{15}$
MK	$-x_{21}$	x_{22}	$-x_{23}$	$-\sum_{i=1}^{\infty} x_{24}^{i}$	$-x_{25}$
C	*	*	x_{33}	*	$-x_{35}$
RM	*	$-x_{42}$	$-x_{43}$	$\sum_{i=1}^{\infty} x_{44}^{i}$	*
ES	$-e_1$	*	*	*	*
W	w_1	w_2	w_3	$-\sum_{i=1}^{\infty}\{w_4^i - w_4^{i+1}\}$	w_5
DE	d_1	d_2	d_3	$\sum_{i=1}^{\infty} d_4^i$	d_5
Fund coordinates					
Capital	K_1	K_2	K_3	K_4	K_5
People	H_1	H_2	H_3	H_4	H_5
Ricardian land	L_1	L_2	L_3	L_4	L_5

*No flow.

In Table 5.1, the only change from Georgescu-Roegen's original formulation (1981) concerns the process P_4 and reinforces his argument. The rationale for this change is as follows.

(i) Other material structures used in the process of recycling will be worn out and hence will themselves have to be recycled in turn. The term w_4^{i+1} represents the waste matter worn out during the ith stage of recycling ($i = 1, 2, \ldots$). The following recursive relations must be satisfied:

$$w_4^1 = w_1 + w_2 + w_3 + w_5, \tag{5.28}$$

$$x_{44}^i = \alpha_i (x_{24}^i + w_4^i), \tag{5.29}$$

$$w_4^{i+1} = (1 - \alpha_i)(x_{24}^i + w_4^i), \tag{5.30}$$

where α_i $(0 < \alpha_i < 1)$ is a technological parameter ($i = 1, 2, \ldots$).

(ii) The theoretical basis of complete recycling is the quasi-static process of the van't Hoff Box, a process which requires infinite time for an infinitesimal movement. Therefore, complete recycling would require infinite time, surely greater than one period of the reproducible process, t. There must be a stage l at which the recycling process must stop.

The energetic dogma that complete recycling is possible with sufficient energy is questionable, due to technological and economic limitations of P_4 and P_1.

4.5.1 Technological and economic limitations of P_4

As Georgescu-Roegen discusses cogently (Georgescu-Roegen 1981), the argument supporting the energetic dogma ignores completely the insurmountable difference between the microscopic and macroscopic operations. While modern knowledge of the microscopic domain of thermodynamics is quite advanced, there is much uncertainty about whether or not it is possible to extrapolate this knowledge of the microscopic domain to a macroscopic domain such as the processes of economic activities. One reason why Georgescu-Roegen proposes his 'Fourth Law' stems from his sincere concern for human survival. The operation of the van't Hoff Box actually requires an infinite time to separate the mixed materials completely. Hence, w_4^{l+1} can never be recycled. Additionally, and paradoxically, in terms of the amounts of controlled energy consumption, it may be better to stop recycling at an earlier stage k than at stage l. Why?

Figure 5.3 illustrates the mixing entropy of two elements X and Y. Theoretically, the work needed to separate X from Y is $T \times \Delta S$, where T is the absolute temperature. The important point is that the slopes of the curve at $x = 0\%$ or $x = 100\%$ have infinite absolute values. This fact implies that a very large amount of energy may be required to recover and recycle the desired mineral elements by removing

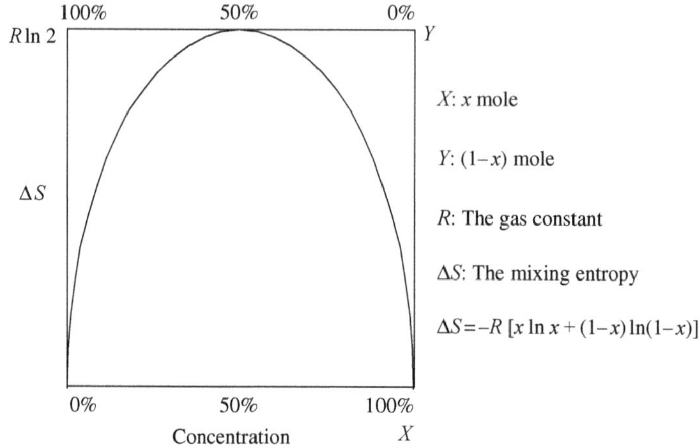

Figure 5.3 The mixing entropy.

a tiny amount of impure element. Hence, there is a trade-off between the amount of energy needed to recycle w_4^{k+1} completely and the amount of w_4^{k+1} itself after x_{44}^k decreases to a low level. The snag in obtaining a general relationship between these two variables is that the shape of this general relationship depends strongly on each element's chemical characteristic and available technology. Finally, there is an economic dimension related to the large scale of the material structure and to the tremendous requirements of matter in bulk and controlled energy in modern industrial society. The quantity of dissipated matter in bulk always increases in line with the increase in stock of material structures to be maintained and preserved. Hence, the amount of controlled energy required in the recycling process necessarily becomes larger and larger with increase in the stock of material structures. Recycling process P_4 cannot escape the limitation of *controlled* energy supply, even if there is an abundant amount of energy *in situ*.

4.5.2 Technological limitations of P_1

The remarks in Section 4.5.1 relate deeply to the technological limitations of P_1. If it is assumed that solar energy is the ultimate source of energy, it is a matter of vital importance to check whether or not all *controlled* energy for economic processes including the recycling process P_4 can be obtained from the sun (Slesser 1980).

Two fundamental factors determining the technological efficiency of P_1 are: (i) density and quality of energy resources; (ii) quantities of matter and controlled energy used for extraction (or capturing in the case of solar energy), transportation, transformation and transmission to obtain and process the controlled energy.

Fossil fuels are optimal in terms of the quantity of matter in bulk required for energy extraction, transformation and transportation to support an industrial society that consumes ever increasing quantities of matter and controlled

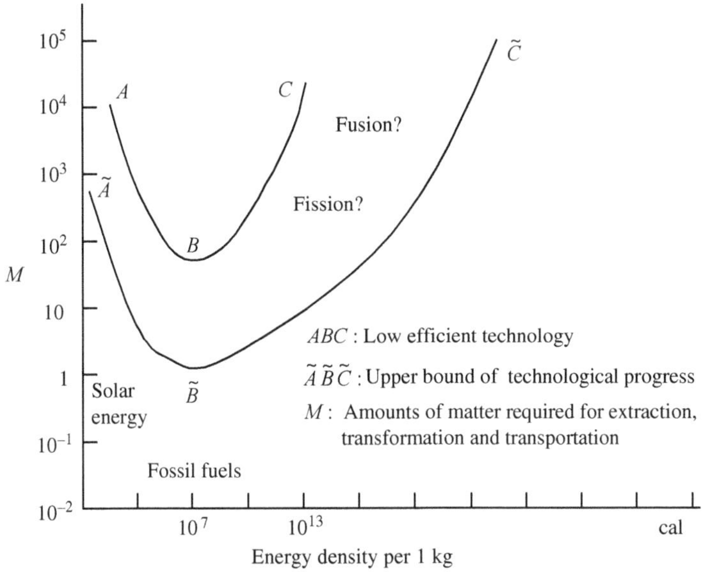

Figure 5.4 The relationship between energy density and the amounts of material requirement.

Source: [Kawamiya 1983: 62].

energy. Kawamiya (1983) calls fossil fuels' superiority as Georgescu-Roegen's Fundamental Proposition (Fig. 5.4), which the latter explains as follows:

> It [the necessary amount of matter for a technology] is high for weak-intensity energy (as is the solar radiation at the ground level) because such energy must be concentrated into a much higher intensity if it is to support the intensive industrial processes as those now supported by fossil fuels. And it is high for high-intensity energy because such energy must be contained (besides being 'sifted' first).
>
> (Georgescu-Roegen 1979: 1050)

Solar energy, although of high quality, has very weak intensity so that the second factor may hamper the secured supply of the controlled energy. This, in turn, reduces the availability of the controlled energy to recycle matter in bulk.

In short, the energetic dogma that complete recycling is possible with sufficient energy ignores: (i) the space and time limitations of human beings, (ii) the insurmountable difference between the microscopic and macroscopic operations, (iii) density and quality of energy resources, (iv) quantities of matter in bulk and controlled energy required for extraction, transportation, transformation and transmission, (v) large-scale material structures in modern industrial society and

(vi) the increasing consumption of matter in bulk and controlled energy on earth.

5 Conclusion: complementary nature of theories of Georgescu-Roegen and Tsuchida

Georgescu-Roegen's view on matter, especially his 'Fourth Law of Thermodynamics', emphasizes the important role played by matter in bulk as a material scaffold in modern production process. 'Matter matters, too' is the apt title of one of Georgescu-Roegen's papers that gives a penetrating insight into the large quantity of matter required by modern manufacturing and agriculture. Georgescu-Roegen's argument that matter on earth will ultimately be degraded is logically convincing. Utilization of low-grade ore is accompanied by a high rate of entropy production, demanding more effective control of disposal of entropy and proving the value of Tsuchida's theory. Air convection and the water cycle play a significant role in discarding thermal entropy production caused by various activities including economic activities.

As far as matter is concerned, the earth is virtually a closed system in the sense of classical thermodynamics. Because the earth is a closed system, special types of matter, e.g. air and water, are not dispersed and lost to outer space due to gravity, so that air and water keep the earth in quasi-steady state by continual thermal entropy disposal. Therefore, matter (air and water) matters, too, in this special sense. While Georgescu-Roegen emphasizes the importance of matter *in general*, the significance of special substances, air and water, and the role of the gravitational field for maintaining quasi-steady state may not have been fully appreciated.

The Entropy Law and the Economic Process shows a very interesting convergence between the Georgescu-Roegen and Tsuchida theories:

> Whether we study the internal biochemistry of a living organism or its outward behavior, we see that it continuously sorts. It is by this peculiar activity that living matter maintains its own level of entropy, although the *individual* organism ultimately succumbs to the Entropy Law. There is nothing wrong in saying that life is characterized by the struggle against the entropic degradation of mere matter.
>
> (Georgescu-Roegen 1971: 192)

Georgescu-Roegen's 'sort' corresponds to the mechanism of entropy disposal in Tsuchida's theory. In a living system, surplus entropy is dispersed through a variety of cycles within the living system, which is an open steady-state system of the second category. Finally, there is disposal of surplus entropy outside the system, keeping the level of entropy within the system at an almost constant and low level. Georgescu-Roegen does not focus on the existence of the second category of an open steady-state system, but he understands the essential property of living systems.

6 Embodied energy analysis, Sraffa's analysis, Georgescu-Roegen's flow–fund model and viability of solar technology

1 Introduction

Peak energy prices triggered by the oil crises of 1970s caused great interest in energy analysis and created several schools of thought, including Embodied Energy Analysis (EEA). Simply put, EEA is a cost-of-production theory in which all costs can ultimately be calculated according to the amount of solar energy necessary to produce commodities directly and indirectly. According to Robert Costanza, a proponent of the theory, '[an] embodied energy theory of value . . . makes theoretical sense and is empirically accurate only if the system boundaries are defined in an appropriate way' (1980: 1224). Georgescu-Roegen (1982) assesses Costanza's thesis in relation to the crucial role played by mineral resources and the fund element (an agent that transforms input into output in the economic process). In view of viability conditions, Georgescu-Roegen (1979) argues against overoptimism in the direct use of solar energy technology, which is still a parasite to fossil and fissile fuels.

This chapter is prompted by recent interest in a possible connection between energy analysis and Sraffa's analysis (SA) (e.g. England 1986; Christensen 1987; Judson 1989; Patterson 1996). The first part of the present chapter: (i) compares the theoretical basis of EEA from the point of view of Piero Sraffa, a view that was not examined by Georgescu-Roegen; (ii) examines EEA critically in terms of Georgescu-Roegen's flow–fund model; and (iii) compares SA and Georgescu-Roegen's flow–fund model. The second part of the chapter is a theoretical analysis of the viability conditions of solar technology for three flow–fund models.

2 Embodied energy analysis, Sraffa's analysis and the flow–fund model

2.1 No-joint-production case

One system of equations in SA (Sraffa 1960: 11) does not consider joint production:

$$(1+r)A^{t}p + P_{H}H = \hat{A}p, \qquad (6.1)$$

where $p = {}^{t}(p_1, p_2, \ldots, p_n)$ is the vector of commodity values (t denotes the transpose) and it is determined together with the wage P_H and the rate of profit r; A is a matrix and element A_{ij} is the quantity of commodity i used in the process j $(i, j = 1, 2, \ldots, n)$; $\hat{A}$ is a diagonal matrix with elements A_i along the diagonal, where A_i is the total quantity of commodity i $(i = 1, 2, \ldots, n)$ annually produced; H is a vector and element H_j is the fraction of the total annual labour employed in the process j $(\sum_{j=1}^{n} H_j = 1)$.

Sraffa assumes that the system of equations (6.1) is in a self-replacing state, so the following inequality should hold:

$$A_{1j} + A_{2j} + \cdots + A_{nj} \leq A_j \quad (j = 1, 2, \ldots, n). \tag{6.2}$$

Sraffa first examines the case in which $r = 0$ and $P_H = 1$,

$$A^{t}p + H = \hat{A}p. \tag{6.3}$$

The system of equations (6.3) is the same as that used in EEA for static analysis (Costanza 1980; Costanza and Hannon 1989; Brown and Herendeen 1996):

$$X^{t}\epsilon + E = \hat{X}\epsilon, \tag{6.4}$$

where X is a matrix and element X_{ij} is input of commodity i to the process j; $\hat{X}$ is a diagonal matrix with elements X_j along the diagonal; E is a vector and element E_j is the external direct energy input to sector j; and ϵ is a vector and element ϵ_j is the embodied energy intensity per unit of X_j.

It is important to discuss the formal similarity between EEA and SA without joint production because the roles of labour and energy inputs in an economic process are the same in both analyses. According to IFIAS (cited in Brown and Herendeen 1996), EEA is the process of determining the energy required directly and indirectly to allow a system (usually an economic system) to produce commodities. EEA claims that 'with the appropriate perspective and boundaries, market-determined dollar values and embodied energy values are proportional' (Costanza 1980: 1224). In SA without joint production, relative commodity values and labour cost have the same proportional relationship: 'the relative values of commodities are in proportion to their labour cost, that is to say to the quantity of labour which directly and indirectly has gone to produce them' (Sraffa 1960: 12). At first sight, EEA and SA without joint production seem to agree on the roles of the net energy input in EEA and of labour in SA because each unit of external energy input has the same embodied energy intensity in EEA and each unit of labour input receives the same wage in SA. However, the two analyses have entirely different aspects of the role played by energy and labour.

Except when $r = 0$ and $P_H = 1$, the commodity values are not proportional to labour cost. Sraffa uses the case of $r = 0$ and $P_H = 1$ as a preliminary step to set up the concept of the Standard Commodity and the Standard System. The Standard Commodity is a composite commodity in which various commodities are represented among its aggregate means of production in the same proportion as various commodities among its products. The Standard System consists of a set of equations corresponding to the Standard Commodity. Sraffa clearly states that 'in the Standard system the ratio of the net product to the means of production would remain the same whatever variations occurred in the division of the net product between wages and profits and whatever the consequent price changes' (1960: 21).

In EEA, energy is the only net input to the economic system, but it is unclear whether Sraffa treats labour as net input to the system. However, Sraffa recognizes two different characteristics of labour: (1) wages consisting of the necessary subsistence of workers as the basic product defined by Sraffa (a commodity enters into the production of all commodities[1]); (2) a share of the surplus product. Sraffa treats labour only as a share of the surplus product and follows the traditional concept of wage, despite noticing drawbacks of this procedure (1960: 10). Georgescu-Roegen's flow–fund approach tries to evade Sraffa's dual nature of labour by establishing an economic sector which maintains all labour power in which the subsistence character of labour is treated.

2.2 *Joint-production case*

The circular nature of joint production involves a complicated theoretical treatment. Both EEA and SA face two central epistemological issues when investigating the case of joint production: (i) since each commodity is produced by several processes, if a commodity Γ enters only one of two different processes but it is produced in the two processes at the same time, it is difficult or impossible to be sure whether it enters directly into the production process; (ii) if commodity Δ is produced by two different processes and a different commodity Γ enters one of the two processes as a means of production, it is difficult or impossible to be sure whether Γ enters indirectly into the production process.

In the case of joint production, there is no operational meaning of 'direct' or 'indirect'. EEA further complicates issues because energy and material flows in ecosystems are measured in different physical units. In order to examine the issue of dimension in EEA, we apply the following equations to the case of joint production (Hannon *et al.* 1986; Costanza and Hannon 1989):

$$q = Ui + w, \tag{6.5}$$

$$q = V^{t}i, \tag{6.6}$$

$$g = Vi, \tag{6.7}$$

where q is the commodity output vector, g the process output vector, w the net system output vector, i a vector of 1's, U the 'use' matrix (commodity × process) giving use of commodities by the processes, and V is the 'make' matrix (process × commodity) giving production of commodities by the processes.

Rewriting (6.5),

$$q = U\hat{g}^{-1}\hat{g}i + w, \tag{6.8}$$

where $\hat{g}$ is a diagonal matrix with elements of g along the diagonal.

Substituting from equation (6.7),

$$q = U\hat{g}^{-1}Vi + w \tag{6.9}$$

and rewriting,

$$q = U\hat{g}^{-1}V\hat{q}^{-1}\hat{q}i + w. \tag{6.10}$$

Defining $U\hat{g}^{-1} = F$ and $V\hat{q}^{-1} = D$ gives

$$q = FDq + w. \tag{6.11}$$

For simplicity, the issue of dimension is explained in terms of a system of three commodities and two processes. Twins T_1, T_2 and T_3 in the matrices indicate dimension (not strictly physical dimension), where the number 1 indicates no dimension:

$$U = \begin{pmatrix} T_1 & T_1 \\ T_2 & T_2 \\ T_3 & T_3 \end{pmatrix}, \tag{6.12}$$

$$V = \begin{pmatrix} T_1 & T_2 & T_3 \\ T_1 & T_2 & T_3 \end{pmatrix} \tag{6.13}$$

and

$$q = Ui + w = V^{t}i = \begin{pmatrix} T_1 \\ T_2 \\ T_3 \end{pmatrix}. \tag{6.14}$$

In order to transform g into a dimensionless quantity, the following path is adopted:

$$g = Vi = \begin{pmatrix} T_1 & T_2 & T_3 \\ T_1 & T_2 & T_3 \end{pmatrix} \begin{pmatrix} T_1^{-1} \\ T_2^{-1} \\ T_3^{-1} \end{pmatrix} = \begin{pmatrix} 1 \\ 1 \end{pmatrix}, \tag{6.15}$$

$$U\hat{g}^{-1} = \begin{pmatrix} T_1 & T_1 \\ T_2 & T_2 \\ T_3 & T_3 \end{pmatrix} \begin{pmatrix} 1 & 0 \\ 0 & 1 \end{pmatrix} = \begin{pmatrix} T_1 & T_1 \\ T_2 & T_2 \\ T_3 & T_3 \end{pmatrix} = F, \tag{6.16}$$

$$V\hat{q}^{-1} = \begin{pmatrix} T_1 & T_2 & T_3 \\ T_1 & T_2 & T_3 \end{pmatrix} \begin{pmatrix} T_1^{-1} & 0 & 0 \\ 0 & T_2^{-1} & 0 \\ 0 & 0 & T_3^{-1} \end{pmatrix} = D = \begin{pmatrix} 1 & 1 & 1 \\ 1 & 1 & 1 \end{pmatrix}. \tag{6.17}$$

Forming FDq

$$FDq = \begin{pmatrix} T_1 & T_1 & T_1 \\ T_2 & T_2 & T_2 \\ T_3 & T_3 & T_3 \end{pmatrix} \begin{pmatrix} T_1 \\ T_2 \\ T_3 \end{pmatrix} = \begin{pmatrix} T_1^2 + T_1T_2 + T_1T_3 \\ T_2T_1 + T_2^2 + T_2T_3 \\ T_3T_1 + T_3T_2 + T_3^2 \end{pmatrix}. \tag{6.18}$$

The dimensions in equation (6.11) are not consistent with dimensions in equations (6.14) and (6.18), making untenable the claim: 'it is indirectly applicable by assuming a set of weights to allow the formation of g and then investigating the properties of these weights' (Hannon *et al.* 1986: 395).

Sraffa's aim of introducing the case of joint production provides the major difference between EEA and SA. Sraffa (1960: Chapter VIII) describes the case of two products jointly produced by two different methods, implying that the same machine at different ages should be treated as being different products with different prices. Thus, the partly worn-out, older machine emerging from the production process may be regarded as a joint product with the year's output of a commodity.

It is important to consider the concept of non-basic and basic commodities. [2] In a system of n productive processes and n commodities (produced jointly or otherwise) a group of m $(1 \leq m < n)$ linked commodities are non-basic if the rank of matrix of n rows and $2m$ columns is less than or equal to m (Sraffa 1960: 51). All other commodities are basic.

A system of equations of the production system can be transformed into a system of equations without non-basic commodities. This transformation produces a set of positive and negative multipliers which, when applied to the original n equations, allows a reduction of the original equations to a smaller number of equations equal in number to basic products. This new system of equations is called the Basic Equations. In each of the smaller number of equations, an equal number of non-basic quantities occur with opposite signs and cancel out, so only basics are included. Sraffa introduces the Basic Equations to show that the relation between relative values of basic commodities and the rate of profit is independent of the relation between relative values of non-basic commodities (if any) and the rate of profit.

A system of equations similar to the Basic Equations in SA may contain negative quantities as well as positive quantities. This is a logical problem, but not one of insufficient data, as claimed by some energy analysts who insist that 'such negative values are mainly a result of flaws in the original data acquisition and aggregation and can be eliminated by judicious further aggregation, or by better data' (Hannon *et al.* 1986: 397); the same view is expressed by Costanza and Hannon (1989: 99).

2.3 Comparison with the flow–fund model

Table 6.1 considers an aggregated economic process:

P_0: transforms matter *in situ* MS into controlled matter CM;
P_1: transforms energy *in situ* ES into controlled energy CE;
P_2: produces maintenance capital goods K;
P_3: produces consumer goods C;
P_4: recycles garbojunk GJ into recycled matter RM;
P_5: maintains population H.

Flows are elements that enter but do not exit the process or, conversely, elements that exit without having entered the process. Funds (capital, people and Ricardian land[3]) are elements that enter and exit the process unchanged, transforming input

Table 6.1 The aggregated economic process

Elements	P_0	P_1	P_2	P_3	P_4	P_5
Flow coordinates						
CM	x_{00}	*	$-x_{02}$	$-x_{03}$	$-x_{04}$	*
CE	$-x_{10}$	x_{11}	$-x_{12}$	$-x_{13}$	$-x_{14}$	$-x_{15}$
MK	$-x_{20}$	$-x_{21}$	x_{22}	$-x_{23}$	$-x_{24}$	$-x_{25}$
C	*	*	*	x_{33}	*	$-x_{35}$
RM	*	*	$-x_{42}$	$-x_{43}$	x_{44}	*
ES	*	$-e_1$	*	*	*	*
MS	$-M_0$	*	*	*	*	*
GJ	W_0	W_1	W_2	W_3	$-W_4$	W_5
DM	s_0	s_1	s_2	s_3	$-s_4$	s_5
DE	d_0	d_1	d_2	d_3	d_4	d_5
RF	r_0	r_1	r_2	r_3	r_4	R_5
Fund coordinates						
Capital	K_0	K_1	K_2	K_3	K_4	K_5
People	H_0	H_1	H_2	H_3	H_4	H_5
Ricardian land	L_0	L_1	L_2	L_3	L_4	L_5

*No flow.

flows into output flows. DM is dissipated matter and DE is dissipated energy. Refuse RF consists, in part, of available matter and available energy, but in a form not potentially useful to people at present.

Georgescu-Roegen's critique of EEA considers double counting of labour. Assuming energy equivalent of labour service e_{L}, one has

$$Yf - e_{\mathrm{L}}H = e, \tag{6.19}$$

$$Y^{\mathrm{t}} = \begin{pmatrix} x_{00} & * & -x_{02} & -x_{03} & -x_{04} \\ -x_{10} & x_{11} & -x_{12} & -x_{13} & -x_{14} \\ -x_{20} & -x_{21} & x_{22} & -x_{23} & -x_{24} \\ * & * & * & x_{33} & * \\ * & * & -x_{42} & -x_{43} & x_{44} \end{pmatrix}, \tag{6.20}$$

where Y is the transposed matrix of the first five rows and five columns of Table 6.1 ($*$ indicates no flow); f the column vector of gross energy equivalents ${}^{\mathrm{t}}(f_0, f_1, f_2, f_3, f_4)$; e the column vector ${}^{\mathrm{t}}(0, e_1, 0, 0, 0)$; and H the column vector ${}^{\mathrm{t}}(H_0, H_1, H_2, H_3, H_4)$.

In a 'static' perspective, there must normally be one monetary equality:

$$\text{Total receipts} = \text{Total cost}. \tag{6.21}$$

Total cost equals cost of input flows plus payments for fund service. So,

$$B_i = P_H H_i + P_K K_i + P_L L_i \quad (i = 0, 1, 2, 3, 4), \tag{6.22}$$

where B is the column vector ${}^{\mathrm{t}}(B_0, B_1, B_2, B_3, B_4)$; and p the column vector of prices ${}^{\mathrm{t}}(p_0, p_1, p_2, p_3, p_4)$ of physical commodities produced by processes (P_i).

The prices must always satisfy, independently of other constraints, the equation

$$Yp = Re + B, \tag{6.23}$$

where R is the price of energy *in situ* corresponding to the conventional royalty income.

If embodied energies are proportional to prices, the factor of proportionality must be R, so

$$p_i = Rf_i. \tag{6.24}$$

Combining equations (6.19), (6.23) and (6.24) produces an absurd result:

$$Re_{\mathrm{L}}H = B. \tag{6.25}$$

Thus, e_{L} should be deleted to avoid double counting of labour. Equation (6.19) should be replaced by

$$Yf = e. \tag{6.26}$$

Combining equations (6.23), (6.24) and (6.26) produces

$$B = 0. \tag{6.27}$$

Equation (6.27) is absurd, based on the flow complex of EEA without the fund element. The flow complex $B = 0$ is similar to that adopted by neoclassical economists dealing with energy analysis (Huettner 1976). In any economic system, B must be a strictly positive vector, even in a socialist system which includes at least some wages and interest.

Georgescu-Roegen never compares his approach with Sraffa's, but such a comparison is worthwhile because recent research (e.g. England 1986) in sustainability issues indicates possible applicability of SA to sustainability issues.

First, Sraffa and Georgescu-Roegen have decidedly different views about the economic process. Sraffa does not consider the creation of the production process and claims that his investigations are 'concerned exclusively with such properties of an economic system as do not depend on changes in the scale of production or in the proportions of factors' (1960: v). On the other hand, Georgescu-Roegen (1974: 251) reports that: 'commodities are *not* produced by commodities, but by processes. Only in a stationary state is it possible for production to be confined to commodities'.[4] Georgescu-Roegen (1974: 252) maintains that 'it is this Π-sector [process production] . . . that constitutes the fountainhead of the growth and further growth'.

Sraffa considers depreciation of capital fund in order to preserve the same efficiency of capital for reproduction of the process. However, SA is essentially a static analysis. Georgescu-Roegen considers the case of a stationary process in which the fund element is intact. Of course, Georgescu-Roegen recognizes the invalidity of this assumption in the long term because of the entropy law: '[a] process by which something would remain indefinitely outside the influence of the Entropy Law is factually absurd. But the merits of the fiction are beyond question' (1971: 229).

Sraffa treats mineral resources and land as non-basic commodities which are not included in the Standard System and having marginal importance. Georgescu-Roegen's approach holds mineral resources to be vital elements for the survival of human beings.

Georgescu-Roegen sees a fundamental difference between the flow and fund elements in the economic process because p_2 is not equal to P_K, p_2 being the price of various maintenance items and P_K the price proper (e.g. renting an automobile). If the rate of profit $r = 0$, then the approaches of both Sraffa and Georgescu-Roegen are identical in a stationary state. The following equation obtained by Sraffa (1960: 66) for the case of capital illustrates the point:

$$Mp\frac{r(1+r)^n}{(1+r)^n - 1} + (C_1 p_1 + \cdots + C_k p_k)(1+r) + P_H H_g = G_g p_g, \quad (6.28)$$

where M is the number of machines of a given type that are required to produce G_g annually.

If r approaches zero, the following equation holds:

$$\frac{Mp}{n} + (C_1 p_1 + \cdots + C_k p_k) + P_H H_g = G_g p_g, \quad (6.29)$$

where $C_1 p_1 + \cdots + C_k p_k$ is the flow cost, Mp/n the fund cost, and $G_g p_g$ the total receipts.

Equation (6.29) is essentially the same as Georgescu-Roegen's for the reproduction system.

3 Viability of solar technology and the flow–fund model

Three types of aggregated reproducible flow–fund models based on solar technology are presented in Tables 6.2–6.4. The analytical framework of these tables has been introduced by Georgescu-Roegen (1978), but little attention has been paid to

Table 6.2 Flow–fund matrix of a viable solar technology

Elements	P_1	P_2	P_3
Flow coordinates			
SE	x_{11}	$-x_{12}$	$-x_{13}$
CL	$-x_{21}$	x_{22}	*
MK	$-x_{31}$	$-x_{32}$	x_{33}
Fund coordinates			
Capital	K_1	K_2	K_3
People	H_1	H_2	H_3
Ricardian land	L_1	L_2	L_3

*No flow.

Table 6.3 Flow–fund matrix of solar collectors produced by solar energy

Elements	P_1	P_2	P_3^*	P_4^*
Flow coordinates				
SE	a_1x_{11}	$-x_{12}$	*	*
CL	$-x_{21}$	x_{22}	*	*
MK	$-x_{31}$	$-x_{32}$	a_2x_{33}	$-x_{34}$
FE	*	*	$-x_{43}$	x_{44}
Fund coordinates				
Capital	K_1	K_2	K_3^2	K_4^2
People	H_1	H_2	H_3^2	H_4^2
Ricardian land	L_1	L_2	L_3^2	L_4^2

*No flow.

Table 6.4 Flow–fund matrix of the present mixed solar technology

Elements	P_1	P_2^*	P_5^*	P_6^*
Flow coordinates				
SE	a_1x_{11}	*	*	*
CL	$-x_{21}$	x_{22}	*	*
MK	$-x_{31}$	$-x_{32}$	$a_2a_3x_{33}$	$-x_{34} - a_2(a_3 - 1)x_{33}$
FE	*	$-x_{12}$	$-a_3x_{43}$	$a_3x_{44} + x_{12}$
Fund coordinates				
Capital	K_1	K_2	K_3^3	K_4^3
People	H_1	H_2	H_3^3	H_4^3
Ricardian land	L_1	L_2	L_3^3	L_4^3

*No flow.

the schematization.[5] The present chapter attempts to show Georgescu-Roegen's flow–fund model to be an indispensable analytical tool for examining the viability of solar technology.

3.1 *Three flow–fund models*

Georgescu-Roegen (1978) identifies a feasible recipe as being any known procedure for manipulating the material environment for some given purpose. 'Technology' can be defined as a set of feasible recipes containing at least one feasible recipe for every commodity necessary for maintaining any fund element involved. A technology is viable if and only if the economic system it represents can operate steadily as long as environmental flows of available energy and matter are forthcoming in necessary amounts (Georgescu-Roegen 1978, 1986).

Table 6.2 is a flow–fund matrix based on the direct use of solar energy:

P_1: collects solar energy SE with the help of collectors[6] CL and other maintenance capital MK;

P_2: produces collectors with the help of solar energy and capital equipment;

P_3: produces capital equipment with the aid of energy.

For the case of Table 6.2, it is appropriate to define the flow–fund matrix of *strong* viability as a matrix where any flow coordinate except collectors has surplus:

$$x_{11} - x_{12} - x_{13} > 0, \qquad -x_{21} + x_{22} = 0, \qquad -x_{31} - x_{32} + x_{33} > 0. \tag{6.30}$$

Here, it is also appropriate to define the flow–fund matrix of *weak* viability as a matrix where only solar energy produces surplus:

$$x_{11} - x_{12} - x_{13} > 0, \qquad -x_{21} + x_{22} = 0, \qquad -x_{31} + x_{32} + x_{33} = 0. \tag{6.31}$$

Table 6.3 concerns a case in which energy made available by solar collectors more than suffices for the reproduction of the system itself, but capital equipment has to be produced by P_3^* using fossil energy FE. Thus, another process is required:

P_4^*: produces FE.

In Table 6.3, a_1, a_2 are technological parameters and, because of the type of technology considered, it is safe to assume that $a_1 < 1$ and $a_2 > 1$. In these tables, identical characters with identical subscripts and superscripts represent identical variables.

Table 6.4 represents the actual case of solar collectors: [7]

P_2^*: produces collectors with the help of fossil energy and capital equipment;
P_5^*: corresponds to P_3^* in Table 6.3;
P_6^*: corresponds to P_4^* in Table 6.3.

Based on the type of technology in question, it is safe to assume that $a_3 > 1$.

3.2 *Analysis and comparisons*

Table 6.2 gives four results. First, a direct calculation shows that

$$\begin{aligned}\det X &= x_{22}(x_{11} - x_{12} - x_{13})(x_{31} + x_{32}) \\ &\quad + x_{22}(x_{33} - x_{31} - x_{32})(x_{11} - x_{12}) > 0,\end{aligned} \tag{6.32}$$

where X represents the flow coordinates matrix of Table 6.2.

Hence, according to Georgescu-Roegen (1966: 323, Theorem 4), the following system has a positive solution $p^{\mathrm{t}} = (p_1^1, p_2^1, p_3^1) > 0$ (p is the column vector of flow prices in Table 6.2):[8]

$$X^{\mathrm{t}} p = B, \tag{6.33}$$

where $B = {}^t(B_1, B_2, B_3) > 0$, $B_i = P_K K_i + P_H H_i + P_L L_i$, P_K is the price of capital service, P_H the price of labour, and P_L the price of Ricardian land.

Thus, for any strong viable technology and fund prices, there exists a set of positive prices for flow coordinates (Georgescu-Roegen 1979).

Second, there exists a case in which equation (6.33) has a positive solution, even when the technology is not viable. Prices of flow coordinates may be calculated using the following example:

$$X = \begin{pmatrix} 4 & -2 & -3 \\ -1 & 1 & 0 \\ -1 & -2 & 5 \end{pmatrix}. \tag{6.34}$$

A direct calculation shows the following results for prices of flow coordinates:

$$p_1^1 = 5(B_1 + B_2) + 3B_3 > 0, \tag{6.35}$$

$$p_2^1 = 2p_1^1 + 2p_3^1 + B_2 > 0, \tag{6.36}$$

$$p_3^1 = 3B_1 + 3B_2 + 2B_3 > 0. \tag{6.37}$$

Third, curiously, when technology is not viable ($x_{11} < x_{12} + x_{13}$ and $x_{33} < x_{31} + x_{32}$), the price of solar energy is negative! In this case, p_3^1, the price of maintenance capital, can also be negative.[9]

Fourth, it is shown easily that the price of solar energy in a strong viable case is lower than that in a weak viable case. Prices of solar energy for cases in Tables 6.2 and 6.3 are easily calculated, assuming weak viability:

$$p_1^1 = \frac{B_1 + B_2 + B_3}{x_{11} - x_{12} - x_{13}}, \tag{6.38}$$

$$p_1^2 = \frac{B_1 + B_2 + cB_3}{a_1 x_{11} - x_{12}}, \tag{6.39}$$

where $cB_3 = B_3^2 + B_4^2$ (c is a parameter), $B_3^2 = P_K K_3^2 + P_H H_3^2 + P_L L_3^2$, and $B_4^2 = P_K K_4^2 + P_H H_4^2 + P_L L_4^2$.

The line segment AE in Fig. 6.1 is represented by the equation[10]

$$\begin{aligned} &a_1(B_1 + B_2 + B_3)x_{11} - cB_3(x_{11} - x_{12} - x_{13}) \\ &\quad - (B_1 + B_2)(x_{11} - x_{13}) - B_3 x_{12} = 0. \end{aligned} \tag{6.40}$$

Figure 6.1 shows two regions Ω_1 and Ω_2: $p_1^1 < p_1^2$ in Ω_1 and $p_1^1 > p_1^2$ in Ω_2.

If c is greater than D, $p_1^1 < p_1^2$ holds true, regardless of the magnitude of a_1. It is not efficient to produce maintenance capital with the help of fossil fuels, so the price of solar energy based on the energy alone is cheaper than the price of solar energy with capital equipment produced through the use of fossil energy. If c is less than D, for each value of c, there exists a lower limit of a_1 above which

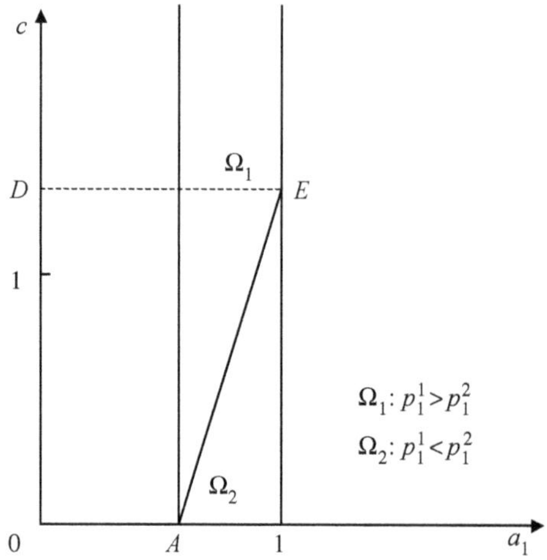

Figure 6.1 Comparison of solar energy for cases in Tables 6.2 and 6.3.

$p_1^1 < p_1^2$ holds true. The price of solar energy based on solar energy alone is cheaper because P_1 produces solar energy efficiently.

The price of solar energy in the case of Table 6.4 is

$$p_1^3 = \frac{B_1 + B_2 + a_3 B_3^2 + (a_3 + x_{12}/x_{44}) B_4^2}{a_1 x_{11}}. \tag{6.41}$$

The equation of hyperbola MJ in Fig. 6.2 can be obtained from (6.39) and (6.41):[11]

$$a_3 = 1 + z_1 + \frac{z_2}{a_1 - x_{12}/x_{11}}, \tag{6.42}$$

where

$$z_1 = \frac{x_{12} B_4^2}{x_{44}(B_3^2 + B_4^2)}, \tag{6.43}$$

$$z_2 = \frac{x_{12} x_{44}(B_1 + B_2 + B_3^2 + B_4^2) + 2x_{12}^2 B_4^2}{x_{11} x_{44}(B_3^2 + B_4^2)}. \tag{6.44}$$

There are two regions Γ_1 and Γ_2: $p_1^3 > p_1^2$ in Γ_1 and $p_1^3 < p_1^2$ in Γ_2.

If a_3 is less than G, $p_1^3 < p_1^2$ always holds true, independently of the value of a_1. When the amount of fossil fuels for producing maintenance capital is small, the price of solar energy is cheaper in the mixed technology of Table 6.4.

As a_1 approaches x_{12}/x_{11}, the range of a_3 in which $p_1^3 < p_1^2$ holds true becomes wider. As the efficiency of producing solar energy becomes lower, the price of solar energy is cheaper in the mixed technology of Table 6.4.

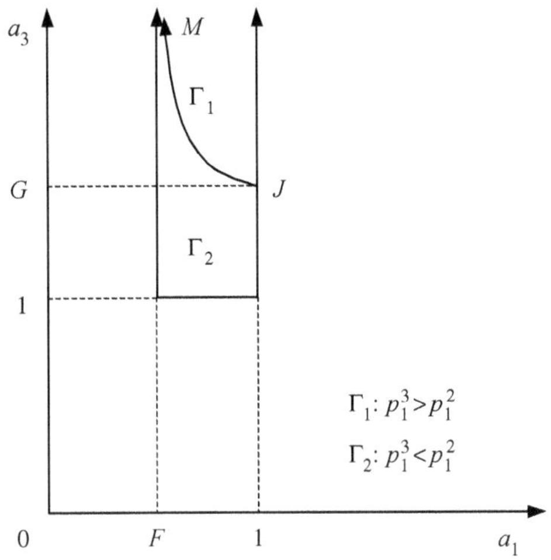

Figure 6.2 Comparison of solar energy: prices for cases in Tables 6.3 and 6.4.

The prices of collectors in Tables 6.2 and 6.3 are

$$p_2^1 = z_3 + \frac{(B_1 + B_2 + B_3)(x_{11}x_{32} + x_{12}x_{31})}{x_{22}(x_{31} + x_{32})(x_{11} - x_{12} - x_{13})}, \tag{6.45}$$

$$p_2^2 = z_3 + \frac{(B_1 + B_2 + cB_3)(a_1x_{11}x_{32} + x_{12}x_{31})}{x_{22}(x_{31} + x_{32})(a_1x_{11} - x_{12})}, \tag{6.46}$$

where

$$z_3 = \frac{B_2x_{31} - B_1x_{32}}{x_{22}(x_{31} + x_{32})}. \tag{6.47}$$

The equation of hyperbola SR in Fig. 6.3 is[12]

$$c = 1 + z_4 - \frac{z_5}{a_1 + (x_{12}x_{31})/(x_{11}x_{32})}, \tag{6.48}$$

where

$$z_4 = \frac{(B_1 + B_2 + B_3)(x_{12}x_{31} + x_{12}x_{32} + x_{13}x_{32})}{(x_{11} - x_{12} - x_{13})B_3x_{32}}, \tag{6.49}$$

$$z_5 = \frac{(B_1 + B_2 + B_3)(x_{11}x_{32} + x_{12}x_{31})^2x_{12}}{(x_{11} - x_{12} - x_{13})B_3x_{11}^2x_{32}^2}. \tag{6.50}$$

Figure 6.3 depicts a case where $x_{31}/x_{32} < 1$. It requires more maintenance capital to produce collectors than to produce solar energy with the help of collectors.

There are two regions Δ_1 and Δ_2: $p_2^1 < p_2^2$ in Δ_1 and $p_2^1 > p_2^2$ in Δ_2.

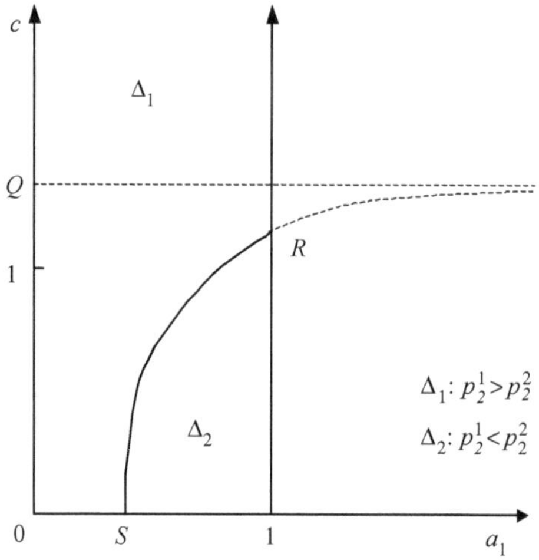

Figure 6.3 Comparison of collectors: prices for cases in Tables 6.2 and 6.3.

If c is greater than R, $p_2^1 < p_2^2$ holds true independently of the value of a_1. It is efficient enough to produce maintenance capital with solar energy, so the price of collectors produced by solar energy is cheaper. If c is less than R, for each value of c there exists a lower limit of a_1, above which $p_2^1 < p_2^2$ holds true. The price of solar collectors based on solar energy alone is cheaper because P_1 produces solar energy efficiently.

4 Conclusion

A recent report in *Oil and Gas Journal* (Campbell 1997: 37) indicates that, by close to the year 2015, real physical shortage of oil supply will begin. Despite the possible exhaustion of oil in the near future, an effective and drastic shift in the use of energy resources has not been and is not being implemented. Abundant coal is more destructive to the environment after energy transformation. Nuclear energy may be much more destructive, considering long-term nuclear waste management. It remains unclear whether or not solar technology can completely replace fossil and fissile fuels. It is an open question as to whether or not solar energy technology will remain a 'parasite' to fossil and fissile fuels.

The analysis presented in this chapter reinforces Georgescu-Roegen's arguments about the issue of solar energy viability; 'viability of a technology requires only that its material scaffold be self-supporting' (1979: 1052). The next issue is to examine the viability of candidates for the direct use of solar energy, particularly the viability of photovoltaic cells.

7 Land: Achilles' Heel of ecology and economy

1 Introduction: two types of efficiency in physical terms

Ever since the Industrial Revolution, successful substitution of land-based resources by fossil fuels and mineral resources has supported the material structure of economic process. This chapter provides an economic and thermodynamic analysis concerning land, focusing mainly on the period since the Industrial Revolution. While the land constraint has eased since the revolution, it is difficult to claim that people have become perfectly emancipated from the land constraint; in fact, this chapter shows that emancipation from the land constraint can be temporary at best.

This introductory section discusses the vitally important characteristic of the present world, namely, the tremendous rate of material and energy degradation causing the rapid depletion of natural resources and the destruction of our environment, including land. Section 2 reconsiders the views of two great minds, Liebig and Marx, who both had prophetic visions concerning the rate of material and energy transformation in modern agriculture and its negative effects on future economy. Section 3 gives a thermodynamic analysis of temporary emancipation from land during the Industrial Revolution in England, dwelling on the substitution of coal for wood, especially in the iron industry, and the growth of the cotton industry. Section 4 shows that, in the United States, temporary emancipation from land is due to the vast quantity of fertile land and the intensive consumption of natural resources, especially oil. This section shows that, even in the United States, the food safety margin will be reduced in the long term, thanks to the law of diminishing returns. Section 5 discusses the essential differences and similarities between farming and manufacturing processes so as to appreciate land constraint properly. Section 6 gives some concluding remarks.

As far as matter and energy transformations are concerned, the economic process can be represented in terms of the relation between low-entropy inputs (inputs of valuable resources) and high-entropy outputs (final outputs of valueless waste). Therefore, an increase in entropy (dS) *per se* is a necessary evil, as long as people are considered as bioeconomic beings. The true problem facing people consists in the choice of the proper speed of increase in entropy (dS/dt) in the long term, as mentioned in Chapter 5. Georgescu-Roegen's emphasis on the large amount of resources required in the economic process, especially on matter in bulk, can best be grasped in terms of the dreadful rate of entropy increase. The rate of entropy increase on the earth has been increasing drastically so that it is not sufficient to talk only about entropy increase. The rate at which entropy increases, in fact, characterizes the destructive aspects of modern technology. While it is virtually impossible to measure this rate exactly for each actual case, the general tendency of entropy increase can be described.

In order to discuss the speed of entropy increase in modern civilization, especially after the 1970s, two types of efficiency in physical terms must be defined as follows:

1 Efficiency of Type 1 (EFT1): It refers to the ratio of output to input. EFT1 does not consider the time required to obtain the output.
2 Efficiency of Type 2 (EFT2): It refers to output per unit time. EFT2 does not consider the amount of inputs to obtain the output.

If the thermal efficiency of an ideal Carnot engine (which has neither friction nor heat loss) is regarded as output, EFT1 is less than 1 because of the Entropy Law. If the speed of a piston of an ideal Carnot engine is regarded as output, EFT2 is infinitesimal, actually zero. Raising EFT2 beyond a certain limit during the transformation process of matter and energy results in a smaller EFT1. For example, to raise the speed of a car beyond an economical speed, gas must be consumed at a higher rate, but even though most drivers know this fact, they prefer to drive fast. Such drivers prefer EFT2 in terms of speed of the car to EFT1 in terms of gas consumption.

Three fundamental substances – fossil fuels, concrete and iron – play indispensable roles in supporting the material structure of modern urban life. These three material bases for urban life are low-entropy resources made with low EFT2 in the past. Fossil fuels result from photosynthesis in plants and animals during the Palaeozoic era. Such results were created over grand scales of time and land, contributing to high EFT2. Limestone, a main element of concrete, comes from the debris of lime algae and iron ore comes from piled ore deposits formed through activities of iron-containing bacteria. People now enjoy high EFT2 by consuming these vast treasures. Therefore, it may perhaps be said that it is very difficult to maintain our civilization without the support of low-entropy resources saved in ecosystems. There is an optimal combination of EFT1 and EFT2 under some technical criterion, but the present state of technology appropriates EFT2 much more than EFT1 and a high level of EFT2 is guaranteed by low-entropy resources stored in the past. Therefore, $\mathrm{d}S/\mathrm{d}t$ necessarily becomes bigger and bigger.

Carter and Dale (1974: 237–8) present an example of the bias of EFT2 over EFT1 on the land problem. There are chemical substances such as Krilium, Loamium and other 'miracle' compounds that are supposed to make productive loam from heavy clay subsoil. These chemicals have only temporary effects (EFT2 complex) without raising land fertility, causing soil particles to cohere, i.e. granulate. This granulation speeds up oxidation in minute organic matter and degrades the soil.

2 Far-sighted views of Liebig and Marx on 'EFT2 complex' of modern agriculture

The natural tendency toward an increase in entropy is equivalent to saying that available matter and energy will be diffused and the rate of diffusion of matter and energy has increased tremendously due to 'EFT2-mania'.

The great minds of Liebig and Marx appreciate the diffusion of matter and energy due to EFT2-mania, especially in agriculture, and both worry about its possible outcome.

Liebig refers to the agricultural methods of his time in Europe as *a spoliation system* because these methods contribute only to further exploitation of the total sum of elements from soils. These methods are directed solely to produce more in a given time period (Liebig 1859). Through his study, Liebig has an insight into the essential characteristic of modern agriculture – the EFT2 complex. Liebig worries about farming based on a spoliation system, where agriculturists ignore the importance of the maintenance of land fertility. Because agriculturists seek to obtain the maximum amount of crops using minimum labour input and a large amount of fertilizer in shorter time (Liebig 1859). For two reasons, Liebig's agronomical view is entirely different from that of the agricultural economists at the time. First, Liebig clearly grasps the fact that the basic cause of degradation of land fertility is the sale of agricultural products and expansion of sewage systems in urban areas without returning residues of agricultural products and excreta to soils. Second, Liebig's contemporary agricultural economists in Europe do not pay sufficient attention to the importance of circulating matter in order to maintain long-term land fertility. Such agricultural economists are primarily interested in increasing the crop yields in a short span of time. Liebig's position is clear:

> Hence, little 'Japhet in search of his Father', the poor child called 'Mineral Theory', was so ill-used and ridiculed, because he was of the opinion that the big purse at least be emptied, by always taking out money without putting any in. But who could have thought twenty years ago, when there was plenty of manure, that it would ever occur to these obstinate and wilful fodder plants to produce no more manure, and no longer to *spare* and *enrich* the ground? The soil is naturally not the cause of this; for they teach that it is inexhaustible, and those still enough believe that the source from which it is derived will always flow. Truly, if this soil could cry out like a cow or a horse which was tormented to give the maximum quantity of milk or work with the smallest expenditure of fodder, the earth would become to these agriculturists more intolerable than Dante's infernal regions. Hence, the advantageous prosecution of this system of modern agriculture is only possible on large estates, for the spoliation of a small one would soon come to an end.
>
> (Liebig 1859: 130–1)

Liebig's critique of the agricultural system is based on his view that land and its natural power are the source of wealth for nations and for the human species as a whole. Liebig's scientific thought places human beings in a natural co-existence with great cycles of nature going on without much intervention, enabling him to posit his view and to differentiate himself from agricultural economics who treat nature as human property.

There is now tremendous degradation of nature and land due to rapid industrial development in both socialist and capitalist countries. Strangely enough, the Marxian economists, assumed to inherit Marx's genius, do not seem to properly appreciate his view on nature and man.[1] The Industrial Revolution caused separation between cities and farm villages (Parsons 1977). In this regard, Marx clearly influenced by Liebig, writes:

> The capitalist mode of production extends the utilization of the excretions of production and consumption. By the former we mean the waste of industry and agriculture, and by the latter partly the excretions produced by the natural exchange of matter in the human body and partly the forms of objects that remain after their consumption. In the chemical industry, for instance, excretion of production are such by-products as are wasted in production on a smaller scale; iron filings accumulating in the manufacture of machinery and returning into the production of iron as raw material, etc. Excretions of consumption are of the greatest importance for agriculture. So far as their utilization is concerned, there is an enormous waste of them in the capitalist economy. In London, for instance, they find no better use for the excretion of four and a half million human beings than to contaminate the Thames with it at heavy expense.
>
> (Marx 1959: 100)

The picture drawn by Marx has much worsened since his time. Marx succinctly grasps the fundamental cause of destruction of nature; in modern society, dialectical relationship between people and nature (material circulation between man and nature) is executed through exchange of economic goods.

Marx writes about Liebig in several places:

> To have developed the point of view of natural science, the negative, *i.e.*, destructive side of modern agriculture, is one of Liebig's immortal merits. His summary, too, of the history of agriculture, although not free from gross errors, contains flashes of light.
>
> (Marx 1936: 555)

Marx's comments on Liebig also appear in a letter to Engels:

> I had to wade through the new agricultural chemistry in Germany, especially Liebig and Schönbein, who are more important in this matter than all the economists put together.
>
> (Marx 1979: 205 and 207)

Liebig's influence on Marx often occurs in *Capital*:

> It [Capitalist production] disturbs the circulation of matter between man and the soil, *i.e.*, prevents the return to the soil of its elements consumed by man in the form of food and clothing; it therefore violates the conditions necessary to lasting fertility of the soil.
>
> (Marx 1936: 554)

Moreover, Marx keenly grasps the syndrome of the EFT2 complex of modern agriculture in the following passages:

> All progress in capitalistic agriculture is a process in the art, not only of robbing the labour, but of robbing the soil; all progress in increasing the fertility of the soil for a given time, is a progress towards ruining the lasting sources of that fertility. The more a country starts its development on the foundation of modern industry, like the United States, for example, the more rapid is this process of destruction. Capitalist production, therefore, develops technology, and the combining together of various processes into a social whole, only by sapping the original sources of all wealth – the soil and the labourer.
>
> (Marx 1936: 555–6)

Marx deeply understands the difference between agriculture and manufacturing:

> It is possible to invest capital here successively with fruitful results, because the soil itself serves as an instrument of production, which is not the case with a factory, as a place and a space providing a basis of operations . . . The fixed capital invested in machinery, etc., does not improve through use, but on the contrary, wears out.
>
> (Marx 1959: 761–2)

Marx also mentions the similar characteristics between large-scale industry and large-scale mechanized agriculture:

> Large-scale industry and large-scale mechanized agriculture work together. If originally distinguished by the fact that the former lays waste and destroys principally labour-power, hence the natural force of human beings, whereas, the latter more directly exhausts the natural vitality of the soil, they join hands in the further course of development in that the industrial system in the country-side also enervates the labourers, and industry and commerce on their part supply agriculture with the means for exhausting the soil.
>
> (Marx 1959: 793)

Clearly, Marx effectively evaluates and appreciates the development process of agriculture and the destructive aspect of modern industry in terms of Liebig's discussion of the circulation of matter between nature and humans.

It seems appropriate to conclude this section with Marx's concern for the forest:

> The long production time (which comprises a relatively small period of working time) and the great length of the periods of turnover entailed made forestry an industry of little attraction to private and therefore capitalist enterprise, the latter being essentially private even if the associated capitalist takes the place of the individual capitalist. The development of culture and of industry in general has ever evinced itself in such energetic destruction of forests that everything done by it conversely for their preservation and restoration appears infinitesimal.
>
> (Marx 1957: 244)

3 The Industrial Revolution in England

Toward the end of the eighteenth century, Liebig and Marx showed the damaging effects of crop sales and sewage system on land fertility, and they worried about the future land situation. Ironically, at that time the Industrial Revolution, providing a temporary relief from the land constraint, had already begun. In order to understand the historical background properly, this section begins with a discussion of land in Europe, especially in England, before the Industrial Revolution.

The Western European civilization has been a dominant influence for over the last 1,000 years. In Western Europe, most of the agricultural land has been cultivated for less than nine centuries. For most part, its climate is conducive to soil conservation, thanks to mild rains and mists, with few torrential downpours and snow that protects the cultivated fields from erosion during winter. The Romans exploited most land in Western Europe by the first century BC, but most of that land recuperated by the time of the Dark Ages. Most of the land north and west of the Alps was nearly as productive as it had been before Phoenician and Greek civilization came to the region during the period of 500 BC. Encouraged by the feudal lords, modern Western civilization developed rapidly from the eleventh century through to the thirteenth century, the amount of cultivated land tripled or quadrupled in most parts of Western Europe. This expansion practically amounted to a recolonization of all Western Europe. Eventually, feudal power collapsed and, by the middle of the fourteenth century, a substantial part of the tillable land of Western Europe was cultivated through the emancipation of the serfs encouraged by the kings in emerging European nations. Although a vast number of Europeans died from the Black Death in the fourteenth century, this period saw the modern systems of crop rotation, manuring, liming and other soil-building methods designed for preserving land fertility. Such more advanced European agriculture allowed the urban population to exceed the rural population for the first time in human history. One farmer could produce more than enough to feed his own family and *another family* in the city (Carter and Dale 1974).

As the population in cities of Western Europe grew, organic raw materials, including food, became scarcer, and the pressure generated by the land shortage began. In England, the pressure was more powerful than on the continent, particularly in Germany and France, because the feudal system in England ended much earlier than in Germany and France. Feudalism in Germany, for instance, 'did not disappear until the Prussian kings came to power about the middle of the seventeenth century' (Carter and Dale 1974: 179). It is important to examine how the Industrial Revolution allowed England to escape this land shortage by the end of the eighteenth century.

The most dramatic change in raw material provision during the Industrial Revolution was the substitution of inorganic sources of supply for organic ones, especially land-based resources (Wrigley 1962). R. G. Wilkinson describes the situation in England before the Industrial Revolution:

> The supply of food and drink depended on agricultural land, clothing came from the wool of sheep on English pasture, and large areas of land were needed for extensive forest: almost all domestic and industrial fuel was firewood, and timber was one of the most important construction materials for houses, ships, mills, farm implements etc. In addition, the transport system depended on horses and thus required large areas of land to be devoted to grazing and the production of feed. Even lighting used tallow candles which depended ultimately on the land supply.
>
> (Wilkinson 1973: 112)

With increase in population, land became increasingly scarce. That this led to a crisis can be seen from the fact that England became a net importer of wheat instead of a net exporter in the late eighteenth century except during 1785–89 (Wilkinson 1973).

The substitution of coal for wood had the most dramatic influence on the progress of the English Industrial Revolution. In some cases, coal was substituted for wood without serious technical difficulties. Where substances were kept separate from the fuel in industries such as smiths, limeburners, salt-boiling, dyeing, soap-boiling, the preparation of alum, copperas, saltpetre and tallow candles, it was quite easy to substitute coal for wood (Wilkinson 1973). However, where coal was in direct contact with raw materials, especially in iron-smelting, the difficulty of substituting coal for wood remained unsolved until Abraham Darby I succeeded in using coke to smelt native ore at his works of Coalbrookdale in 1709 (Armytage 1961).

The quality of coke pig iron was inferior to charcoal pig iron because wood is a raw material of low entropy. Therefore, the refining process was still dependent on charcoal. In addition, coke furnaces required a site near large coal mines, iron mines and water mills. Another great difficulty was that coal mining reached depths at which the then existing methods of drainage became impracticable (Wilkinson 1973).

A secured supply of water was a prerequisite for building large-scale water mills and much water was necessary to turn water mills using Newcomen's engine. Newcomen's engine had an overall thermal efficiency of only 0.2 per cent.

Therefore, a water shortage problem began. Watt's steam engine, with a thermal efficiency of 2 per cent, solved the problem of drainage in coal mines and enabled the construction of water mills that are not so dependent on location and seasonal variation in water flow. Thanks to the increased thermal efficiency of Watt's steam engine, transportation of raw materials and final goods was eased dramatically so that it became possible to construct iron works in areas remote from coal mines and consuming cities.

Through the development of Watt's steam engine, the English iron industry shifted to coke furnaces (blast furnaces) and subsequently established industrial supremacy for about a century. During this period, the refining process was also transformed to use cokes, thanks to the puddling process patented by H. Cort in 1783 (Armytage 1961).

By using a reverberatory furnace, pig iron was heated indirectly, so that the impure elements in coal did not diffuse into iron. However, the reduction in thermal efficiency due to indirect heating was a burden, although there was plenty of coal available. A dramatic improvement in the balance of thermal efficiency was achieved by the Siemens–Martin process in 1865 (Armytage 1961).

The development process of the (coke) blast furnace can be regarded as a typical example of resource substitution. First, there occurs a scarcity problem of low-entropy resource (e.g. wood). A substitutable resource is of high entropy (coal) so that a roundabout process is needed to remove mixing entropy due to poor-quality raw material (coal). Unless a new resource is itself of low entropy (e.g. oil) or there is another low-entropy material available to reduce the entropy of the new resource of high entropy, the latter cannot be available to mankind by technological progress. Technology cannot produce something from nothing; it is merely a catalyst, as it were, to induce the emergence of latent ability of a resource.

Another important technological aspect of the Industrial Revolution came from a change in the transportation system. The secure supply of raw materials is key in carrying out large-scale production. As E. A. Wrigley indicates, 'production of the former (mineral production) is a punctiform; of the latter (vegetable and animal production) areal' (Wrigley 1962: 3). In England, the expansion of the transportation system was necessary due to increase in population. It became impossible for a growing eighteenth-century population within a local area to sustain an adequate standard of living. Instead of horses, canals and later steam railways became major means of transportation.

Growth of the cotton industry, one of the dominant features of the revolution, shows a different aspect of raw material supply. In England, shift from the wool to cotton industry benefited from two land-saving factors. First, while cotton is a land-based resource, England could exploit land in India and America and it was relatively easy for the cotton industry to expand production without causing a land shortage in England. Second, while the wool industry had a process 'solar energy + water ⇒ meadow ⇒ wool', the cotton industry followed 'solar energy + water ⇒ cotton' (Kawamiya 1983). The latter did not require part of the roundabout process, i.e. 'meadow ⇒ wool'. However, as the production of cotton expanded dramatically, working hours increased greatly because more labour was required to process cotton into a piece of cloth. At the same time, only water mills and horse power were available as sources of motive power before the invention of the steam engine. Mechanization by utilizing steam engines solved these problems successfully, so the rapid expansion of the cotton industry became possible subsequently.

The Industrial Revolution in England was supported by two thermodynamic improvements and changes – first, the transition from organic materials, especially wood (scarce and of low entropy) to coal (high entropy) and second, the transition from good-quality wool (but dependent on land in England) to poor-quality cotton (but abundant in India and America) (Kawamiya 1983).

The Industrial Revolution seemed to be a panacea for the land problem. However, coal itself is a land-based resource and to use a past heritage created by plants over a long period of time means that people are totally dependent on land. In addition, there is a similarity between the scarcity of wood before the revolution and the resource problems facing mankind today and in the near future. Transition from wood (charcoal) to coal in the iron industry means transition from a 'clean resource' (low entropy of mixing) to a 'dirty resource' (high entropy of mixing). Today there is a similar transitional problem because oil and natural gas are superior to coal. By the 1970s, oil was used intensively all over the industrial world. Rapid shift of a fundamental resource has been rather unusual in the modern history of humans. The transition from coal to oil means transition from a 'dirty resource' to a 'clean resource'. One of the features of modern technologies is an intensive use of oil, which was produced on land in the past. The consumption of oil increased exponentially during 1860–1980. Oil is now used at an accelerated rate, consumption doubling about every ten years (Tsuchida 1982: 76). Truly, in the process of the industrial revolution, the land shortage has been reduced by shifting from wood to coal. However, it would be absurd to claim that the present crisis can be overcome based on the past success.

4 Temporary emancipation from land: the United States

'It is the quantity of the land, not its quality, which is decisive here' (Marx 1959: 656) in the development of America in the colonial times, as Marx correctly indicates. Carter and Dale agree:

> The area now known as the United States contained nearly two billion acres of land. Two-thirds of the country was covered with magnificent forests or lush grass, wildlife of all types abounded, rainfall was adequate for agriculture over more than one-half the area, and all this land was occupied by less than two million people.
>
> (Carter and Dale 1974: 222)

A peculiar aspect of the American Revolution is that, after independence, the European settlers had only American Indians as competitors for the vast expanse of land. At first, successive American presidents obtained land by entering into treaties with the American Indians. During these early years of US history, most lands in the middle and west parts of the US were American Indian territory. Later, colonists started a westward expansion with the tacit consent and support of the American government. Commenting on the land situation in the United States, Liebig writes:

> As men began to till the soil, and as fast as they exhausted one locality of such elements of God's bounty as were in a condition, from their solubility, to act as food for plants, they moved to new places rather than to properly work or fertilize old ones. They were not the servitors of their grandchildren, but with a vast country before them they chose to skim it, and as they drove the Red Men westward, they found new fields for planting, and they 'skimmed' the land. Here the great mistake was made, that of overrunning the soil to reap a few good crops that ended in impoverishing it, and this bad example has followed to the present day. Thus the Atlantic slope became a depleted expanse, and unprofitable with the modes of culture in practice.
>
> (Liebig 1859: 243)

With respect to the tendency of decrease in yields, Liebig writes:

> A writer in the 'Year Book of Agriculture for 1855', on the 'Alarming Deterioration of the Soil' referred to various statistics of great significance in connection with this subject. Some of them regarded Massachusetts, where the hay crop declined *twelve* per cent. from 1840 to 1850, notwithstanding the addition of 90,000 acres to its mowing lands, and the grain crop absolutely depreciated 6,000 bushels, although the tillage lands had been increased by the addition of 60,000 acres.
>
> (Liebig 1859: 243)

Marx, who fully understands that sales of agricultural products to remote areas without returning crop residues place stress on the natural circulation of matter and cause the decreased land fertility, pays special attention to J. F. W. Johnston's *Notes on North America: Agricultural, Economical, and Social* and calls him the English Liebig (Marx and Engels 1982: 476). Johnston reaches a similar conclusion about American agriculture, as Liebig does – that export of large quantities of agricultural products is nothing less than the export of land fertility itself, without compensation. Johnston also sees clearly that the virgin lands in America do not have limitless fertility, while vast stretches of land enable America to export a large quantity of agricultural products *temporarily*:

> The power of exporting large quantities of wheat implies neither great natural productiveness, nor permanently rich land . . . And yet, such a country as I have described – like the interior uplands of western New York – will give excellent first crops, even of wheat, and will supply, to those who *skim the first*

> *cream off the country*, a large surplus of this grain to send to market (italics added).
>
> (Johnston 1851: 223–4)

Johnston predicts the situation of America:

> When a tract of land is thinly peopled – like the newly settled districts of North America, New Holland, or New Zealand – a very defective system of culture will produce food enough not only for the wants of the inhabitants, but for the partial supply of other countries also. But when the population becomes more dense, the same imperfect system will no longer suffice.
>
> (Johnston 1847: 4)

By the end of World War I mistreatment of land in the United States took the form of shipment of furs and skins of wildlife, export of as much timber as foreign markets would take and burning of much of what was not wanted, and transfer of soil fertility through export of tobacco, cotton, wheat, corn, beef, pork and wool. Americans tried to extract land products as quickly as possible and caused ruin in a shorter time (EFT2 complex) than any earlier society because there was more land to exploit and better tools for exploitation (Carter and Dale 1974). This situation did not change much until 'agribusiness' came to the temporary rescue after World War II. B. Commoner notes:

> [A]gribusiness is founded on several technological developments, chiefly farm machinery, genetically controlled plant varieties, feedlots, inorganic fertilizers (especially nitrogen), and synthetic pesticides. But much of the new technology has been an ecological disaster; agribusiness is a main contributor to the environmental crisis.
>
> (Commoner 1971: 148)

The environmental crisis identified by Commoner, especially erosion and degradation of land, is a result of the EFT2 complex, which typifies modern industry including agriculture. Agribusiness is interested in increasing crop yields as much as possible in the shortest span of time instead of increasing total agricultural produce by maintaining land fertility for future generations. Continued abuse of land by agribusiness contributed to land exhaustion. It misunderstood the meaning of culture, as H. Maron, who visited Japan in the last days of the Tokugawa shogunate as a member of the Prussian East Asian Expedition, correctly observed:

> If by 'culture' is meant the capability of the soil to give permanently high produce, by way of *real interest on the capital of the soil*, I must altogether deny that our farms (with perhaps a few exceptions), can properly be said to be in a satisfactory state of culture. But we have by excellent tillage and a peculiar method of manuring, put them in a condition to make the entire productive power of the soil available, and thus to give immediately full crops.

> It is not, however, the interest that we obtain in such crops, but the capital itself of the soil upon which we are drawing. The more largely our system enables us to draw upon this capital, the sooner it will come to an end.
>
> (Liebig 1972: 369–70)

It is useful to discuss intensive petroleum utilization and some of its consequences. With the possible exception of iron ore, a general trend of resource substitution is the movement toward resources of high entropy after first exhausting the resources of low entropy. A typical example is the gold ore. Pure gold was mined in ancient times but, in modern gold mining, only about seven grams of pure gold per one ton of gold ore is usually mined. Transition from wood to coal during the Industrial Revolution was a similar resource substitution. However, as discussed before, the transition from coal to oil is an entirely different substitution. It is an exceptionally rare case of substitution of a main resource which supports the motive power of a whole industrial system (Kawamiya 1983).

Oil has three distinctive characteristics. First, oil is made of high-purity hydrocarbons and it has very low mixing entropy, making oil superior to coal. Second, oil is a liquid and has low entropy *per unit volume*, making it better than natural gas because transportation and storage of natural gas requires more equipment. Third, the environmental pollution is relatively mild when oil is burned, making oil superior to coal and nuclear energy (Kawamiya 1983).

Oil is an excellent raw material in manufacturing and products such as plastics and polythenes provide an important group of new materials to substitute for wooden products. 'Polythene sheet is replacing cellophane and paper (both made from wood pulp) for bags and wrapping as well as for a number of other uses, and heavier plastics are being substituted for wood in moulding where rigidity and heat resistance are unnecessary' (Wilkinson 1973: 185). These are a few examples of substitution of minerals for land-based resources. A most important distinction between modern technology and technology in the Industrial Revolution era is that substitution of minerals for land-based resources is now accelerated vastly in scale and variety.

The intensive use of energy, especially oil and oil-related products, in modern agriculture has been examined in terms of energy balance in corn production in the United States, considering the energy required for the production of agricultural machines, fertilizers, pesticides and other management tools as indirect input to corn production (Pimentel *et al.* 1973). Between 1945 and 1970, corn yield increased from 3.4 to 8.2 billion kcal (238%), and the total energy inputs increased from 0.9 to 2.9 billion kcal (312%). But, the ratio of return kcal to input kcal was reduced from 3.70 to 2.82.

The United States seems to have escaped the land trap by the intensive use of machinery and chemicals, but the law of diminishing returns on land has already begun to work, as Commoner writes:

> Between 1949 and 1968 total United States agricultural production increased by about 45 per cent. Since the United States population grew by 34 per cent

> in that time, the overall increase in population was just about enough to keep up with population; crop production *per capita* increased 6 per cent. In that period, the annual use of fertilizer nitrogen increased by 648 per cent, surprisingly larger than the increase in crop production.
>
> (Commoner 1971: 149)

Liebig answers the question why modern agricultural methods cannot escape the trap of the law of diminishing returns. His answer is *Gesetz des Minimums* (*the Doctrine of Minimum*):

> [E]very field contains a *maximum* of one or several, and a *minimum* of one or several other nutritive substances. It is by the *minimum* that the crops are governed, be it lime, potash, nitrogen, phosphoric acid, magnesia, or any other mineral constituent; it regulates and determines the amount or continuance of the crops.
>
> (Liebig 1972: 207)

When soil has one or more abundant mineral constituents (e.g. nitrogen), the rate at which that mineral constituent is removed by the crops is small so that, temporarily, the effect of the law of diminishing returns is not obvious. Therefore, intensive use of chemicals can temporarily keep soil from suffering from the trap of the law of diminishing returns of the 'rate' type (Mayumi 1990). However, other elements, especially the rare ones, are removed as crops are harvested. The relative decrease in the quantity of these elements profoundly influences the succeeding crop yields, resulting in a decrease in land fertility. That is to say, the law of diminishing returns of the 'stock' type for these elements begins to take effect and the crop yields decrease dramatically in the long term. It is important to know fully the condition and composition of soil, which, ironically, vary in different fields. A general principle cannot be applied to different soils. The condition and composition of soil depends on geography, precipitation, temperature, etc., so it is necessary to revalue indiscriminate application of machinery and chemicals to different soils.

5 Farming vs. manufacturing

This section examines the similarities and the essential differences between farming and manufacturing by noting the fundamental asymmetry of the two sources of low entropy, sunlight and fossil fuels. It is shown that, due to this asymmetry, agriculture cannot be more productive than manufacturing and that modern agriculture is nothing but manufacturing, which is against the pattern of ecological succession (Mayumi 1994).

5.1 Viability, and similarities between farming and manufacturing

According to Georgescu-Roegen, 'a viable technology is a complex of techniques that can support the life of the associated biological species as long as some specific "fuel" is forthcoming' (Georgescu-Roegen 1992). Human history shows only three viable technologies: agriculture, the mastery of fire, and the steam engine (the internal-combustion engine). Georgescu-Roegen calls these technologies Promethean:

> With just the spark of a match we can set on fire a whole forest, nay, all forests. This property, although not as violent, characterizes the other two Promethean recipes. It is a commonplace that a seeded grain of corn will normally yield a surplus of a handful of grains.
>
> (Georgescu-Roegen 1992: 150)

This explosive characteristic of Promethean technique shared by agriculture and manufacturing shows a tendency for humans to speed up the depletion of the special fuels for these Promethean techniques. Land is the special fuel for agriculture. Fossil fuels are the special fuels for modern industry. It is a matter of vital importance both for agriculture and for manufacturing to secure sufficient amounts of these special fuels.

Each agricultural operation performed by people and machinery consists mostly of *mechanical movements*. In the case of agriculture, basic work done by people and machinery is nothing but an attempt to move or to transport materials. So, in a sense, people must wait while nature works. Even in modern manufacturing industrial society, the situation is essentially the same. Without moving or transporting raw materials and labour on a large scale, industrial society could never even temporarily undertake large-scale production. In other words, without the fossil fuels such as oil and coal, which are the motive sources of modern civilization, large-scale production could never occur, even if other mineral resources are abundant. Modern civilization is based entirely on *motive power and transportation*. For example, most oil is used for transportation and motive power. After Georgescu-Roegen's expression, our civilization is based on Prometheus II (T. Savery and T. Newcommen, N. Otto and R. Diesel): clearly, *no coal and oil, no modern civilization*. These two fossil fuels are contributed by animals and plants who lived *in vast stretches of land over thousands of millions of years* and guaranteed the essential merits of modern industry, i.e. *land saving and time saving*. Modern civilization consumes these natural gifts at a rate much faster than the rate at which coal and oil were created naturally. Hence it still depends heavily on land-based resources in manufacturing as well as in agriculture. Thus, in terms of such a dependence, there is no difference between farming and manufacturing.

There is another similarity between farming and manufacturing concerning future water shortage. Theoretically, about 500 tons of water are required to produce one ton of carbohydrate. Japan, for example, imports eighty million tons of agricultural products every year, amounting to forty billion tons of water, far more than the water use for all urban areas in Japan. This situation implies that exporting countries are losing ecological capacity to preserve their water resources (Kawamiya 1983). Water plays a crucial role in the disposal of waste heat and materials, after transforming low-entropy inputs into high-entropy outputs in the production process (Tsuchida 1982).

In the United States, for instance, more than 45 per cent of the total end use of water was directed to stream electric use in 1980 (US Department of Commerce 1987). Soon, severe competitions for water resources will emerge between agriculture and industry, as well as between developed and developing countries.

5.2 *Source of differences between farming and manufacturing*

It is useful to represent a process using Georgescu-Roegen's analytical tool, namely, the flow–fund model. The boundary of such a process must have two analytical components, one being the frontier of the process which sets the process against its environment at any point in time, and the other the duration of the process. The boundary is a void by which there is a partial process and another partial process, i.e. its environment. Georgescu-Roegen's scheme allows investigation of what happens on the boundary.

To understand the essential difference between farming and manufacturing requires introduction of the concept of an elementary process. An elementary process 'is the process defined by a boundary such that only one unit or only one normal batch is produced. The most instructive illustration is the sequence of operations by which an automobile is produced on an assembly line' (Georgescu-Roegen 1984). The individual elementary process may be arranged in series, in parallel, or in line. Partial processes arranged in series are such that no process overlaps another in time. Partial processes arranged in parallel are such that a certain number of elementary processes start at the same time and repeat after they are finished. Partial processes arranged in line are such that the time of production is divided into equal intervals and one elementary process starts at each division point, i.e. the elementary processes are uniformly staggered in time so that the arrangement of this type can eliminate *technical idleness* completely.

Georgescu-Roegen writes:

> Since processes are arranged in line (and in a proper fashion), the flow that moves through the process moves without any waste of time from one agent to another. The agents [funds] are thus never idle. In this lies the essential difference between manufacturing and farming processes. In agriculture elementary processes cannot be started at any time of the year as is ordinarily the case in manufacturing.
>
> (Georgescu-Roegen 1984: 25)

Georgescu-Roegen expounds his analysis of the difference between the two processes by noting the fundamental asymmetry of the two sources of low entropy, sunlight and fossil fuels. There are three disadvantages in agriculture. First, 'nature dictates the time when an agricultural elementary process must be started if it is to be successful at all' (Georgescu-Roegen 1971: 297). Second, because of the impossibility of mining the stock of solar energy at a rate people want, they must wait and be patient. As Adam Smith notes, 'in agriculture too *nature labours* along with man' (Smith 1937: 344). People must wait for nature to work. Third, the most important element of the asymmetry is that there is a lasting obstacle to manipulating living matter as efficaciously as inert matter due to the impossibility of attaining the microcosmic as well as the cosmic dimension of space and time.

Owing to these three disadvantages, from the outset, agriculture cannot achieve higher production than manufacturing. The productivity difference stems from two sources: First, manufacturing can go beyond natural cycles (day and night, seasons, change in climatic conditions, nature and rhythm of animals, plants, food chain, interaction between water and soils, etc.). It can produce more goods than farming in terms of scale and variety. Second, manufacturing is usually independent of soil productivity, so the production per unit area can be raised dramatically.

To sum it up, it is unrealistic to expect agriculture to have the same essential merits as manufacturing, i.e. *land saving and time saving.*

5.3 Ecological succession and modern farming

In order to fully understand the disadvantages of agriculture compared with manufacturing, it is necessary to investigate the characteristics of ecological succession (Kurihara 1975). During the early stages, changes in structure and composition of a community are rapid, slowing gradually until a point of dynamic equilibrium (climax) when it is almost stable.

The characteristics of ecological succession are:

1 In early stages of ecological succession, the variety of living things is limited, becoming complex with progressive stages of ecological succession.
2 Quantities of organic and inorganic elements are the same, except in early stages of ecological succession when the quantities of inorganic elements are very small. Therefore, utilization of nourishment is higher in early stages and fertilizers also work better.
3 The weight of living things per unit area is smaller in early than in mature stages.
4 The rate of increase in total production is higher in early than in mature stages.
5 After dynamic equilibrium is reached (climax), it is almost stable unless disturbed.

In a certain sense, agriculture demands artificial creation of early stages of ecological succession, so that its advantageous characteristics can be exploited. A simple community, full of only plants and animals people want, can promote a strong effect of fertilizers on crops and higher land productivity. However, there are some troublesome characteristics about early stages of ecological succession. First, the weight of plants per unit area is relatively small, so it is impossible to expect large yields from land. Second, simplified flora in the early stages of ecological succession results in a simplified fauna, which depends on the size and variety of the flora. Hence, the number of a particular group of herbivora tends to dominate because of favourable conditions for them. Third, early stages of ecological succession are not stable and easily succumb to disturbances from the environment. These unfavourable characteristics are the original source of the disadvantages of agriculture compared with manufacturing. In order to increase the weights people use fertilizers and improve plant breeding in an attempt to overcome the first troublesome characteristic. The second characteristic above means that a particular group of herbivora becomes more and more dominant. The frequent occurrence of harmful insects is due in part to the intensive use of chemical fertilizers. Furthermore, people need extra matter, energy and labour to maintain agricultural land at early stages of ecological succession. The third characteristic implies sustained labour for cultivation, control and weeding need to spread fertilizers, pesticides and herbicides. Contrary to commonsense view, agriculture itself is *not in tune with the pattern of nature through ecological succession.*

In traditional agriculture, matter and energy within a particular area circulate properly so that no waste matter is actually produced. However, in modern agriculture, most matter and energy are introduced from the outside of the area. It is also difficult to circulate the matter and energy harmoniously within the area so that waste matter and polluted substances flow inside as well as outside of the area. Modern agriculture in industrial society is nothing but a manufacturing process. In this respect, there is no fundamental difference between the two processes in modern era.

6 Conclusion

As long as Homo sapiens remains dependent on land as a source of organic substances, what happens when land deteriorates is a critical question. The crucial role played by land in early Greece and the result of the ill-treatment of land in the fourth century BC appears in one of Plato's dialogues. Critias states:

> You are left (as with little islands) with something rather like the skeleton of a body wasted by disease; the rich, soft soil has all run away leaving the land nothing but skin and bone. But in those days the damage had not taken place, the hills had high crests, the rocky plain of Phelleus was covered with rich soil, and the mountains were covered by thick woods, of which there are some traces today.
>
> (Plato: 134)

Critias' lamentation can be applied to any civilization. *Civilization* has a tendency to expand beyond the endurable limit of reproduction level, resulting in a reduction of land productivity and an increase in deserts.

It must not be forgotten that modern material structure and the EFT2 complex have been supported by the abundance of fossil fuels and mineral resources during the last one hundred years or so, as Georgescu-Roegen states:

> Now, economic history confirms a rather elementary fact – the fact that the great strides in technological progress have generally been touched off by a discovery of how to use a new kind of accessible energy. On the other hand, a great stride in technological progress cannot materialize unless the corresponding innovation is followed by a great mineralogical expansion. Even a substantial increase in the efficiency of the use of gasoline as fuel would pale in comparison with a manifold increase of the known, rich oil fields.
>
> This sort of expansion is what has happened during the last hundred years. We have struck oil and discovered new coal and gas deposits in a far greater proportion than we could use during the same period. Still more important, all mineralogical discoveries have included a substantial proportion of *easily* accessible resources.
>
> (Georgescu-Roegen 1975: 362)

It is essential to note that fossil fuels, especially oil and coal, are contributions made by animals and plants over vast stretches of land and over several thousands of millions of years. These fossil fuels guarantee the essential merits of modern industry (land saving and time saving) and support the EFT2 complex. People continue to depend on land completely in manufacturing as well as in farming. If it were not for fossil fuels such as oil and coal, which provide modern civilization with motive power and transportation, large-scale production would never have been possible, even though other mineral resources are abundant.

Modern society cannot follow the past patterns. 'The pattern of the past – use up the natural [land-based] resources and move to new land – is no longer an adequate solution. The time has arrived when all peoples must take stock of their resources and plan their future accordingly' (Carter and Dale 1974: 23). In the United States alone, an estimated fifty million acres will erode in the next twenty-five years. In 1970, it had about 400 million acres of cropland (Carter and Dale 1974). However, even in the US, the most powerful country today, the food safety margin will grow thin at the end of the twenty-first century. It is imperative that we build economic systems which do not stress land so much.

8 Environment and North–South trade: another view

1 Introduction

Economic growth and advancement of science and technology result in increased production and consumption but also have negative side-effects, e.g. (i) natural-resource depletion and environmental degradation, such as deforestation, soil erosion and pollution, and (ii) increasing disparity between rich and poor both within and across national borders. The most conspicuous ecological degradation is in Third World nations:

> [T]he last thirty years have been the most disastrous in the history of most, if not all, Third World countries. There has been massive deforestation, soil erosion and desertification. The incidence of floods and droughts has increased dramatically as has their destructiveness, population growth has surged, as has urbanization, in particular the development of vast shanty-towns, in which human life has attained a degree of squalor probably unprecedented outside Hitler's concentration camps.
>
> (Goldsmith 1985: 210)

Ecological degradation is today most catastrophic in Third World countries. Developed countries cannot face the unpleasant fact that the environmental problems in the Third World are also problems for developed countries. One important cause of environmental crisis in the Third World lies in the political and economic structure of North–South trade. Developing countries produce mainly raw materials and monocultural products for export to developed countries. Monocultured lands are agro-ecosystems similar to ecological communities in early stages of ecological succession discussed in Chapter 7.

Present North–South trade enhances the risk of land deterioration and accelerates degradation of ecosystems in the Third World. In fact, large-scale land abuse in developing nations results from the current structure of North–South trade. Developing countries interacting with more advanced socioeconomic systems must abandon traditional, mainly subsistence economic systems (Martinez-Alier 1996). Unfortunately, the traditional economy is being abandoned very quickly, with devastating loss of ecological viability and cultural heritage in the Third World.

This chapter reconsiders the neoclassical economic paradigm of growth through trade and suggests that, in view of sustainability, it is vital to acknowledge: (i) the importance of preserving the identity and integrity of economic systems in each region of the world by enlarging as much as possible self-sufficiency and equity of their economic systems assessed at national and regional levels; and (ii) the importance of biospheric equilibria as one criterion to be used to regulate world economic activity. Section 2 discusses differences and similarities of past and present ecological degradation. Section 3 briefly discusses the standard theory of international trade and then presents an entropy theoretical approach to North–South trade issues and promotion of sustainability. Section 4 examines the historical relationship of humans with nature, showing that the ecological crisis is rooted in the extraordinary acceleration of the exosomatic mode of human evolution. Dramatic acceleration of economic activity started by the Industrial Revolution has not been accompanied by adequate cultural controls on human development. Cultural, scientific and economic paradigms are much slower to evolve than material processes of production and consumption. Section 5 uses a hierarchy theory to touch upon the problem of perception of ecological decline.

2 Ecological degradation and drive toward unsustainability: Jevons' paradox

Ancient people felt '[i]ntimacy with nature and sensitivity to its cycles [and they felt] more direct dependence on the natural world' (Hughes 1975). This attitude toward nature dramatically altered when there was a switch from the endosomatic mode of evolution to the exosomatic mode of evolution. '[Humans] transgressed the biological evolution by entering into a far faster evolutionary rhythm [exosomatic evolution] – the evolution in which organs are manufactured, instead of being inherited somatically' (Georgescu-Roegen 1986: 249). Dramatic change in the mode of human evolution together with the rise of 'Western Materialism' since the seventeenth century led to rapid depletion of mineral resources and fossil fuels (Norgaard 1995: 478) and to serious global environmental damage. In thermodynamic terms, the present situation is characterized by a tremendous increase in the rate of entropy generation of modern economies. Presently, annual economic activity consists of transporting and transforming six billion tons of fossil fuels, four billion tons of minerals, wood, etc., and one trillion tons of water. If this situation continues for another five hundred years, even with zero growth rate, waste matter of five trillion tons will accumulate in our environment. This quantity is equal to spreading 500 kg of waste matter per square metre all over the United States (Kawamiya 1983: 9).

In order to understand better the current rate of matter and energy degradation, it is useful to recall two types of efficiency introduced in Chapter 7. EFT1 is the output/input ratio and does not consider the time required to obtain one unit of output. EFT2 is the output obtained per unit time (the speed of throughput) and does not consider the amount of input required to obtain one unit of output.

Thermodynamic considerations indicate which type of efficiency is optimized by social and economic systems. A lower input requirement, implied by an increase in EFT1, has beneficial effects on the stability of the boundary conditions. This lower requirement of input is ecologically benign, since it decreases depletion of natural resources and stress on the environment. A higher speed of throughput, implied by an increase in EFT2, has beneficial effects on the ability to maintain more complexity and hierarchy in society. This higher speed is benign to the economic process, since it can be related to a higher level of production and consumption of goods and services.

EFT1 is related to the scale of the system (e.g. the size of the economic system is compared with ecosystems). Therefore, EFT1 should be considered more carefully when 'natural capital' becomes a limiting factor in economic growth (Daly 1995). In thermodynamic terms, EFT1 is concerned with the minimum energy throughput needed for a particular structure/function in society. Prigogine formalizes this efficiency as 'Minimum Entropy Production Principle' (Glansdorff and Prigogine 1971; Nicolis and Prigogine 1977). This principle states that 'linear systems obey to a general inequality implying that at a steady nonequilibrium state, entropy production becomes a minimum, compatible with the constraints applied on the system' (Nicolis and Prigogine 1977: 45). However, this principle applies only to steady-state situations occurring sufficiently close to equilibrium, for which the state of the system depends on the set of constraints imposed by the given associative context (e.g. for lower-level system components operating under a controlled set of boundary conditions). Scientists use a Liapunov function, typical of control theory, to formalize this kind of stability. Clearly, all living and economic systems are dissipative; they must be open and exchange flows of energy and matter with their environment. The higher the EFT1, the lower the quantity of input taken from the environment (less depletion of natural resources) and also the lesser the waste released into the environment (less environmental pollution).

On the other hand, lowering the flow of throughput implies lowering the complexity that can be sustained within the system (e.g. a lower standard of living in economic systems) and an increased risk of collapse in case of perturbations. Consequently, even in ecological theory, an increase in EFT2 in energy terms has been proposed as one of the general principles of evolution for self-organizing systems, such as Lotka's maximum energy flux (Lotka 1956: 357).

The parallel functioning of self-organizing adaptive systems over various hierarchical levels can be used to reconcile these two contrasting principles.

When describing a system at higher levels (evolutionary view), the maximum power principle indicates the continuous process of generation of new complexity through co-evolution, i.e. increasing compatibility and adaptability for the nested hierarchical system. On a larger scale, unpredictable behaviours can be expected from a system away from thermodynamic equilibrium. 'When a dissipative structure is near such instability its entropy production reaches a relative maximum and it becomes sensitive to small fluctuations' (O'Neill *et al.* 1986: 105).

A description of lower-level systems (quasi-steady state view – types operating within a given associative context) requires dealing with dissipative components subjected to a strict set of constraints within a stable set of boundary conditions (e.g. cells within an organism). Under these conditions, it is reasonable to assume a trend toward a continuous reduction of quantities of energy and matter required to sustain a particular function – an increase in efficiency. However, this increase in efficiency at lower levels (reduction of entropy generation per unit mass of the dissipative adaptive system) results in a higher stability of that function in the long term, only if the energy (free energy) 'spared' at lower levels by higher efficiency is then moved up in the hierarchy (Margalef 1968) and invested in adaptability (in the emergence of new structures/functions) in higher levels of the nested hierarchical system.

In other words, the trends of maximization of power for the whole system and minimization of entropy production per unit lower-level component – resulting from describing the process at a lower hierarchical level – occur simultaneously on different scales. The final outcome of these two parallel contrasting trends is a larger integration of the self-organizing adaptive system with its environment. This implies an increased compatibility between various control systems on different space–time scales. They operate on different scales within both the adaptive system under analysis and its environment determining the favourable boundary conditions upon which the system relies for its survival.

Unfortunately, when a short-term economic objective is aimed only at growth of GDP, the main concern is an increase in EFT2 (the speed of throughput in terms of production and consumption); there is little concern with EFT1 (less depletion of natural resources and less environmental pollution). The definition of value is generated by the system itself, such as when humans are concerned with their standard of living. Such a definition of value ignores long-term environmental effects, especially when costs and benefits for the environment are not easy to define (Giampietro 1994*a*). The final result of the optimization is a myopic rule: the higher the speed of throughput (e.g. GDP), the better.

In *The Coal Question* of 1865, William Stanley Jevons discusses the trend of future coal consumption and argues against contemporary predictions about future reduction in the consumption of coal due to technological progress. He explains an intrinsic human addiction to the comfort offered by exosomatic instruments related to 'EFT2 fetishism': an increase in efficiency in using a resource leads to increased use of that resource rather than to a reduction in its use. This can be termed 'Jevons' paradox' (Jevons 1965: Chapter VII of the economy of fuel; Jevons 1990).

'Jevons' paradox' proves true when applied to the demand for coal and other fossil energy resources. Doubling the efficiency of food production per hectare over the last fifty years (thanks to the Green Revolution) did not solve the problem of hunger. An increase in efficiency worsened the problem because of the resulting increase in population (Giampietro 1994*b*). Similarly, building new roads did not solve the traffic problem because increasing use of personal vehicles was encouraged (Newman 1991). Rising oil prices resulted in more energy-efficient automobiles, which in turn led to increased leisure driving (Cherfas 1991). Car performance has improved and people drive much more than before. Now, in the United States, for instance, bigger and more sophisticated vehicles such as mini-vans, pick-up trucks and four-wheel-drive vehicles have become very popular. Similarly, another common example is technological improvement in efficiency leading to bigger refrigerators (Khazzoom 1987).

In economic terms, an increase in supply combined with higher efficiency boosts demand. Technological improvement in the efficiency of a process (e.g. an increase in miles travelled per unit consumption of gasoline) represents improvement in intensive variables. However, when technological improvement occurs, there is usually room for expansion in the size of the system (e.g. more people make more use of their cars). Expansion in the size of the system represents a change in extensive variables, the dimension of the process. Unless there is a comprehensive analysis of change induced by technological improvement, there is possible misunderstanding caused by counter-intuitive behaviour of evolving complex systems.

The limited ability of controlling energy and matter flows prevented early tool-making societies from encountering 'Jevons' paradox' or 'EFT2 fetishism'. Still, pre-industrial societies faced environmental decline in a form analogous to modern environmental decline, the only important difference being the scale of such predicament. Earlier civilizations caused stress on natural ecosystems, but were unable to disturb, on a global scale, bio-geochemical cycles such as water and nitrogen cycles or the composition of the atmosphere such as accumulation of green-house gases. Nevertheless, study of the past can teach us how to formulate better policy for sustainable use of natural resources and environmental management.

Until the transition to agricultural society about 10,000 years ago, 'a combination of gathering foodstuffs and hunting animals' had been a basic form of subsistence with little damage to the environment in part due to 'a number of accepted social customs' (Ponting 1991). This transition to agriculture made possible the emergence of complex and hierarchical societies. In fact, agriculture was responsible for increase in population density and accumulation of sufficient surpluses to sustain armies and administrators (Tainter 1988).

As in the past, despite technological advance, modern civilization continues to depend on the ecological viability of agricultural base. More than ninety-eight per cent of food consumed by people is obtained by land production still based on factors that cannot be substituted for by injection of technical capital, factors like availability of fresh water, fertile soil, pollination by insects (Ehrlich *et al.* 1993; Kendall and Pimentel 1994). Industrialized society, heavily dependent on fossil fuels and mineral resources, still depends on ecological flows for its food security. In this regard, industrialized society differs from subsistence society only in terms of the global scale of operations and rate of ecological degradation.

As in ancient times, 'it is in the area distant from the centers of powers . . . the first indicators of ecological catastrophe become apparent' (Weiskel 1989). Areas remote from power are characterized by weaker economies and often by more fragile ecosystems. In those remote areas, environmental degradation is an early warning signal indicating lack of respect for the stability of biospheric equilibria.

Even in the 1990s, a major reason for conflict between Bangladesh and India had been the dispute over land and water, crucial renewable resources (Homer-Dixon *et al.* 1993). Arguments over land and water cause many local conflicts throughout the Third World.

3 North–South trade and ecological crisis

The character of ancient trade is still debated by anthropologists. For example, K. Polanyi emphasizes institutionalized reciprocity and redistribution. R. McC. Adams reevaluates innovative, risk-taking, profit-motivated behaviour of traders (Adams 1992). Free-trade dogma based on international specialization supported by comparative advantage is a cornerstone of standard economics. It is used to argue, for example, that England established world supremacy through overseas commerce. Standard economics teaches that 'free trade in goods between different regions is always to the advantage of each trading country, and therefore the best arrangement from the point of view of the welfare of the trading world as a whole, as well as of each part of the world taken separately' (Kaldor 1980: 85). Thus, Friedrich List's infant-industry argument is an exception to the standard theory (Røpke 1994). The traditional theory of free trade is refined theoretically in the Heckscher–Ohlin theory and the Stolper–Samuelson theorem (Kaldor 1980; Røpke 1994).

The General Agreement on Tariffs and Trade (GATT) shows a fundamental commitment to unrestricted trade based on the free-trade dogma of standard economics. Three central principles of the GATT system provide the framework for international trade: (i) non-discrimination, (ii) reciprocity and (iii) general prohibition of non-tariff trade measures (Watkins 1992). However, N. Kaldor states (1980) that standard trade theory 'rests on a number of artificial assumptions'. Free trade is subject to actual conditions. Thus, the possibility of increasing returns in the field of manufactured goods led to concentration of industry in developed countries – a polarization process. This polarization resulted in the present world situation in which 'differences in wealth and living standards became considerably larger' (Kaldor 1980). Developing Arthur Lewis' argument, Graciera Chichilnisky (1986) also shows that the policy of export expansion in the South leads to lower terms of trade and to lower export revenues in the South. Several important issues, not properly treated within the traditional framework of standard theory including 'forced specialization' and 'absolute advantage' of developed countries (Daly 1993; Røpke 1994), are not discussed here. Rather, our concern is biophysical and sustainable issues resulting mainly from North–South trade.

Basically, North–South trade may be analysed using the following entropy theoretical approach. If a system absorbs low entropy from its environment and releases high entropy of matter and heat, the system can maintain a quasi-steady state. Suppose there are two subsystems A and B. If subsystem A extracts low-entropy resources from subsystem B and releases high-entropy waste into its environment including B, entropy saturation in A can be avoided, at least locally and temporarily, at the expense of B. There is some 'freedom' for subsystems to share total entropy production in the whole system and exchange entropy with their environment. Thus, to picture the world economy, it is necessary to specify subsystem relationships.

The case of Japan's trade with the rest of the world reinforces this theoretical approach. As discussed in Chapter 7, Japan imports some eighty million tons of forest and agricultural resources such as timber, fodder and foods. Since about 500 tons of water is usually required to produce one ton of carbohydrate, in a sense, Japan imports forty billion tons of water resources, more than the water required in all Japanese cities (Kawamiya 1983: 23). Thus, Japan exploits low-entropy resources from exporting countries. When a country subsystem (e.g. USA) produces monocultural products for Japan, relying on intensive use of oil-based inputs, it experiences, as a side-effect, increased deterioration of its land (Pimentel *et al.* 1995). Recall that monocultural agricultural systems are based on an excessive simplification of agro-ecosystems which imitate early stages of ecological succession. When a country subsystem (e.g. a timber exporter in South Asia) cuts and exports forest resources at competitive prices for Japan, a side-effect that country subsystem experiences is loss of habitats and biodiversity, soil erosion and other environmental damage (Farber 1995).

Without transfer of capital and trade, developed countries would accelerate their own environmental crisis. With autarky, a high standard of living coupled with high population density in developed countries would encounter environmental constraints. For example, the need to mechanize agriculture and rely heavily on petrochemicals for food production could exacerbate even more the ecological predicament of developed countries. As R. U. Ayres (1995) correctly observes, with the current rapid international capital movement, developed countries such as Japan export part of the production process as well as industrial wastes to developing countries. In this way, developed countries escape the negative environmental side-effects and high-entropy generation (see Martinez-Alier (1996) for a splendid account of NAFTA issues).

Unfortunately, no GATT articles impose trade restrictions for biophysical and sustainability reasons. In addition, GATT outlaws 'use of trade controls, such as import tariffs and quotas, designed to prevent cheap food imports' from developed countries into developing countries (Watkins 1992: 69). A difficult situation is created:

> In the North, the energy intensive production systems which have sustained economic growth and trade expansion have contributed to industrial pollution, global warming and ozone depletion. These problems now constitute a profound threat to the future welfare of the citizens of developed and developing countries alike. In the South, the lethal combination of debt-service obligations and falling commodity prices has deepened a more immediate ecological crisis. Forced to export an ever increasing volume of commodities to compensate for declining prices, many countries, as the 1985 Brundtland Report noted, have over-exploited fragile ecological bases, sacrificing long-term sustainability for short-term trade gains.
>
> (Watkins 1992: 98–9)

The most devastated is Africa, which imported 'two-fifths of its food supply and [where] about a third of its people depended wholly or partly on imported food' in 1985, resulting in complete loss of self-sufficiency (cited in Weikel 1989). The only choice appears to be a global reallocation of existing wealth, if aggregate growth beyond carrying capacity is unsustainable in the long term and the poor are harmed more by both resource depletion and environmental decline (Colby 1991; Daly 1992*a*). However, the reality is: 'a political attempt to move the ecological agenda away from the issue of Raubwirtschaft by the wealthy. Thus, in the wake of the Brundtland Report, the study of poverty as a cause of environmental degradation has become more fashionable than the study of wealth as the main human threat to the environment' (Martinez-Alier 1991: 123).

Modern agriculture based on Green Revolution technology is not a solution for the famine problem in the Third World, particularly in tropical areas (Norgaard 1981). Green Revolution technology depends on extensive availability of petrochemical products, imposing a financial burden on Third World governments and creating a wide range of health hazards. Given the possible shortage of oil, development schemes based on this technology can probably not be sustained indefinitely (Weiskel 1989). Yet, Third World nations faced with short-term food shortage must rely on this technology in order to avoid the Malthusian population growth trap, even though such reliance is not sustainable in the long term (Giampietro and Bukkens 1992).

The following three points deserve attention in promoting sustainability in developing countries:

(1) It is necessary to empower local communities with the principle of distributional equity in the decision-making process, avoiding the so-called 'top-down' decision-making process. In developing countries, traditional socioeconomic systems are affected by a powerful drive toward dramatic social change. This drive is generated by interaction with socioeconomic systems of more highly developed societies. Huge disparities in the standard of living between developed and developing nations generate friction that pushes less developed societies to rapid change of their internal organization. Socioeconomic systems in developing countries must adapt as quickly as possible to the new set of risks and opportunities. Obviously, more privileged social groups must involve in this modernization process. Later, further friction within the socioeconomic system occurs at the national level. Social changes tend to pass from upper class to lower class.

The social changes alter the perspectives of the developed world in a way that threatens diversity of cultural experiences, values, knowledge and alternative economic paradigms. The developed world tries to propagate and amplify its value systems everywhere. Ironically, the loss of cultural diversity occurs precisely when developed countries themselves discover that their own value systems might not achieve sustainability.

Therefore, it is vital to preserve respect for different cultural identities. Actions to promote sustainable development should enhance the preservation of socioeconomic systems that can counter the strong driving force toward unsustainability.

To repeat, an effort must be made to empower local communities in the decision-making process. Approaches based on grassroots development schemes together with help from NGOs deserve top priority, allowing local people to use indigenous farming knowledge and inherent natural resource management skills (Altieri and Masero 1993). Such approaches, implemented at local levels by NGOs, can increase pressure on governments of both developed and developing countries, leading to more altruism in trade negotiations (Røpke 1994).

To implement a development project requires resolution of 'discount rate dilemma': 'natural resources are most likely to be over-exploited at high discount rates than at low ones, whereas low discount rates discriminate against projects with an environmental dimension that have a long gestation period' (Barbier and Markandya 1990: 668).

There are also additional issues of environmental risk and irreversible nature of impacts (Markandya and Pearce 1988; Barbier and Markandya 1990).

(2) It is necessary to reorient the world economy toward increased local self-sufficiency and social equity defined and assessed at the level of national and regional economic systems. This implies abandoning a myopic view of growth through unlimited trade. John Gowdy (1995: 494) aptly remarks that 'a regionally based economy is not a sufficient condition for sustainability'. However, an effort must be made to increase self-sufficiency and social equity of economic systems at national or regional levels as a prerequisite for sustainability. There are several reasons why:

(i) Reducing the space–time scale for making decisions about sustainability makes it easier to involve local people in the decision-making process and to increase the responsibility of local communities for resources management (Røpke 1994).[1] Except when resources available to a community are well below some threshold level, decisions related to sustainability should be made as close as possible to the local people and with the participation of all major stake-holders. This would allow local people to utilize their indigenous knowledge in the decision-making process.

(ii) Internalizing most external services on which economic systems rely makes it easier for the system to respond quickly to intricate changes and the variety of signals from surrounding ecosystems (Norgaard 1981).

(iii) The goal of harmonizing energy and material circulation with local ecosystems is achievable. However, the space–time range of production and consumption in the socioeconomic system should be similar to the space–time range of the material cycles occurring in local ecosystems. Energy expenditures for transportation from distant ecosystems can be justified only if there is no sufficient access to energy resources in the area. So, it is necessary to assess directly the possible negative effects of increased trade on the stability of the biosphere and on the integrity of local socioeconomic systems.

(3) It is necessary to amend GATT's articles to promote sustainability on a global level by reducing the impact on the biosphere caused by rapid expansion of

the world economy. These amendments will enhance the integrity of national and regional economies and the degree of self-sufficiency and equity at the national and regional level (Watkins 1992): (i) restrictions on the volume of trade of defined commodities should be considered in view of environmental protection; (ii) developing countries should have subsidies and *ad hoc* regulation imposing a minimum level of processing of natural resources before export; (iii) tariff systems should retain as much as possible of the value in developing countries to slow the trend of excessive exploitation of natural resources (e.g. tropical timber).

4 Relationship of humans with nature

Natural systems tend to evolve by balancing the goals of (i) increasing their complexity (the activity of their process of self-organization); and (ii) increasing their stability by harmonizing internal activities with environmental boundary conditions (Odum 1971). On the other hand, modern people seem more concerned with only the first of these two goals ('EFT2 fetishism').

A progressive change in the perception of the relationship that humans should have with nature may lead to sudden departure from sustainable pattern of socioeconomic activities. Thus, an excessive priority on industrial activities is based on a world view that perceives humans, nature and environment as separate. Parts of nature that are useful for human activity (e.g. parts that provide raw materials for economic consumption) are viewed as resources and, therefore, as belonging to economy, and not as belonging to nature.

According to Lynn White (1967), the first clear change in the perception of humans and nature occurred in the late seventh century AD, with the introduction of new technology for plowing. The ability of socioeconomic systems to generate surplus for self-organization changed them from being part of nature to being exploiters of nature. The advent of monotheistic religions like Judaism, Christianity and Islam in the Mediterranean basin – the heart of western civilization – accentuated such an anthropocentric view. Humans viewed themselves as 'special' creatures of God, distinct from the environment in which they operate. This view, sharply contrasting with pagan animism, legitimized exploitation of nature for improvement of human life. This anthropocentric view of technical development was further reinforced by the Baconian creed: 'scientific knowledge means technological power over nature' (White 1967: 1203).

Western hedonism is partly responsible for the modern ecological crisis, since 'for more complex forms of society a dynamic equilibrium is stabilized only at a high level of energy [and mineral resources] expenditure per capita' (Giampietro and Bukkens 1992: 45). Hence, the current ecological crisis has been generated not only by changes in the perception of the relation of humans to nature, but also by sudden access to immense stocks of fossil energy made possible by the Industrial Revolution. As Georgescu-Roegen states:

> The fossil-fuels bonanza of the past century has raised the exosomatic production to a miraculous level in the developed nations, and somewhat indirectly a little in the rest of the world as well.
>
> (Georgescu-Roegen 1986: 273)

5 Conclusion

Historical accidents, differences in natural resource allocation and geographical characteristics give to certain regions an initial advantage in the process of development. Initial advantages are then amplified during the process, resulting in ever increasing gaps between developed and developing countries if corrective policies are not applied. Evolving systems follow the law, 'the survival of the first', identified by Hopf (1988). Through stimulated trade, developed countries with favourable terms of trade can actually increase rather than decrease the existing gap.

Environmental impacts caused by local people in developing countries are relatively low compared with those caused by developed countries. People faced with aggravated environmental conditions are forced to exploit immediate economic benefits at the expense of long-term sustainability of livelihood. Barbier and Markandya (1990: 668) write: 'one of the consequences of deforestation and the depletion of fuelwood supplies is that it forces poor households to divert dung for use as fuel rather than for fertilizer. The "present value" of the dung as fuel is higher than its value as a oil nutrient'.

The basic difficulty in coping with ecological decline lies in the problem of perception. For example, deforestation of tropical areas affects both local weather and global climatic conditions. At present, the Third World suffers the most ecological degradation. However, problems in the Third World are problems of the developed world. The present situation in West Africa mirrors a near anarchy that will soon confront the developed countries as well (Kaplan 1994).

Giampiertro and Bukkens state the essential point correctly:

> The separation between the developed and developing worlds is mainly due to the perception/description of Western socioeconomic culture; in biophysical terms these two worlds are linked together by the existence of a hierarchical structure. When dealing with a hierarchical system, the essential ethical problem is the correct definition of the boundaries and therefore of the goals of the system. This definition, together with the knowledge of the constraints operating in the system, may then allow discussion of the mechanism with which decisions should be made.
>
> (Giampietro and Bukkens 1992: 49)

Each level of hierarchy – individual, societal (local, national and international) and biophysical – must be analysed scientifically and ethically in relation to the other levels, allowing us to assess the overall issues of sustainability.

9 Modelling relation, hierarchical systems and bioeconomic approach to sustainability issues

1 Introduction

Sustainability issues imply a new role for scientists in relation to human progress because issue-driven research takes precedence over curiosity-driven research and because of the need to adopt a much more integrated approach for describing the interplay between economic systems and ecological systems. 'The objective of scientific endeavour in this new context may well be to enhance the process of the social resolution of the problem, including participation and mutual learning among the stakeholders, rather than a definite "solution" or technological implementation. This is an important change in the relation between the problem identification and the prospects of science-based solutions' (Funtowicz *et al.* 1998: 104). Funtowicz and Ravets (1990) have developed a new epistemological framework, 'Post-Normal Science' in which uncertainty, stakeholders and their value conflicts play a central role in the process of decision-making. 'Post-Normal' indicates a departure from curiosity-driven or puzzle-solving exercises of normal science, in the Kuhnian sense (Kuhn 1962). Normal science, so successfully extended from the laboratory of core science to the conquest of nature through applied science, is no longer appropriate for the solution of sustainability problems. The social, technical and ecological dimensions of sustainability problems are so deeply connected that it is simply impossible to consider these dimensions as separated into conventional disciplinary fields.

It is argued that traditional scientific activity cannot guide sustainability issues using Robert Rosen's modelling relation (1985; 1991) as a starting point. Some object lessons are extracted from Rosen's arguments for scientists working on sustainability issues. Then the general framework of a methodological tool based on hierarchy theory is presented. This methodological tool establishes a relation between the description of socioeconomic systems on one particular level (the focal level) with that of the corresponding higher (e.g. ecological) and lower (e.g. individual perspectives of humans operating within the society) levels. For the most comprehensive account of this approach, together with a complete list of equations and applications, see the two special issues of *Population and Environment*, 2000, vol. 22(2) and 2001, vol. 22(3).

2 Modelling relation by Robert Rosen in theoretical science

Without getting into philosophical arguments, I share Rosen's view that science requires fundamental duality between 'self' and its 'ambience' – between 'the internal, subjective world of the self' and 'an external, objective world of phenomena'. Science is a way of importing the external world of phenomena into the internal, subjective world that can be perceived in some way. The duality between self and its ambience, according to Rosen, is a manifestation of 'Natural Law' consisting of two parts: one permits science to exist in the abstract, i.e. there are relations (including causal relations) manifest in the external world of phenomena. The other allows scientists themselves to exist, i.e. the relations among phenomena (supposed to exist within the external world) are partly perceived by the cognitive self.

The first duality separates the universe into self and its ambience. If self refers to a scientist, in order for the scientist to manage their own perceptions of the external world, the scientist needs the second dualism between 'a natural system' and its 'environment' in the external world. A natural system is a mental construct originated by the scientist, but both a natural system and its environment belong to the external world. Also, the choice of the definition of an identity for a particular natural system depends entirely on the scientist's interest in the general sense of the word. So, such pre-analytical choice itself, in principle, has nothing to do with the objective and directly perceptible property of the external world.

A natural system in the external world is an identified entity reflecting a scientist's interest in studying it. The identity of this entity may be expressed in terms of: (i) a collection of qualities believed to induce the perception of various phenomena (observable attributes of the natural system recorded by a scientist); and (ii) mechanisms establishing possible structural/functional linkages among this collection. According to Rosen, relations among phenomena within a natural system are supposed to reflect causal entailment (or implication) occurring within that system.

The first step of model generation for a scientist is to identify a 'sub-natural system' consisting only of the set of qualities and possible structural/functional linkages reflecting the interests of the scientist in relation to the real world. This first step implies selecting only a limited set of observable behaviours of a particular natural system, among a virtually infinite universe of observable behaviours. So, a natural system in the external world can generate a large number of different sub-natural systems, depending on the collection of qualities according to a scientist's interest. In Rosen's own expression, 'a complex system [a natural system] is one which allows us to discern many subsystems [sub-natural systems]' (Rosen 1977: 229). However, Rosen's theoretical scheme does not distinguish between a natural system and a sub-natural system.

The second step in the modelling by a scientist is using a set of measurement systems and external references (semantic scheme including languages). In this way, the scientist can 'interact' with a selected sub-natural system and transform a set of qualities and linkages considered relevant by the scientist into a set of quantifiable observables reflecting an internal relationship hypothesized by the scientist's pre-analytical vision (Schumpeter 1954: 41–2).

This second preliminary data collection step is required for the third step, i.e. to construct a 'formal system' within which a scientist's hypothesized internal relationships are formalized *consistently* using *meaningless* symbols in terms of: (i) a finite set of axioms, (ii) a finite set of production rules and (iii) a finite set of algorithms. Consistent formalization means that 'P' and 'not P' never co-exists, but this is impossible even within mathematics: Gödel's incompleteness theorem (Wilder 1952: 256–61). Observable quantities and pre-analytic relationships are represented in mathematical forms, generating a purely syntactic system. As Kleene states, formalization of a theory means 'it should be possible to perform the deductions treating the technical terms as words in themselves without meaning' (Kleene 1952: 59).

To summarize, a scientist has to make three steps to 'encode' a sub-natural system into a formal system. First, a sub-natural system must be identified. Then, preliminary data collection using a system of measurements and a semantic scheme must be made. This second step is required to interact with the sub-natural system in order to identify quantifiable observables and pre-analytic relationships. Finally, a consistent formal system, together with axioms, production rules and algorithms, must be produced.

In Rosen's word, each theorem derived from axioms, production rules and algorithms is 'a state of a [sub-]natural system' or 'a prediction within a formal system'. 'Predictions' are theorems or propositions derived within the formal system using axioms, production rules and algorithms. Making predictions in the above sense is called 'mathematical decoding' of a formal system into a sub-natural system. Each prediction may correspond to a particular aspect of a sub-natural system. However, within a purely formal system, there is freedom for a scientist to interpret any theorem in any way. Thus, the scientist may lose contact with any external reference and any quality thereof existing in a sub-natural system.

Experiments using a set of measurement systems and a semantic check must be made to see whether or not predictions, obtained using the formal system of inference, correspond to values of observables and their relationships associated with a sub-natural system. If observed quantities and their relationships are those predicted within the formal system, a scientist 'theoretically decodes' predictions based on the formal system into a sub-natural system. Mathematical decoding and theoretical decoding must be differentiated because the mathematical decoding step can be logically independent of the encoding step insofar as theorems derived from axioms, production rules and algorithms are internally consistent.

In Fig. 9.1 there are two separate paths: 6 and $(1 \vee 2) + 3 + (4 \vee 5)$. Each path takes a scientist from phenomena in SN (sub-natural system) to those in SN. Path 6 represents causal entailment within SN. Path $(1 \vee 2) + 3 + (4 \vee 5)$ involves encoding, formal entailment within F (a consistent formal system) and theoretical decoding. If a scientist obtains almost always the same answer without having to revise the formal system regardless of whether path 6 is followed, or path $(1 \vee 2) + 3 + (4 \vee 5)$ is followed, the formal system is called 'a model' of

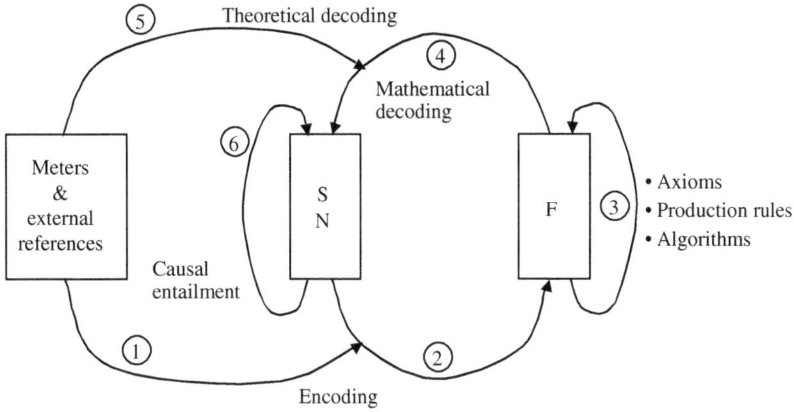

Figure 9.1 Modelling relation.

the sub-natural system SN with respect to the encoding and the formal system. A theoretical decoding that establishes commutative relations between the two paths is called 'complete decoding' of the formal system into the sub-natural system.

3 Lessons from the modelling relation for sustainability issues

The so-called 'models' used in social sciences, including economics, are not models in the sense defined above. Such models are at best a 'simile' of a sub-natural system.

According to Georgescu-Roegen (1971), in physics, 'a model must be accurate in relation to the sharpest measuring instrument [and] there is an objective sense' in comparing accuracy among different formal systems representing a particular physical model. Economists do not have measurement schemes that can effectively test the validity of an economic 'model'. So, economists have to deal with a sub-natural system using external references including value judgements and an avoidable process of 'introspection'. Finally, they can 'simile encode' the sub-natural system into a formal system with the help of 'dialectics' which means that 'P' and 'not P' can co-exist (FD in Fig. 9.2). This encoding occurs only provided that the sub-natural system is stable during a given time horizon. Every time their models failed to predict the energy demand, econometricians found a ready, yet self-defeating, excuse: 'history has changed the parameters' (Georgescu-Roegen 1976). Georgescu-Roegen writes: if 'history is so cunning, why persist in predicting it? What quantitative economics needs above all are economists such as Simon Kuznets, who would know how to pick up a small number of relevant variables, instead of relying upon the computer to juggle with scores of variables and thus losing all mental [introspective] contact with the dialectical nature of economic phenomena'.

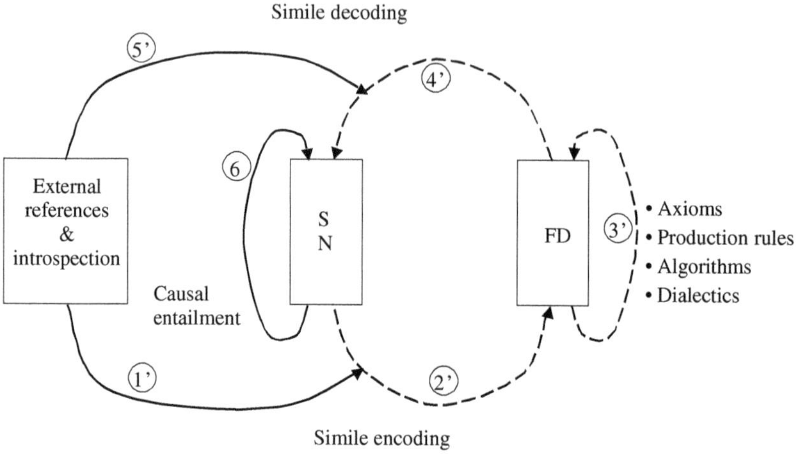

Figure 9.2 Theoretical simile.

Economic 'model', being a simile, can guide experts equipped with analytical and dialectical minds. Economists need an excellent 'delicacy and sensitivity of touch' that may be called art. Because of this peculiar aspect of economic analysis, economists who deal with sustainability issues must pay due attention to 'transparency' to promote dialogue with stakeholders and policy makers. Transparency means that certain details for the model must be clearly spelt out to laypersons: (i) assumptions, (ii) the process of application of a particular methodology, (iii) data collection process, (iv) criteria to measure improvements, (v) choice of indicators and their feasibility domains, (vi) goals, (vii) boundary conditions including choice of interest groups, (viii) initial conditions and (ix) time horizon.

Rosen's (1991) modelling relation in Fig. 9.1 leads to the conclusion: there is no 'final cause' in Aristotelian discussion of causal categories. If a theorem P is an 'effect', it is possible to identify Aristotle's idea of 'material cause' of P with axioms, his idea of 'efficient cause' of P with production rules, and his idea of 'formal cause' of P with a particular algorithm, producing a corresponding trajectory of propositions from axioms to the theorem P. In complete formal terms (without resorting to mysterious 'teleology'), final causation does not appear in the modelling relation diagram: (i) something is a final cause of P requires P itself to entail (or imply) something; (ii) a final cause of P must entail the entailment of P itself. This peculiar 'reflexive' character of final cause implies that the effect of P acts back on the causal process that is generating it. So, the future actively affects the present and the past. Dealing with sustainability issues (everything is always changing) requires dealing with finality into our theoretical scheme and putting finality in the centre stage of analysis. A reflexive system or an anticipatory system can change its present internal structures/functions for survival. It uses the internal (or endogenous) modelling effort of future scenarios within itself to foresee its possible goals and states in the future. Of course, a reflexive system can change its structures/functions based on past experience. Another peculiar aspect of a reflective system is that the announcement to be taken by other reflexive systems may change the internal modelling effort of that particular reflexive system. According to Georgescu-Roegen (1971: 335), 'no process in which the Oedipus effect is at work can be represented by an analytical model [a purely formal system]'.

A reflexive system treated as a sub-natural system in the modelling relation creates a new type of difficulty. As noted above, a final causation is absent in a purely formal system. The statement that there is no internal mechanism within the formal system for changing any axiom, any production rule or any algorithm may be superfluous. However, this seemingly trivial statement explains why the mathematical game theoretic approach faces serious limitations when applied to any real situation. As reflexive systems, humans always try to change the rules of a game.

Dealing with sustainability issues requires the admission that it is impossible to know 'what is the question?' (Peet 1998). It cannot be known how to put a shared question in a proper perspective, especially in a situation (Post-Normal situation) where 'facts are uncertain, values in dispute, stakes high and decisions urgent' (Funtowicz and Ravetz 1993: 744). The cases allow certain courses of action.

First, the people concerned (scientists, stakeholders and decision-makers) must reach a kind of consensus about the sub-natural system to be considered and the direction that should be followed in the long term for the pursuit of happiness (Peet 1998; Shingu 1998). Of course, this consensus must be revised through the process of dialogue among us. Identification of a sub-natural system includes the determination of factors such as a space–time scale adopted, choice of relevant stakeholders, present status of distribution of wealth among people, decision members at each level of organization, appropriate institutional and political settings, available technological matrix, a reasonable understanding of the whole spectrum of resources and the environmental situation. At the risk of accusation of being a Utopian concerning the question of direction of societies, it is reasonable to share the view with Peet (1998) that all people should be 'able to live in dignity with the minimum adverse impact on Nature, now and in the future'. However, it is necessary to clarify the meaning of Peet's statement through continual dialogue. Dialogue among members of a society helps create a process by which people recognize and understand unavoidable trade-offs necessary for reaching a specified goal.

The next issue is to select a set of criteria or indicators that can show whether or not there is progress towards given goals. Choice of indicators has technical aspects, but the process of determining those indicators must be transparent to laypersons. Scientists must explain to stakeholders such details as underlying assumptions, a method of calculation of indicators, limitations of indicators and the trade-off relations among the indicators. In particular, interaction between scientists and the rest of the stakeholders must focus on how to assess: (i) values taken by indicators reflecting trade-offs with other indicators; (ii) resource supply constraint; (iii) environmental capacity constraint; (iv) institutional constraint; and (v) distribution of cost and benefits among stakeholders in relation to particular values taken by the various indicators.

However, at this point, it is difficult for scientists to devise a set of indicators typical in the Post-Normal situation when there is neither encoding nor decoding available. Unfortunately, there is no guide, even for the so-called 'experts', on how to devise suitable indicators, so the wisdom of laypersons may surpass that of scientists in many respects, requiring continuous dialogue and transparency concerning the nature of the issue involved. On this point, Georgescu-Roegen's advice seems helpful: people 'seem to forget not only that science emerged from unidirectional observation but that some pre-scientific thought always precedes the scientific one' (Georgescu-Roegen 1971). Scientists must reach a workable body of descriptive propositions for a given sub-natural system by observing the system. This should not be done by collapsing its description into a pre-defined collection of standard indicators. Whenever a situation has special features, scientists must be able to include such a peculiarity in their representation. Standard sophisticated methodologies do not help in this task; a simple analysis with a few but well-chosen factors is a less deceptive guide for scientists.

4 Hierarchical system perspectives for sustainability issues

As shown in the previous two sections, there are several formidable problems in applying traditional scientific methodologies to sustainability issues. Global problems such as climate changes caused by increased releases of carbon dioxide into the earth's atmosphere demand the development of methodological tools to link small-scale phenomena at lower levels to large-scale phenomena at higher levels. Then, it may be possible to obtain an operational basis of integrated assessment that can apply to the decision making process under conditions of uncertainty. A proper understanding of sustainability issues requires 'translation of information between scales and methods to relate findings at different scales' (O'Neill 1989: 150).

Hierarchical system perspectives offer a valuable clue to understanding relevant phenomena and their relationships within a system out of the total complexity of the system itself. In agreement with some scientists (Allen and Starr 1982; O'Neill *et al.* 1986) working in hierarchy theory, it seems inappropriate to imply that 'reality, independent of our cognizance, is in its nature hierarchical' (Allen and Starr 1982: 6). Hierarchical structure is a consequence of human's epistemological nature because if 'there are important systems in the world that are complex without being hierarchic, they may to a considerable extent escape our observation and our understanding' (Simon 1962: 477).

A system is hierarchical when it operates on multiple spatiotemporal scales, i.e. when different process rates are found in the system (O'Neill 1989). Systems are hierarchical when they are analysable into successive sets of subsystems (Simon 1962: 468) or when alternative methods of description exist for the same system (Whyte *et al.* 1969). Human societies and ecosystems are perfect examples of complex hierarchical systems, difficult to analyse, especially when dealing with the issue of sustainability (Giampietro 1994*a*,*b*). The basic idea underlying the approach in this chapter is that behaviour within a system can be described on three adjacent levels of 'Triadic Structure' (Koestler 1967; Salthe 1985; O'Neill

1989). The focal level is the level of interest for a particular research and once the appropriate focal level is identified, dynamic behaviour can be explained by the behaviour of components belonging to the next lower level. Functional or adaptive relevance of larger-scale behaviour can be explained by reference to components belonging to a higher level.

A component of one hierarchy level is a 'holon' introduced by Koestler (1969). A holon has a dual nature (Allen and Starr 1982: 8–16) being at the same time a 'whole' made of smaller parts (e.g. a human being is made of organs, tissues, cells, molecules, etc.) and a 'part of some greater whole' (an individual human being is part of a family, a community, a country, the global economy, etc.). Hierarchical systems have an implicit duality: holons have their own composite structure at the focal level, but because of interaction with the rest of the hierarchy, they perform functions that contribute to the so-called 'emergent properties' that can only be seen from higher levels of analysis. The problem in dealing with holons is that the space–time closure of their structure (the holon seen on the focal level from the lower level) does not coincide with the space–time closure of their role (the holon seen on the focal level from the higher level).

Because of peculiar functioning on parallel scales, hierarchical systems can be studied either in terms of structures or in terms of functional relationships. Established scientific disciplines rarely acknowledge that this unavoidable and prior choice of 'perspective' implies a bias in the description of the behaviour of complex systems (Giampietro 1994*a*). For example, analysing complex systems in terms of structures implicitly assumes: (i) initial conditions (a history of the system which affects its present behaviour) and (ii) a stable higher level on which functions are defined for these structures in order to make them meaningful and stable in time. Similarly, to possess functions at a certain level requires the assumption of stability at the lower levels where there is the structural support for the function (Simon 1962). Hence, no description of the dynamics of a focal level (e.g. society as a whole) can escape the issue of structural constraints (what happens at lower levels?) or functional constraints (what happens at the higher level?).

The hierarchical nature of socioeconomic systems implies a complex behaviour of parallel processes whose effects can be detected with time lags on different space–time scales. So, dealing with the sustainability of socioeconomic systems requires analysis of society's self-organization process in a dual way: (i) on the process side, under the assumption that a society is in quasi-steady state, the pattern of investment of useful energy can be studied; and (ii) on the control side, the profile of human time allocation can be studied from an evolutionary perspective.

Based upon hierarchical system perspectives, the society is seen as the focal level that can be described by variables such as level of energy use, GNP, population size and life expectancy. These variables are defined and assessed at the hierarchical level of the entire society. The corresponding higher level, the ecological level, is seen as the ensemble of biophysical processes on which society depends. At this higher level of ecological systems, it is possible to assess the scale of the processes of natural self-organization of ecosystems seen as dissipative systems based on solar energy. This assessment can be made using a set of variables that are defined only on a scale larger than that used for describing the society. This class of systems was first investigated by Prigogine's school (e.g. Nicolis and Prigogine 1977). The variables for the assessment of ecosystems include the amount of solar energy and biomass in the self-orgnaization, and the size of ecosystems directly or indirectly exploited. The lower hierarchical level could contain individual economic sectors, specific social groups, or individuals using variables describing the characteristics of the interaction with the focal level of society.

5 Theoretical framework

Humans alter the ecosystems in which they live through their technology which is used to increase the efficacy of the process of production and consumption of goods and services in society. They attempt to stabilize and 'improve' the structures and functions of society according to a set of internally generated values given a set of boundary conditions. The process of self-organization of society can be described in terms of two different types of activities that are related to 'efficiency' or to 'adaptability'. This has to do with two functions in the evolution of the system (Schneider and Kay 1994): (i) sustaining the short-term stability of the process by taking advantage of existing favourable gradients (i.e. efficiency according to present boundary conditions) (Conrad 1983); and (ii) sustaining the long-term stability of such a process by maintaining a high compatibility in the face of a changing environment (i.e. adaptability defined as the ability to be efficient according to unknown future boundary conditions) (Conrad 1983).

The main idea of the model of analysis presented here is that the technological development of a society can be described in terms of an acceleration of energy throughput in the primary sectors of economy generating a decoupling between the profile of human time allocation (human time seen as a proxy for the available capability of control) and the profile of exosomatic energy (exosomatic energy seen as a proxy for investment of useful energy). Exosomatic energy proposed by Georgescu-Roegen (1971) is the useful energy throughput outside human bodies as opposed to endosomatic energy (the energy metabolized by humans). In modern societies, a smaller and smaller fraction of total human time is used for running the primary sectors of the economy (e.g. food security, energy and mining and manufacturing), whereas the material throughput in these sectors has increased dramatically.

A scheme presenting an overview of the parallel allocation of (i) exosomatic energy (ET) and (ii) total human time (THT) over different compartments of the economy is given in Fig. 9.3. The overall flow of ET and THT are variously used:

(i) to procure and transform energy input in the energy sector and to procure raw materials;
(ii) to build and maintain exosomatic devices (manufacturing sector);
(iii) to guarantee food and environmental security;

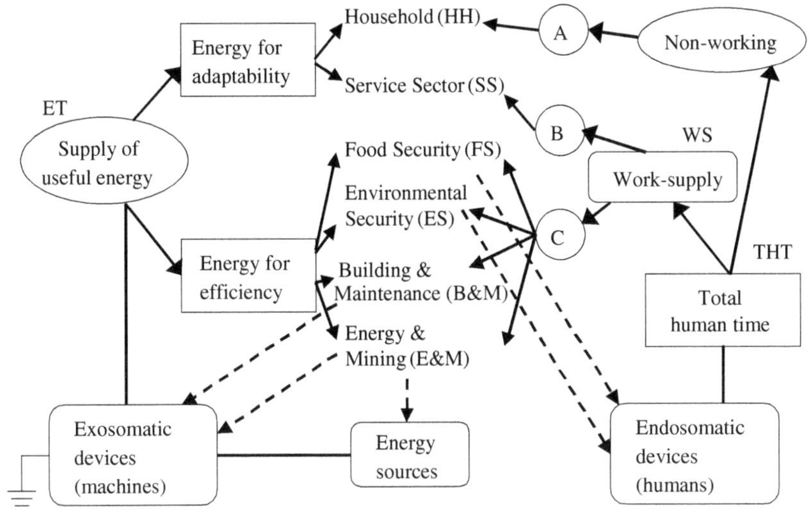

Figure 9.3 Parallel allocation of exosomatic energy and human time.

(iv) to provide services in the service sector; and
(v) to support human activities outside work in the household sector.

Activities (i)–(iii) have been defined as CI activities (Circulating Investment that stabilizes the steady state). The sectors using exosomatic energy used in CI activities are indicated as: E&M (Energy and Mining), B&M (Building and Maintenance), FS (Food Security) and ES (Environmental Security). Altogether, these sectors absorb an amount of working time assessed by C. Activities (iv) and (v) have been defined as FI activities (Fixed Investment that increases adaptability). The flows of exosomatic energy in FI activities are indicated as SS (Service Sector) and HH (Household Sector), whereas the human time allocated in these two sectors is, respectively, B and A. Clearly,

$$\text{E\&M} + \text{B\&M} + \text{FS} + \text{ES} + \text{SS} + \text{HH} = \text{ET} \qquad \text{on the energy side,}$$

$$A + B + C = \text{THT} \qquad \text{on the human time side.}$$

By assessing the flows and parameters presented in Fig. 9.3, it is possible to describe, for any defined society, the particular autocatalytic loop of exosomatic energy in terms of demand of labour WS = B + C (determined by the labour productivity in different economic sectors) related to the stabilized flow ET. A variable called SEH (Strength of the Exosomatic Energy Hypercycle) measures the supply of energy accessible to society per unit of working time in the primary sector of the economy. SEH can be expressed as a combination of technical coefficients.

On the other hand, to change perspective, moving from a biophysical analysis of technical coefficients (the matrix of inputs and outputs of energy and labour in different sectors of the economy as depicted in Fig. 9.3) to a socioeconomic perspective, it is still possible to describe the relation between energy demand and labour supply, but this implies an inversion of the terms 'demand' and 'supply' with respect to 'useful energy' and 'labour time'. The demand of exosomatic energy consumed by society per unit of working time allocated in the primary sectors of the economy has been called BEP (Bioeconomic Pressure). Several variables (referring to different perspectives of the socioeconomic system) can be used to characterize such a pressure and they can be aggregated into this numerical indicator (e.g. age structure, level of education, labour load, etc.). Such a pressure is generated by societal activity aimed at improving the material standard of living. BEP tends to push faster and faster energy and matter throughputs within the economic process (e.g. producing and consuming more goods and services per capita).

According to the scheme in Fig. 9.3, the energy throughput (the level of energy dissipation – ET) at which society's energy budget can be stabilized (when requirement is equal to supply) is defined by: (i) characteristics of the society determining the level of consumption of energy per unit of human time; and (ii) characteristics of the interaction technology/natural resources determining the supply of energy per unit of human time.

Putting all this into a hierarchical perspective, at the focal level, society can be seen as a dissipative system whose energy budget must be balanced: the energy consumed by society to stabilize its structure and functions must be made available through its interaction with the environment. However, simply matching energy demand and supply does not necessarily guarantee stability for the system. The energy balance defined on the focal level is stable only if it is compatible with: (i) lower-level constraints related to the 'biophysical' (food requirements and labour supply) and cultural dimensions (material standard of living and social equity acceptable to members of society) of socioeconomic organization; and (ii) higher-level constraints, i.e. compatibility with 'ecological' boundary conditions.

5.1 Interface focal/lower-level (intensive variables only)

Is current material standard of living (i) technically feasible and (ii) culturally acceptable? By using the hierarchical model presented in this chapter, it is possible to translate this question into a problem of congruence of two indicators: (i) is it possible to have BEP (wanted by people) = SEH (achieved by technology)? (ii) is the current BEP above the minimum acceptable value (BEP*) defined by current cultural identity?

It should be noted that BEP, even if defined in terms of a set of measurable characteristics defined at the level of society, provides indications about material standard of living as perceived by lower-level holons (Pastore *et al.* 1996).

5.2 Interface focal/higher-level (intensive and extensive variables)

Is the dimension of the total energy throughput dissipated by society compatible with the stability of boundary conditions? Alternatively, is the amount of inputs taken from the ecosystems and the amount of wastes dumped into the ecosystems compatible with the stability of the processes of self-organization occurring in the ecosystems with which the society is interacting?

In order to answer this question, it is necessary to first define the concepts of 'environmental loading' and 'critical environmental loading'. The concept of environmental loading was first introduced by H. T. Odum (1996) as an attempt to put in perspective human interference with the activity of self-organization of natural systems.

1. *Environmental loading* – indices of environmental loading, defined as human interference on the activity of natural systems, can be obtained by comparing (i) the assessments of the scale of human activity (e.g. input demand and waste production) with (ii) the assessments of the scale of ecosystem activity (e.g. regenerative capacity and absorbing capacity); or alternatively, by comparing (i) densities of matter or energy flows induced in the ecosystems as a result of alterations by humans with (ii) densities of matter or energy flows in the natural ecosystem in the absence of alterations by humans.
2. *Critical environmental loading* – the maximum level of environmental loading which is still compatible with the stability of the process of self-organization of ecosystems.

Note that any attempt to compare the scale of activity of human societies with the scale of activity of ecosystems implies a combined use of intensive variables (such as level of energy dissipation per unit of control – e.g. *W*/kg of humans in society and *W*/kg of biomass in ecosystems) – and extensive variables (such as 'control capability' available in the information system – e.g. population size for human society and total biomass for ecosystems).

The check on this interface is totally different from the one made about the focal or lower-level check. In that case, the optimization is related only to what happens within the system (optimal allocation of economic resources according to marginal costs). This is the point made by Daly (1992*b*) about standard economic analysis which focuses mainly on optimum allocation. This carries the risk of overlooking the effects of the size of the economic system on the stability of boundary conditions.

5.3 The dynamic system

The model looks at human societies as dynamic systems based on the resonance between controls generating useful energy and vice versa. This follows the intuition of Simon (1962) about the functioning of complex systems – recipes inducing processes and processes making recipes – and that of Prigogine (1978), namely,

DNA making metabolism and metabolism making DNA. This conceptualization fits perfectly with the conceptual model of resonating self-entailment proposed by Rosen (1991) for living systems.

Describing the process of self-organization of human society in terms of a dynamic system provides a direct link between the input–output characteristics of the economic process (technical coefficients achievable on the process side according to technology and natural resources) determining SEH and the set of cultural and social characteristics of the society determining BEP.

The balancing of the energy budget implies that the exosomatic energy consumption must be met by the exosomatic energy supply. Therefore, the two readings of the socioeconomic system according to the concepts of BEP and SEH establish a link among variables referring to different types of analysis: (i) physiological variables, (ii) socioeconomic variables, (iii) technological variables and (iv) indicators of environmental stress (Giampietro 1997; Giampietro *et al.* 1997).

6 Society seen as in a steady state

In his analysis of ecosystem structure, Ulanowicz (1986) finds that the network of matter and energy flows making up an ecosystem can be divided into two parts: one that generates a hypercycle and the other that has a purely dissipative nature.

The part that generates a hypercycle is a net energy producer for the rest of the system. Since some dissipation is always 'necessary to build and maintain structures at sub-compartment level' (Ulanowicz 1986: 119), the net energy producing part comprises activities that generate a positive feedback by taking advantage of sources of free energy outside the system (e.g. solar energy). The role of the hypercyclic part is to drive and keep the whole system away from thermodynamic equilibrium.

The dissipative part comprises activities that are net energy degraders. However, this part is not necessarily useless for the system. It provides control over the entire process of energy degradation and stabilizes the whole system. An ecosystem made of a hypercyclic part alone cannot be stable in time. Without the stabilizing effect of the dissipative part, a positive feedback 'will be reflected upon itself without attenuation, and eventually the upward spiral will exceed any conceivable bounds' (Ulanowicz 1986: 57).

A similar approach can be used to describe society from the process side. Society consists of two compartments, one of which is hypercyclic (a net producer of useful energy for the rest of society) and the other purely dissipative (a net consumer of useful energy). Getting back to Fig. 9.3, where the total flow of exosomatic energy consumed by society (ET) is divided into two types of investments: CI, necessary to stabilize the steady state (efficiency) and FI ($=$ HH $+$ SS), necessary to make the system adaptive in the face of changing boundary conditions (adaptability).

The different nature of the use of the energy flows FI and CI can also be seen in terms of the hierarchy theory. The energy in the energy-supply system (CI flow) maintains the dynamic energy budget in the short term on the time scale of operation of the energy converters through feeding and replacing them. The spare useful energy allocated to activities elsewhere (FI flow) affects the dynamic equilibrium of society in the long term by accumulation of knowledge, capital and expansion of human potentialities. The CI flow refers to energy spent directly in the primary and other sectors responsible for guaranteeing the steady state whose effects are detectable on shorter time scales, whereas the FI flow refers to energy spent in the maintenance of the activities of the rest of the society whose effects are detectable only on longer time scales.

It may be clear that the quantity of useful energy that any society can allocate to the stabilization of its structure in the long term (FI flow) depends on the efficiency of the energy-supply system (ET/CI). Hence, for given boundary conditions and available technology, there is a biophysical constraint on the fraction of useful energy that can be allocated to 'adaptability' at the level of society. A higher efficiency of the energy-supply system is indicated by a lower demand of useful energy consumed for its own operation and maintenance per unit of ET.

7 Society seen as an evolving system

In order to use an analogy between ecosystems and human societies, it is necessary to define an equivalent of 'species' in ecosystems for the organization of human society. A reasonable candidate would be 'labour positions' or 'roles'. In fact, a labour position in society, like a species in an ecosystem, reflects the ability to perform an encoded activity that has proved useful for the system from past experience. However, labour positions alone are not sufficient to regulate flows of matter and energy in society. During labour time, humans control only the flows of resources that are used in the economic process of production (the supply side). In ecosystems, it is well known that autotrophs (primary producers) need heterotrophs (herbivores, carnivores and detritus feeders) to degrade their by-products (e.g. preventing accumulation of oxygen in the atmosphere) and to recycle nutrients such as nitrogen. The rate and the pattern of primary production in ecosystems are controlled not only by the activity of primary producers, but also by the activity of consumers and decomposers. So, there is a direct biophysical relation between autotrophs and heterotrophs in ecosystems. Actually, the more developed is the ecosystem, the more consumers and decomposers play a key role in the regulation of the overall flow of solar energy (Odum 1971). In order to produce more, autotrophs must be 'eaten' at a higher rate by heterotrophs.

The same analogy applies to the economic process. In order to be able to produce more, society must be able to consume more. As with the heterotrophs, the amount and pattern of human consumption directly affects the amount and pattern of production. In order for society to be more productive and efficient, labour hours must be partially 'eaten' by expanding HH. In other words, at the level of society, labour time has to be sacrificed in favour of consumption if more products and services and higher wages are to be obtained. Here, the distinction between 'roles' and 'incumbents' (Bailey 1990) is particularly useful: when a society goes through a phase of economic development, it can change the allocation of human time among different roles (e.g. decreasing time in production and increasing it in consumption) with the same endowment of incumbents (same structure of population) by changing socioeconomic variables (e.g. work load). Then, the distribution of the population among age classes will eventually change (Giampietro and Bukkens 1996; Giampietro and Mayumi 1996; Giampietro *et al.* 1997).

In order to increase the performance of an economic system, more diversity and efficiency in labour positions (roles) and more diversity and efficiency in consumption roles are necessary. Labour positions and consumption roles must be defined at the hierarchical level of society, since their existence is independent of the incumbent at the particular moment (Bailey 1990).

Increasing leisure time plays an important role in increasing consumption and production (Zipf 1941). Moreover, labour roles due to organization can be seen as replicated actions (Bailey 1990: 179) and, therefore, reflect what happened in the past. Also, leisure time tends to be allocated to an established set of leisure roles, i.e. individual choices are constrained by cultural identity (e.g. Europeans play soccer whereas Americans prefer football). However, the fidelity to leisure roles is less strictly enforced by society than for labour roles. This allows more freedom of decision for individuals and, hence, more variability in the set of activities performed during leisure time.

8 The double autocatalytic loop: human control, exosomatic power and environmental services

The autocatalytic loop of human activity can be described from a hierarchical perspective in terms of division of human control over 'efficiency' (short time scale, regulating the focal/lower-level interface assuming fixed boundary conditions) and 'adaptability' (long time scale, regulating the focal/higher-level interface assuming a given history of the system). Such a 'triadic' reading (Salthe 1985) is illustrated in section (i) of Fig. 9.4.

The human control (time/activity) available to the socioeconomic system can be allocated to three levels, the focus, higher and lower level. Indeed, humans must pay a tribute, in the form of time allocation, to all three hierarchical levels:

1. Tribute paid to the higher hierarchical level in the form of *A* activities, necessary to guarantee adaptability in the long term. This higher level relates to society in a historical perspective. *A* activities provide society with 'initiating conditions' (cultural identity, knowledge, technological capital and reproduction of humans). The present generation must take care of the initiating conditions for future generations.
2. Tribute paid to the focus level in the form of *B* activities, to ensure the everyday maintenance of the structure of human mass. *B* activities provide the system of controls over the network of matter and energy consumed by society.
3. Tribute paid to the lower hierarchical level in the form of *C* activities, to guarantee efficiency in the set of everyday operations. These activities guarantee the necessary input flows from the environment.

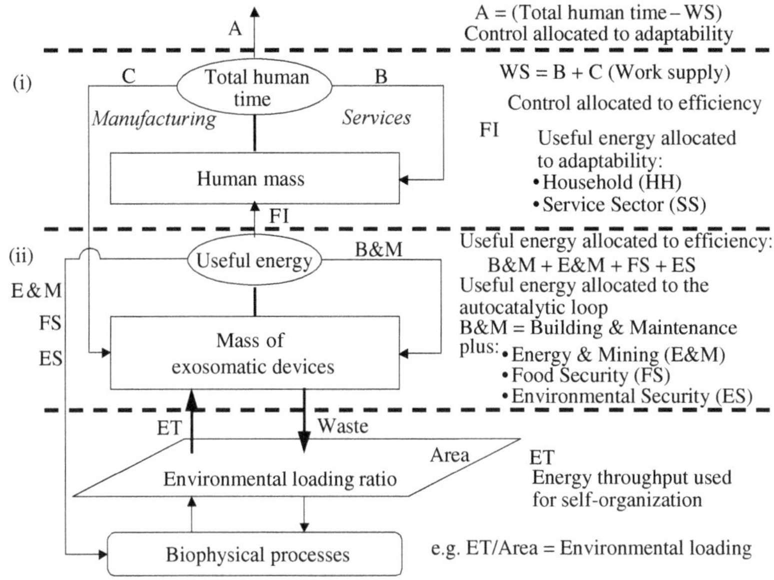

Figure 9.4 The double autocatalytic loop: (i) human time; (ii) exosomatic energy.

The autocatalytic loop generated by exosomatic devices (machines) has two distinct interfaces (see section (ii) in Fig. 9.4), one with humans and the other with the environment. Regarding the former, machines represent a cost for humans in terms of human labour demand, but machines pay back in terms of a net supply of useful energy for humans. Regarding the latter, machines alter boundary conditions with their activity through the withdrawal of inputs and disposal of wastes. Given a particular area, the scale of machine activity (exosomatic energy dissipation which measures the amount of energy conversions controlled by machines) relative to the scale of ecological activity defines a certain environmental loading ratio.

When describing the autocatalytic exosomatic loop from a hierarchical perspective, as is illustrated in section (ii) of Fig. 9.4, exosomatic devices have to pay a tribute to the three hierarchical levels:

1 Tribute paid to the higher hierarchical level in the form of FI consisting of HH and SS. This is the disposable useful energy that humans obtain in return for the construction and maintenance of machines.
2 Tribute to the focus level in the form of B&M. This is the useful energy generated by machines to build and maintain their own structure.
3 Tribute paid to the lower hierarchical level in the form of E&M, FS and ES. This is the useful energy generated by machines required for the stabilization of energy and material inputs and waste disposal into the environment.

Within the hierarchical framework, the following indicators can be defined:

(i) An indicator of technological development equal to the exo/endo energy ratio – this indicator assesses the ability of technology for making a better use of natural resources by amplifying the societal metabolism well above the sum of energy controlled through human metabolism.
(ii) An indicator of technological efficiency equal to the ratio FI/ET – this indicator assesses the fraction of useful energy to be considered as 'disposable energy income' for adaptability.
(iii) An indicator of the relative weight of adaptability and efficiency in society equal to the ratio $(A + B)$/THT – this indicator assesses, on the control side, the allocation of the capability for control on long-term and short-term investments.
(iv) An indicator of material standard of living or technological development BEP – this indicator correlates well with all the major indicators of development (Pastore *et al.* 1996) and, therefore, assesses, at the societal level, the material standard of living coupled to a particular combination of socioeconomic characteristics.
(v) A family of indicators of environmental stress (environmental loading ratios) – these indicators can be chosen according to the limiting set of resources (either on the input or the sink side) in the analysis of environmental compatibility.

9 Conclusion

From an anthropocentric point of view, it is desirable for technology to continuously increase ET/C so as to continuously improve the standard of living. However, labour productivity in the energy sector is also affected by limited supply of resources and limited ability of natural systems to absorb waste disposal and be resilient to other perturbations associated with technological processes. The scales of economics systems are fundamental in determining the feasibility of possible solutions.

Low labour productivity and low standard of living are basic problems facing developing societies which exploit mainly the energy funds. In developed, oil-based economies labour productivity and standard of living are high, due to the use of fossil energy stocks and abundant technology leading to unsustainability (Giampietro and Mayumi 1998). The desire for high Western-like standards of living and the desire for improvement in BEP (more than 500 NJ/hour) are rapidly spreading across the world. Adoption of such a high material standard of living must be coupled to a high level of labour productivity and excessive use of fossil energy. This rapidly spreading desire for a high standard of living harms the traditional energy sector of developing societies, which is based on energy fund exploitation.

Inevitably, the friction is generated by the interaction of two types of socioeconomic system operating at widely different rates of energy throughput, one based on stock exploitation and the other on fund exploitation. Interaction with oil-based economic activities provides members of developing societies with the opportunity to amplify the return of labour (SEH) well above traditional labour based on biophysical conversions. When such amplification occurs, farmers abandon labour-intensive and low-remuneration jobs, even if natural resources are used much less efficiently and even if there are much higher environmental loading ratios.

It is much easier to reach a high exo/endo energy ratio (a larger SEH) by depleting energy stocks and consequently ignoring the sustainability issues than by managing the available energy funds in a sustainable way. This fact favours Western economies over subsistence economies because, despite better ecological performance and higher sustainability in many traditional subsistence economies, job opportunities in subsistence economies provide inadequate return per hour of labour. Subsistence societies cannot afford high BEP.

Subsistence societies which operate at a low population density are ecologically sustainable (low EL), but economically unsustainable (too low BEP) when they can interact with the Western world. Western societies are economically competitive (high BEP), but ecologically unsustainable (too high EL) in the long term.

The methodological tool developed in this chapter is an attempt to deal with the biophysical roots of contrasts between traditional and modern economies. Clearly, the tool does not provide a definite answer to solve these contrasts, but it at least establishes a link between different perspectives (e.g. ecological, social, economic, etc.). I believe that this link provides useful information for dealing with sustainability issues of human development in the era of Post-Normal Science.

Appendix A. Integral curves around a saturation point

For the sake of simplicity, let us assume that there is only one saturation point (s_1, s_2) in the plane. We define the sign of S as positive for all regular points,

$$S = \varphi_1(x_1, x_2)(s_1 - x_1) + \varphi_2(x_1, x_2)(s_2 - x_2). \tag{1}$$

Suppose the saturation point is located at the origin in the plane. Then, in a small region around the saturation point, we can obtain the following inequality:

$$x_1\varphi_1(x_1, x_2) + x_2\varphi_2(x_1, x_2) < 0. \tag{2}$$

The following stability condition is imposed on functions $\varphi_1(x_1, x_2)$ and $\varphi_2(x_1, x_2)$:

$$\begin{vmatrix} \varphi_1 & \varphi_2 \\ \dfrac{\partial}{\partial x_1}\left(\dfrac{\varphi_2}{\varphi_1}\right) & \dfrac{\partial}{\partial x_2}\left(\dfrac{\varphi_2}{\varphi_1}\right) \end{vmatrix} < 0. \tag{3}$$

Under the assumption that $\varphi_1(x_1, x_2)$ and $\varphi_2(x_1, x_2)$ are regular functions in a domain around the saturation point, total differentiation of (2) produces

$$\varphi_{11}^0\, \mathrm{d}x_1^2 + (\varphi_{12}^0 + \varphi_{21}^0)\, \mathrm{d}x_1\, \mathrm{d}x_2 + \varphi_{22}^0\, \mathrm{d}x_2^2 < 0. \tag{4}$$

In a small domain around the origin equation $\varphi_1(x_1, x_2)\mathrm{d}x_1 + \varphi_2(x_1, x_2)\mathrm{d}x_2 = 0$ can be replaced by

$$(x_1\varphi_{11}^0 + x_2\varphi_{12}^0)\, \mathrm{d}x_1 + (x_1\varphi_{21}^0 + x_2\varphi_{22}^0)\, \mathrm{d}x_2 = 0. \tag{5}$$

Owing to (4), when $\varphi_{12}^0 \neq \varphi_{21}^0$ the integral curve for (5) is

$$\log\left[x_1^2 T\left(\frac{x_2}{x_1}\right)\right] + \frac{2(\varphi_{21}^0 - \varphi_{12}^0)}{\eta} \arctan\left[\frac{1}{\eta}\frac{\mathrm{d}T(x_2/x_1)}{\mathrm{d}(x_2/x_1)}\right] = \text{const.}, \tag{6}$$

where

$$\begin{aligned} T(x) &= \varphi_{11}^0 + (\varphi_{12}^0 + \varphi_{21}^0)x + \varphi_{22}^0 x^2, \\ \eta^2 &= 4\varphi_{11}^0\varphi_{22}^0 - (\varphi_{12}^0 + \varphi_{21}^0)^2. \end{aligned} \tag{7}$$

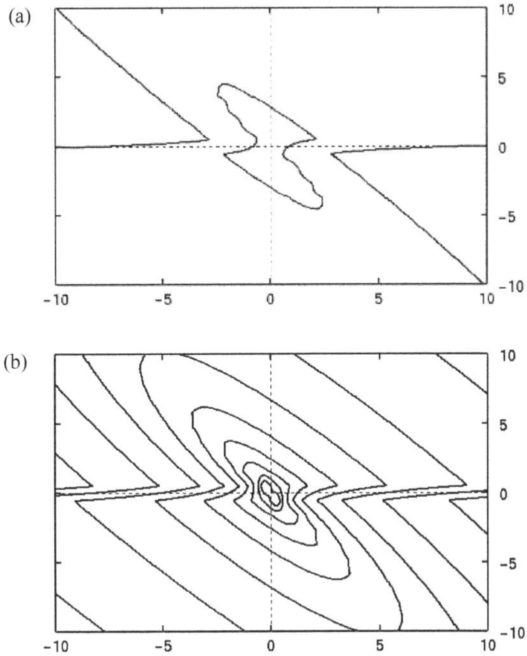

Figure A.1 Integral curves of Georgescu-Roegen's solution.

Georgescu-Roegen claims that the integral curves (6) 'envelope the saturation point'. Georgescu-Roegen (1936: 560) adopts the transformation between the plane (x_1, x_2) and the plane (x_1, y_2) where $x_2 = x_1 y_2$. The Jacobian determinant of this transformation is zero at the saturation point. Therefore, this transformation is not locally invertible at the saturation point. Thus, the integral curves (6) have peculiar forms shown in Fig. A.1.

There is yet another way of proving that there is no simple closed curve satisfying (5) using Bendixson's test (Andronov *et al.* 1973: 207)

Bendixson's Test

If the system

$$\frac{dx}{dt} = P(x, y), \qquad \frac{dy}{dt} = Q(x, y) \tag{8}$$

is analytic and the function

$$\frac{\partial P}{\partial x} + \frac{\partial Q}{\partial y} \tag{9}$$

has fixed sign in a simply connected region G, then G contains no simple closed curves.

For the purpose of using Bendixson's test, equation (5) can be written in the following way:

$$\frac{\mathrm{d}x_1}{\mathrm{d}t} = -x_1\varphi_{21}^0 - x_2\varphi_{22}^0, \tag{10}$$

$$\frac{\mathrm{d}x_2}{\mathrm{d}t} = x_1\varphi_{11}^0 + x_2\varphi_{12}^0. \tag{11}$$

Applying Bendixson's test to equations (10) and (11),

$$\frac{\partial(-x_1\varphi_{21}^0 - x_2\varphi_{22}^0)}{\partial x_1} + \frac{\partial(x_1\varphi_{11}^0 + x_2\varphi_{12}^0)}{\partial x_2} = -\varphi_{21}^0 + \varphi_{12}^0 \neq 0. \tag{12}$$

Thus, it is proved that (5) has no closed paths.

There exists an easier way to obtain integral curves of spiral form conjectured by Georgescu-Roegen. Rewriting (10) and (11) in vector form,

$$\frac{\mathrm{d}\vec{X}}{\mathrm{d}t} = A\vec{X}, \tag{13}$$

where $\vec{X} = (x_1, x_2)$ and

$$A = \begin{bmatrix} -\varphi_{21}^0 & -\varphi_{22}^0 \\ \varphi_{11}^0 & \varphi_{12}^0 \end{bmatrix}. \tag{14}$$

The two eigenvalues λ_1 and λ_2 of A are conjugate to each other, due to (4). Putting $\lambda_1 = \mu + \mathrm{i}\nu$ and $\lambda_2 = \mu - \mathrm{i}\nu$, matrix A can be diagonalized,

$$\exp At = \mathrm{e}^{\lambda_1 t}P_1 + \mathrm{e}^{\lambda_2 t}P_2, \tag{15}$$

where

$$P_1 = \frac{A - \lambda_2 I}{\lambda_1 - \lambda_2} = \frac{A - \bar{\lambda}_1 I}{\lambda_1 - \bar{\lambda}_1}, \tag{16}$$

$$P_2 = \frac{A - \lambda_1 I}{\lambda_2 - \lambda_1} = \bar{P}_1. \tag{17}$$

From (16) and (17), we can see that each element of matrix P_2 is conjugate with the corresponding element of matrix P_1. Now we can rewrite (15) in the following form:

$$\exp At = \mathrm{e}^{\lambda_1 t}P_1 + \mathrm{e}^{\bar{\lambda}_1 t}P_2 = 2\,\mathrm{Re}(\mathrm{e}^{\lambda_1 t}P_1). \tag{18}$$

If we put $P_1 = Q_1 - \mathrm{i}Q_2$, we can change (18) further into the form

$$\exp At = 2\mathrm{e}^{\mu t}(Q_1 \cos \nu t - Q_2 \sin \nu t). \tag{19}$$

So, we can obtain the integral curves for (13):

$$\vec{X}(t) = \exp At \cdot \vec{X}_0 = 2e^{ut}(Q_1 \cos \nu t - Q_2 \sin \nu t)\vec{X}_0. \tag{20}$$

If we transform (20) using the two lines $2Q_1\vec{X}_0$ and $2Q_2\vec{X}_0$ as new axes into the plane (u_1, u_2), we can obtain

$$u_1 = c_1 e^{\mu t} \cos \nu t, \tag{21}$$

$$u_2 = c_2 e^{\mu t} \sin \nu t. \tag{22}$$

Equations (21) and (22) are the spiral forms predicted by Georgescu-Roegen. These can be further transformed into another new plane (y_1, y_2) where $y_1 = u_1/c_1$ and $y_2 = u_2/c_2$:

$$y_1^2 + y_2^2 = e^{2\mu t}. \tag{23}$$

Appendix B. Conditions for balanced sustained growth of the open dynamic Leontief model

The open Leontief dynamic model is

$$z_1(t) = y_1(t) - M_{11}\frac{\mathrm{d}y_1(t)}{\mathrm{d}t} - M_{12}\frac{\mathrm{d}y_2(t)}{\mathrm{d}t}, \tag{1}$$

$$z_2(t) = y_2(t) - M_{21}\frac{\mathrm{d}y_1(t)}{\mathrm{d}t} - M_{22}\frac{\mathrm{d}y_2(t)}{\mathrm{d}t}. \tag{2}$$

Let

$$M = \begin{bmatrix} M_{11} & M_{12} \\ M_{21} & M_{22} \end{bmatrix}.$$

Then

$$\begin{bmatrix} \frac{\mathrm{d}y_1(t)}{\mathrm{d}t} \\ \frac{\mathrm{d}y_2(t)}{\mathrm{d}t} \end{bmatrix} = M^{-1}\begin{bmatrix} y_1(t) \\ y_2(t) \end{bmatrix} - M^{-1}\begin{bmatrix} z_1(t) \\ z_2(t) \end{bmatrix}, \tag{3}$$

because

$$\begin{aligned} \frac{1}{\det(M^{-1})} = \det(M) &= M_{11}M_{22} - M_{12}M_{21} \\ &= (B_{11}B_{22} - B_{12}B_{21})(a_{11}a_{22} + a_{12}a_{21})/D^2 \\ &> 0. \end{aligned}$$

Since $M_{11} > 0$, $M_{22} > 0$ and $\det(M^{-1}) > 0$, the two eigenvalues of M^{-1} must be positive. So, the solution of (3) given below diverges:

$$\begin{bmatrix} y_1(t) \\ y_2(t) \end{bmatrix} = \mathrm{e}^{M^{-1}t}\begin{bmatrix} y_1(0) \\ y_2(0) \end{bmatrix} - \int_0^t \mathrm{e}^{M^{-1}(t-\tau)}M^{-1}\begin{bmatrix} z_1(\tau) \\ z_2(\tau) \end{bmatrix}\mathrm{d}\tau, \quad t \geq 0. \tag{4}$$

We will prove the following proposition.

Proposition 1 *If $\rho_1, \rho_2, \rho_5, \rho_6 \neq 0$, then there exists no solution of (3) satisfying both $\mathrm{d}y_1(t)/\mathrm{d}t > 0$ and $\mathrm{d}y_2(t)/\mathrm{d}t > 0$, where*

$$\rho_1 = y_1(0) - \frac{a - d - \sqrt{(a-d)^2 + 4bc}}{2c} y_2(0), \tag{5}$$

$$\rho_2 = \frac{d - a + \sqrt{(a-d)^2 + 4bc}}{2b} y_1(0) + \frac{\left(a - d - \sqrt{(a-d)^2 + 4bc}\right)^2}{4bc} y_2(0), \tag{6}$$

$$\rho_5 = z_1(t) - \frac{a - d - \sqrt{(a-d)^2 + 4bc}}{2c} z_2(t), \tag{7}$$

$$\rho_6 = \frac{d - a + \sqrt{(a-d)^2 + 4bc}}{2b} z_1(t) + \frac{\left(a - d - \sqrt{(a-d)^2 + 4bc}\right)^2}{4bc} z_2(t). \tag{8}$$

Proof Let $A = M^{-1}$, then the solution (4) becomes

$$\begin{bmatrix} y_1(t) \\ y_2(t) \end{bmatrix} = \mathrm{e}^{At} \begin{bmatrix} y_1(0) \\ y_2(0) \end{bmatrix} - \int_0^t \mathrm{e}^{A(t-\tau)} A \begin{bmatrix} z_1(\tau) \\ z_2(\tau) \end{bmatrix} \mathrm{d}\tau, \quad t \geq 0. \tag{9}$$

Let ξ_1, ξ_2 be the two eigenvalues of matrix A, then matrix A becomes

$$A = P \Lambda P^{-1}, \tag{10}$$

where

$$\Lambda = \begin{bmatrix} \xi_1 & \\ & \xi_2 \end{bmatrix} \tag{11}$$

and

$$A = \frac{1}{\det(M)} \begin{bmatrix} M_{22} & -M_{12} \\ -M_{21} & M_{11} \end{bmatrix} := \begin{bmatrix} a & b \\ c & d \end{bmatrix}. \tag{12}$$

Here, it should be noted that $a > 0$, $b < 0$, $c < 0$ and $d > 0$.

Elementary calculations produce

$$\xi_1 = \frac{a+d+\sqrt{(a-d)^2+4bc}}{2}, \tag{13}$$

$$\xi_2 = \frac{a+d-\sqrt{(a-d)^2+4bc}}{2}, \tag{14}$$

$$P = \begin{bmatrix} 1 & \dfrac{a-d-\sqrt{(a-d)^2+4bc}}{2c} \\ \dfrac{-a+d+\sqrt{(a-d)^2+4bc}}{2b} & 1 \end{bmatrix}, \tag{15}$$

$$P^{-1} = \frac{1}{\det(P)} \begin{bmatrix} 1 & -\dfrac{a-d-\sqrt{(a-d)^2+4bc}}{2c} \\ -\dfrac{-a+d+\sqrt{(a-d)^2+4bc}}{2b} & 1 \end{bmatrix}, \tag{16}$$

and

$$\begin{aligned} e^{At} &= Pe^{\Lambda t}P^{-1} \\ &= P\begin{bmatrix} e^{\xi_1 t} & \\ & e^{\xi_2 t} \end{bmatrix} P^{-1} \\ &= \frac{1}{\det(P)} \begin{bmatrix} 1 & \dfrac{a-d-\sqrt{(a-d)^2+4bc}}{2c} \\ \dfrac{-a+d+\sqrt{(a-d)^2+4bc}}{2b} & 1 \end{bmatrix} \\ &\quad \times \begin{bmatrix} e^{\xi_1 t} & \\ & e^{\xi_2 t} \end{bmatrix} \\ &\quad \times \begin{bmatrix} 1 & -\dfrac{a-d-\sqrt{(a-d)^2+4bc}}{2c} \\ -\dfrac{-a+d+\sqrt{(a-d)^2+4bc}}{2b} & 1 \end{bmatrix}. \end{aligned} \tag{17}$$

Three cases are considered to prove Proposition 1.

Case 1 $z_1(t) = 0, \; z_2(t) = 0$. The solution becomes

$$\begin{bmatrix} y_1(t) \\ y_2(t) \end{bmatrix} = e^{At} \begin{bmatrix} y_1(0) \\ y_2(0) \end{bmatrix}, \quad t \geq 0. \tag{18}$$

Substitution of (17) into (18) produces

$$\begin{aligned}
\begin{bmatrix} y_1(t) \\ y_2(t) \end{bmatrix} &= Pe^{\Lambda t}P^{-1}\begin{bmatrix} y_1(0) \\ y_2(0) \end{bmatrix} \\
&= \frac{1}{\det(P)}\begin{bmatrix} e^{\xi_1 t} + \frac{a-d-\sqrt{(a-d)^2+4bc}}{4bc}e^{\xi_2 t} & \frac{a-d-\sqrt{(a-d)^2+4bc}}{2c}(e^{\xi_2 t}-e^{\xi_1 t}) \\ \frac{d-a+\sqrt{(a-d)^2+4bc}}{2b}(e^{\xi_1 t}-e^{\xi_2 t}) & e^{\xi_2 t} + \frac{a-d-\sqrt{(a-d)^2+4bc}}{4bc}e^{\xi_1 t} \end{bmatrix}\begin{bmatrix} y_1(0) \\ y_2(0) \end{bmatrix} \qquad (19) \\
&= \frac{1}{\det(P)}\begin{bmatrix} \left(y_1(0) - \frac{a-d-\sqrt{(a-d)^2+4bc}}{2c}y_2(0)\right)e^{\xi_1 t} + \left(\frac{\left(a-d-\sqrt{(a-d)^2+4bc}\right)^2}{4bc}y_1(0) + \frac{a-d-\sqrt{(a-d)^2+4bc}}{2c}y_2(0)\right)e^{\xi_2 t} \\ \left(\frac{d-a+\sqrt{(a-d)^2+4bc}}{2b}y_1(0) + \frac{\left(a-d-\sqrt{(a-d)^2+4bc}\right)^2}{4bc}y_2(0)\right)e^{\xi_1 t} + \left(y_2(0) - \frac{d-a+\sqrt{(a-d)^2+4bc}}{2b}y_1(0)\right)e^{\xi_2 t} \end{bmatrix} \\
&= \frac{1}{\det(P)}\begin{bmatrix} y_1(0) - \frac{a-d-\sqrt{(a-d)^2+4bc}}{2c}y_2(0) \\ \frac{d-a+\sqrt{(a-d)^2+4bc}}{2b}y_1(0) + \frac{\left(a-d-\sqrt{(a-d)^2+4bc}\right)^2}{4bc}y_2(0) \end{bmatrix}e^{\xi_1 t} \\
&\quad + \frac{1}{\det(P)}\begin{bmatrix} \frac{\left(a-d-\sqrt{(a-d)^2+4bc}\right)^2}{4bc}y_1(0) + \frac{a-d-\sqrt{(a-d)^2+4bc}}{2c}y_2(0) \\ y_2(0) - \frac{d-a+\sqrt{(a-d)^2+4bc}}{2b}y_1(0) \end{bmatrix}e^{\xi_2 t} \qquad (20) \\
&:= \underbrace{\frac{1}{\det(P)}\begin{bmatrix} \rho_1 \\ \rho_2 \end{bmatrix}e^{\xi_1 t}}_{\text{Part 1}} + \underbrace{\frac{1}{\det(P)}\begin{bmatrix} \rho_3 \\ \rho_4 \end{bmatrix}e^{\xi_2 t}}_{\text{Part 2}}. \qquad (21)
\end{aligned}$$

In order to prove Proposition 1 one requires that $y_1(t)y_2(t) < 0$ when $t \to \infty$. Because $\xi_1 > \xi_2 > 0$ according to (20), Part 1 determines the signs of $y_1(t)$ and $y_2(t)$ when $t \to \infty$ provided that $\rho_1, \rho_2 \neq 0$. So, if $\rho_1\rho_2 < 0$, Proposition 1 is satisfied. We prove the following lemma.

Lemma 1 *If $\rho_1 > 0$, then $\rho_2 < 0$, or if $\rho_2 > 0$, then $\rho_1 < 0$.*

Proof Suppose that $\rho_1 > 0$ and $\rho_2 > 0$; we have

$$y_1(0) - \frac{a - d - \sqrt{(a-d)^2 + 4bc}}{2c} y_2(0) > 0, \tag{22}$$

$$\frac{d - a + \sqrt{(a-d)^2 + 4bc}}{2b} y_1(0) + \frac{\left(a - d - \sqrt{(a-d)^2 + 4bc}\right)^2}{4bc} y_2(0) > 0. \tag{23}$$

Since $ad - bc > 0,\ b,\ c < 0$ and $d - a + \sqrt{(a-d)^2 + 4bc} > 0$. Thus, (22) and (23) become

$$y_1(0) + \frac{d - a + \sqrt{(a-d)^2 + 4bc}}{2c} y_2(0) > 0, \tag{24}$$

$$y_1(0) + \frac{d - a + \sqrt{(a-d)^2 + 4bc}}{2c} y_2(0) < 0. \tag{25}$$

Inequalities (24) and (25) show a contradiction. Thus, Lemma 1 is proved. However, if $\rho_1 = \rho_2 = 0$, then Part 2 in (21) determines the signs of $y_1(t)$ and $y_2(t)$. Because the signs of ρ_3 and ρ_4 are the same, there exist solutions such that both $\mathrm{d}y_1(t)/\mathrm{d}t$ and $\mathrm{d}y_2(t)/\mathrm{d}t$ have the same sign under the following condition:

$$y_1(0) = \frac{a - d - \sqrt{(a-d)^2 + 4bc}}{2c} y_2(0).$$

Case 2 $y_1(0) = 0,\ y_2(0) = 0$. The solution becomes

$$\begin{bmatrix} y_1(t) \\ y_2(t) \end{bmatrix} = -\int_0^t \mathrm{e}^{A(t-\tau)} A \begin{bmatrix} z_1(\tau) \\ z_2(\tau) \end{bmatrix} \mathrm{d}\tau, \quad t \geq 0. \tag{26}$$

Substitution of (17) into (26) results in

$$
\begin{aligned}
\begin{bmatrix} y_1(t) \\ y_2(t) \end{bmatrix} &= -\int_0^t P e^{\Lambda(t-\tau)} P^{-1} P \Lambda P^{-1} \begin{bmatrix} z_1(\tau) \\ z_2(\tau) \end{bmatrix} \mathrm{d}\tau \\
&= -\int_0^t P \begin{bmatrix} \xi_1 e^{\xi_1(t-\tau)} & \\ & \xi_2 e^{\xi_2(t-\tau)} \end{bmatrix} P^{-1} \begin{bmatrix} z_1(\tau) \\ z_2(\tau) \end{bmatrix} \mathrm{d}\tau \qquad (27)
\end{aligned}
$$

$$
\begin{aligned}
&= -\frac{1}{\det(P)} \int_0^t \begin{bmatrix} \xi_1 e^{\xi_1(t-\tau)} + \frac{a-d-\sqrt{(a-d)^2+4bc}}{4bc}\xi_2 e^{\xi_2(t-\tau)} & \frac{a-d-\sqrt{(a-d)^2+4bc}}{2c}(\xi_2 e^{\xi_2(t-\tau)} - \xi_1 e^{\xi_1(t-\tau)}) \\ \frac{d-a+\sqrt{(a-d)^2+4bc}}{2b}(\xi_1 e^{\xi_1(t-\tau)} - \xi_2 e^{\xi_2(t-\tau)}) & \xi_2 e^{\xi_2(t-\tau)} + \frac{a-d-\sqrt{(a-d)^2+4bc}}{4bc}\xi_1 e^{\xi_1(t-\tau)} \end{bmatrix} \\
&\quad \times \begin{bmatrix} z_1(\tau) \\ z_2(\tau) \end{bmatrix} \mathrm{d}\tau \qquad (28)
\end{aligned}
$$

$$
\begin{aligned}
&= \underbrace{-\frac{1}{\det(P)} \int_0^t \begin{bmatrix} z_1(\tau) - \frac{a-d-\sqrt{(a-d)^2+4bc}}{2c} z_2(\tau) \\ \frac{d-a-\sqrt{(a-d)^2+4bc}}{2b} z_1(\tau) + \frac{\left(a-d-\sqrt{(a-d)^2+4bc}\right)^2}{4bc} z_2(\tau) \end{bmatrix} \xi_1 e^{\xi_1(t-\tau)} \mathrm{d}\tau}_{\text{Part 3}} \\
&\quad \underbrace{-\frac{1}{\det(P)} \int_0^t \begin{bmatrix} \frac{\left(a-d-\sqrt{(a-d)^2+4bc}\right)^2}{4bc} z_1(\tau) + \frac{a-d-\sqrt{(a-d)^2+4bc}}{2c} z_2(\tau) \\ z_2(\tau) - \frac{d-a+\sqrt{(a-d)^2+4bc}}{2b} z_1(\tau) \end{bmatrix} \xi_2 e^{\xi_2(t-\tau)} d\tau}_{\text{Part 4}} \qquad (29)
\end{aligned}
$$

$$
:= -\frac{1}{\det(P)} \int_0^t \begin{bmatrix} \rho_5 \\ \rho_6 \end{bmatrix} \xi_1 e^{\xi_1(t-\tau)} \mathrm{d}\tau - \frac{1}{\det(P)} \int_0^t \begin{bmatrix} \rho_7 \\ \rho_8 \end{bmatrix} \xi_2 e^{\xi_2(t-\tau)} \mathrm{d}\tau. \qquad (30)
$$

Part 3 determines the signs of $y_1(t)$ and $y_2(t)$ when $t \to \infty$ provided that $\rho_5, \rho_6 \neq 0$. The similar argument as used for Lemma 1 also applies, without proof, to Lemma 2 in the following.

Lemma 2 *If $\rho_5 > 0$, then $\rho_6 < 0$, or if $\rho_6 > 0$, then $\rho_5 < 0$.*

However, if $\rho_5 = \rho_6 = 0$, then Part 4 in (29) determines the signs of $y_1(t)$ and $y_2(t)$. Because the signs of ρ_7 and ρ_8 are the same, there exist solutions such that both $\mathrm{d}y_1(t)/\mathrm{d}t$ and $\mathrm{d}y_2(t)/\mathrm{d}t$ have the same sign under the following condition:

$$z_1(t) = \frac{a - d - \sqrt{(a-d)^2 + 4bc}}{2c} z_2(t).$$

Case 3 (General case) The solution becomes

$$\begin{bmatrix} y_1(t) \\ y_2(t) \end{bmatrix} = \frac{1}{\det(P)} \begin{bmatrix} \rho_1 \\ \rho_2 \end{bmatrix} \mathrm{e}^{\xi_1 t} + \frac{1}{\det(P)} \begin{bmatrix} \rho_3 \\ \rho_4 \end{bmatrix} \mathrm{e}^{\xi_2 t} - \frac{1}{\det(P)} \int_0^t \begin{bmatrix} \rho_5 \\ \rho_6 \end{bmatrix} \xi_1 \mathrm{e}^{\xi_1 (t-\tau)}\, \mathrm{d}\tau - \frac{1}{\det(P)} \int_0^t \begin{bmatrix} \rho_7 \\ \rho_8 \end{bmatrix} \xi_2 \mathrm{e}^{\xi_2 (t-\tau)}\, \mathrm{d}\tau \tag{31}$$

$$= \underbrace{\frac{1}{\det(P)} \begin{bmatrix} \underbrace{\rho_1 \mathrm{e}^{\xi_1 t} - \int_0^t \rho_5 \xi_1 \mathrm{e}^{\xi_1 (t-\tau)}\, \mathrm{d}\tau}_{\eta_1} \\ \underbrace{\rho_2 \mathrm{e}^{\xi_1 t} - \int_0^t \rho_6 \xi_1 \mathrm{e}^{\xi_1 (t-\tau)}\, \mathrm{d}\tau}_{\eta_2} \end{bmatrix}}_{\text{Part 5}} + \underbrace{\frac{1}{\det(P)} \begin{bmatrix} \rho_3 \mathrm{e}^{\xi_2 t} - \int_0^t \rho_7 \xi_2 \mathrm{e}^{\xi_2 (t-\tau)}\, \mathrm{d}\tau \\ \rho_4 \mathrm{e}^{\xi_2 t} - \int_0^t \rho_8 \xi_2 \mathrm{e}^{\xi_2 (t-\tau)}\, \mathrm{d}\tau \end{bmatrix}}_{\text{Part 6}} \tag{32}$$

It is evident that Part 5 determines the signs of $y_1(t)$ and $y_2(t)$ when $t \to \infty$ provided that $\rho_1, \rho_2, \rho_5, \rho_6 \neq 0$. We prove the following lemma.

Lemma 3 *If $\eta_1 > 0$, then $\eta_2 < 0$, or if $\eta_2 > 0$, then $\eta_1 < 0$.*

Proof Suppose that $\eta_1 > 0,\ \eta_2 > 0$, then we have

$$\rho_1 \mathrm{e}^{\xi_1 t} - \int_0^t \rho_5 \xi_1 \mathrm{e}^{\xi_1 (t-\tau)}\, \mathrm{d}\tau > 0, \tag{33}$$

$$\rho_2 \mathrm{e}^{\xi_1 t} - \int_0^t \rho_6 \xi_1 \mathrm{e}^{\xi_1 (t-\tau)}\, \mathrm{d}\tau > 0. \tag{34}$$

ρ_1 and ρ_2 have the following relation:

$$\rho_2 = \frac{d - a + \sqrt{(a-d)^2 + 4bc}}{2b}\rho_1. \tag{35}$$

On the other hand, ρ_5 and ρ_6 have the following relation:

$$\rho_6 = \frac{d - a + \sqrt{(a-d)^2 + 4bc}}{2b}\rho_5. \tag{36}$$

Substitution of (35) and (36) into (34) produces

$$\frac{d - a + \sqrt{(a-d)^2 + 4bc}}{2b}\left(\rho_1 e^{\xi_1 t} - \int_0^t \rho_5 \xi_1 e^{\xi_1 (t-\tau)}\,d\tau\right) > 0. \tag{37}$$

Because $((d - a + \sqrt{(a-d)^2 + 4bc})/2b < 0)$, (37) becomes

$$\rho_1 e^{\xi_1 t} - \int_0^t \rho_5 \xi_1 e^{\xi_1 (t-\tau)}\,d\tau < 0. \tag{38}$$

Relations (38) and (33) contradict each other. Thus, Lemma 3 is proved.

Assuming $\rho_1 = \rho_2 = \rho_5 = \rho_6 = 0$ in (32) and differentiating both sides of (32) with respect to t, we obtain

$$\begin{bmatrix} \dfrac{dy_1(t)}{dt} \\ \dfrac{dy_2(t)}{dt} \end{bmatrix} = \frac{\xi_2}{\det(P)} \begin{bmatrix} \rho_3 e^{\xi_2 t} - \int_0^t \rho_7 \xi_2 e^{\xi_2 (t-\tau)}\,d\tau - \rho_7(t) \\ \rho_4 e^{\xi_2 t} - \int_0^t \rho_8 \xi_2 e^{\xi_2 (t-\tau)}\,d\tau - \rho_8(t) \end{bmatrix}. \tag{39}$$

Because $\rho_3 = q\rho_4$ and $\rho_7 = q\rho_8$, where

$$q = \frac{a - d - \sqrt{(a-d)^2 + 4bc}}{2c} > 0, \tag{40}$$

the differential equation (39) can be rewritten as follows:

$$\begin{bmatrix} \dfrac{dy_1(t)}{dt} \\ \dfrac{dy_2(t)}{dt} \end{bmatrix} = \frac{\xi_2}{\det(P)} \begin{bmatrix} \rho_3 e^{\xi_2 t} - \int_0^t \rho_7 \xi_2 e^{\xi_2 (t-\tau)}\,d\tau - \rho_7(t) \\ 1/q(\rho_3 e^{\xi_2 t} - \int_0^t \rho_7 \xi_2 e^{\xi_2 (t-\tau)}\,d\tau - \rho_7(t)) \end{bmatrix}. \tag{41}$$

Rewriting A and dividing by $e^{\xi_2 t}$,

$$A = \rho_3 e^{\xi_2 t} - \int_0^t \rho_7 \xi_2 e^{\xi_2 (t-\tau)}\,d\tau - \rho_7(t), \tag{42}$$

we obtain the following condition for balanced sustained growth of the open Leontief dynamic model:

$$p\left[y_1(0) - z_1(0) - \int_0^t \frac{dz_1(\tau)}{d\tau} e^{-\xi_2\tau}\, d\tau\right] + q\left[y_2(0) - z_2(0) - \int_0^t \frac{dz_2(\tau)}{d\tau} e^{-\xi_2\tau}\, d\tau\right] > 0, \tag{43}$$

where

$$p = \frac{(a - d - \sqrt{(a-d)^2 + 4bc})^2}{4bc} > 0. \tag{44}$$

Thus, we have established the following proposition.

Proposition 2 *The necessary and sufficient condition for balanced sustained growth are the following:*

$$y_1(0) - z_1(0) - \int_0^t \frac{dz_1(\tau)}{d\tau} e^{-\xi_2\tau}\, d\tau > 0, \tag{45}$$

$$y_2(0) - z_2(0) - \int_0^t \frac{dz_2(\tau)}{d\tau} e^{-\xi_2\tau}\, d\tau > 0, \tag{46}$$

$$y_1(0) = q y_2(0), \tag{47}$$

$$z_1(t) = q z_2(t). \tag{48}$$

Appendix C. A Leontief dynamic model with two delays

We investigate the condition of existence of the inverse Laplace transform of a Leontief dynamic model with two delays:

$$z_1(t) = a_{11}x_1(t) - a_{12}x_2(t) - B_{11}\frac{\mathrm{d}x_1(t-\tau_1)}{\mathrm{d}t} - B_{12}\frac{\mathrm{d}x_2(t-\tau_2)}{\mathrm{d}t}, \tag{1}$$

$$z_2(t) = -a_{12}x_1(t) + a_{22}x_2(t) - B_{21}\frac{\mathrm{d}x_1(t-\tau_1)}{\mathrm{d}t} - B_{22}\frac{\mathrm{d}x_2(t-\tau_2)}{\mathrm{d}t}. \tag{2}$$

The Laplace transforms of (1) and (2) are

$$\begin{aligned}\begin{bmatrix} X_1(s) \\ X_2(s) \end{bmatrix} = \frac{1}{f(s)} &\begin{bmatrix} a_{22} - B_{22}s\mathrm{e}^{-\tau_2 s} & a_{12} + B_{12}s\mathrm{e}^{-\tau_2 s} \\ a_{21} + B_{21}s\mathrm{e}^{-\tau_1 s} & a_{11} - B_{11}s\mathrm{e}^{-\tau_1 s} \end{bmatrix} \\ &\times \begin{bmatrix} Z_1(s) + B_{11}P_1(s) + B_{12}P_2(s) \\ Z_2(s) + B_{21}P_1(s) + B_{22}P_2(s) \end{bmatrix},\end{aligned} \tag{3}$$

where

$$P_1(s) = -x_1(-\tau_1) + s\mathrm{e}^{-\tau_1 s}\int_{-\tau_1}^{0} x_1(\xi)\mathrm{e}^{-\xi s}\,\mathrm{d}\xi, \tag{4}$$

$$P_2(s) = -x_2(-\tau_2) + s\mathrm{e}^{-\tau_2 s}\int_{-\tau_2}^{0} x_2(\xi)\mathrm{e}^{-\xi s}\,\mathrm{d}\xi, \tag{5}$$

$$f(s) = \alpha - \beta s\mathrm{e}^{-\tau_1 s} - \gamma s\mathrm{e}^{-\tau_2 s} + \delta s^2\mathrm{e}^{-(\tau_1+\tau_2)s}, \tag{6}$$

$$\alpha = a_{11}a_{22} - a_{12}a_{21}, \tag{7}$$

$$\beta = a_{12}B_{21} + a_{22}B_{11}, \tag{8}$$

$$\gamma = a_{11}B_{22} + a_{21}B_{12}, \tag{9}$$

$$\delta = B_{11}B_{22} - B_{12}B_{21}. \tag{10}$$

In relation (3), $X_i(s)$ is the Laplace transform of $x_i(t)$ and $Z_i(s)$ is the Laplace transform of $z_i(t)$.

The necessary condition for the existence of the inverse Laplace transform of (3) is that $f(s) = 0$ does not have any root over the half-plane $\mathrm{Re}(s) > 0$.

Multiplying by $e^{(\tau_1+\tau_2)s}$, relation (6) becomes

$$g(s) = \alpha e^{(\tau_1+\tau_2)s} - \beta s e^{\tau_2 s} - \gamma s e^{\tau_1 s} + \delta s^2. \tag{11}$$

In order to derive the necessary condition for equation $g(s) = 0$ to have no zeros over the half-plane $\mathrm{Re}(s) > 0$, the theory concerning the distribution of zeros of transcendental function is useful. A quasi-polynomial is a transcendental function as follows:

$$H(\mathrm{i}z) = \sum_{\mu,\nu} c_{\nu\mu} z^{\nu} e^{-\mathrm{i}\lambda_\mu z}. \tag{12}$$

The term $c_{mn} z^m e^{-\mathrm{i}\lambda_n z}$ is called the principal term of the quasi-polynomial $H(\mathrm{i}z)$ if $c_{mn} \neq 0$ and exponents m and λ_n each attain their maximum (Čebotarev and Meǐman 1949: 254). The following theorem was proved first by Pontryagin (1955 originally published in 1942) and extended to a general case by Čebotarev and Meǐman (1949: 255).

Theorem 1 *The quasi-polynomial $H(\mathrm{i}z)$ without the principal term has an infinite number of roots in the lower half-plane and their imaginary parts attain arbitrarily large values.*

If Theorem 1 is applied to $g(s)$, $\alpha = 0$ and $\delta = 0$ are necessary to obtain the inverse Laplace transform of $(X_1(s), X_2(s))$. Under these restrictions on α and δ, the following proposition is easily derived.

Proposition 1 *In order for $f(s) = 0$ to have no zeros over the half-plane $\mathrm{Re}(s) > 0$, if $\tau_1 > \tau_2$, then $\gamma > \beta$, or if $\tau_1 < \tau_2$, then $\gamma < \beta$.*

Proof Let $s = x + \mathrm{i}y$, $f(s)$ becomes

$$\begin{aligned} f(x+\mathrm{i}y) = {} & [\beta e^{-\tau_1 x}\cos(\tau_1 y) + \gamma e^{-\tau_2 x}\cos(\tau_2 y)] \\ & + \mathrm{i}[\beta e^{-\tau_1 x}\sin(\tau_1 y) + \gamma e^{-\tau_2 x}\sin(\tau_2 y)]. \end{aligned} \tag{13}$$

Let $f(x+\mathrm{i}y) = 0$, then we have

$$\begin{aligned} &\beta e^{-\tau_1 x}\cos(\tau_1 y) + \gamma e^{-\tau_2 x}\cos(\tau_2 y) = 0, \\ &\beta e^{-\tau_1 x}\sin(\tau_1 y) + \gamma e^{-\tau_2 x}\sin(\tau_2 y) = 0. \end{aligned} \tag{14}$$

If $\tau_2 = k\tau_1$ with $k > 1$, we have

$$\begin{aligned} &e^{-\tau_1 x}[\beta\cos(\tau_1 y) + \gamma e^{-(k-1)\tau_1 x}\cos(\tau_2 y)] = 0, \\ &e^{-\tau_1 x}[\beta\sin(\tau_1 y) + \gamma e^{-(k-1)\tau_1 x}\sin(\tau_2 y)] = 0. \end{aligned} \tag{15}$$

Eliminating the term $e^{-\tau_1 x}$ and combining the two terms of (15),

$$\beta^2 = \gamma^2 e^{-2(k-1)\tau_1 x}. \tag{16}$$

Then, we obtain

$$x = -\frac{1}{2(k-1)\tau_1} \ln \left(\frac{\beta}{\gamma}\right)^2. \tag{17}$$

In order to have $x < 0$, $\beta > \gamma$ must be satisfied. If $k < 1$, then $\gamma > \beta$ must be satisfied. Thus, Proposition 1 is proved.

Notes

2 Foundations of consumer choice theory for environmental valuation in view of Georgescu-Roegen's contribution

1 G. S. Becker extended the neoclassical utility maximizing approach to endogenous preferences, including personal and social capital (e.g. Stigler and Becker 1977; Becker 1996). According to Becker, this extended utility function remains the same over time and, for different individuals, includes addictive, social, advertising capital as arguments. However, Becker and other neoclassical analysts do not seriously consider the issue of relevant choices of the axioms underlying utility theory as discussed in this chapter.

2 When Georgescu-Roegen (1954*b*) discussed this particular set of axioms, he did not consider their relationship to environmental valuation.

4 Information, pseudo-measures and entropy: an elaboration on Georgescu-Roegen's critique

1 However, L. D. Landau, a Nobel prize winner in physics, conjectured the quantum mechanical origin of irreversibility: 'quantum mechanics does in fact involve an important non-equivalence of the two directions of time. This appears in connection with the interaction of a quantum object with a system which with sufficient accuracy obeys the laws of classical mechanics, a process of fundamental significance in quantum mechanics. If two interactions *A* and *B* with a given quantum object occur in succession, then the statement that the probability of any particular result of process *B* is determined by the result of process *A* can be valid only if process *A* occurred earlier than process *B*.... Thus in quantum mechanics there is a physical non-equivalence of the two directions of time, and theoretically the law of increase of entropy might be its macroscopic expression' (Landau and Lifshitz 1980: 32).

5 A critical appraisal of two entropy theoretical approaches to resources and environmental problems: Georgescu-Roegen and Tsuchida

1 In thermodynamic current theory, a system is classified into three categories. A system through which neither matter nor energy is exchanged is called an isolated system. A system through which only energy is exchanged is called a closed system. A system through which both matter and energy are exchanged is called an open system.

2 If the relations between the thermodynamic flows such as a flow of heat, chemical reaction rates, etc., J_i $(i = 1, \dots, n)$, and the thermodynamic forces such as temperature gradient, chemical affinities, etc., X_i $(i = 1, \dots, n)$, may be expected to be linear, this part of non-equilibrium thermodynamics is called the linear thermodynamics of irreversible processes. We can write these relations as $J_i = \sum_{j=1}^{n} L_{ij} X_j$ for n flows and n forces. The coefficients L_{ij} are called the phenomenological coefficients. Onsager

reciprocity relations express that $L_{ij} = L_{ji}$. For non-linear systems, the principle of minimum entropy production does not hold. If the integral of the second-order variation of entropy production is positive, the system is stable. However, the converse does not hold. Furthermore, since we do not know about the integral of the first-order variation of entropy production, we cannot determine whether or not entropy production reaches an extremum in a stable state (Glansdorff and Prigogine 1971).

3 A. J. Lotka stated, concerning the direction of evolution, in 1922: '*natural selection* tends to make the energy [entropy] flux through the system a maximum, so far as compatible with the constraints to which the system is subject' (Lotka 1922: 148).

4 B. Commonor reached the same conclusion concerning the nested-hierarchical structure of living things without using an entropy theoretical approach: '[w]ithin every living thing on the earth, indeed within each of its individual cells, is contained another network – on its own scale, as complex as the environmental system – made up of numerous, intricate molecules, elaborately interconnected by chemical reactions, on which the life-properties of the whole organism depend' (Commonor 1971: 21).

5 There was no atmospheric compositional difference among the Earth, Mars and Venus 4,500 million years ago. With respect to what happened since then, see Gribbin (1980).

6 Embodied energy analysis, Sraffa's analysis, Georgescu-Roegen's flow–fund model and viability of solar technology

1 This definition is not precise for the case of joint production to be introduced later in this chapter.

2 Manara (1980) and Steedman (1980) adopt another definition of basic and non-basic commodities. Their definition is based on the fact that the definition adopted by Sraffa may result in the case of no solution or the case of multiple solutions. The present author follows Sraffa's definition because that definition should not be changed purely for analytical convenience. Pasinetti (1980) gives yet another definition.

3 In this representation, outflows of any kind are represented by positive coordinates and inflows by negative ones.

4 The meaning of commodities adopted by Georgescu-Roegen is slightly different from that of Sraffa. Sraffa considers the worn-out machine as a commodity with an appropriate age.

5 An exception is Morroni (1992).

6 Collectors are devices of any kind used by presently known feasible recipes for the direct use of solar energy.

7 $K_3^3 = a_3K_3^2$, $H_3^3 = a_3H_3^2$, $L_3^3 = a_3L_3^2$. $K_4^3 = (a_3 + x_{12}/x_{44})K_4^2$, $H_4^3 = (a_3 + x_{12}/x_{44})H_4^2$ and $L_4^3 = (a_3 + x_{12}/x_{44})L_4^2$. a_2 and a_3 are related to each other by the equation $x_{44}x_{34} + a_2a_3x_{33}x_{44} - a_2x_{33}x_{44} = a_3x_{34}x_{44} + x_{34}x_{12}$.

8 Vector notation $\lambda > \mu$ means $\lambda_i > \mu_i$ for every i.

9 $p_1^1 = [B_3(x_{31} + x_{32}) + (B_1 + B_2)x_{33}]/[x_{33}(x_{11} - x_{12}) - x_{13}(x_{31} + x_{32})]$ and $p_3^1 = [B_3(x_{11} - x_{12}) + (B_1 + B_2)x_{13}]/[x_{33}(x_{11} - x_{12}) - x_{13}(x_{31} + x_{32})]$.

10 $A = [(B_1 + B_2)(x_{11} - x_{13}) + B_3x_{12}]/(B_1 + B_2 + B_3)$ and $D = 1 + [(B_1 + B_2 + B_3)x_{13}]/[B_1(x_{11} - x_{12} - x_{13})$.

11 $F = x_{12}/x_{11}$, $G = 1 + Y$ and $Y = x_{12}[x_{44}(B_1 + B_2 + B_3^2 + B_4^2) + (x_{11} + x_{12})B_4^2]/[(x_{11} - x_{12})x_{44}(B_3^2 + B_4^2)]$.

12 $S = -x_{12}x_{31}/(x_{11}x_{32}) + z_6/z_7$, $z_6 = (B_1 + B_2 + B_3)(x_{11}x_{32} + x_{12}x_{31})^2x_{12}$, $z_7 = [(x_{11} - x_{12} - x_{13})B_3x_{32} + (B_1 + B_2 + B_3)(x_{12}x_{31} + x_{12}x_{32} + x_{13}x_{32})]x_{11}^2x_{32}$, $Q = 1 + z_8/z_9$, $z_8 = (B_1 + B_2 + B_3)[(x_{12}x_{31} + x_{12}x_{32} + x_{13}x_{32})x_{11}x_{31} - (x_{11}x_{32} + x_{12}x_{31})^2]$, $z_9 = (x_{11} - x_{12} - x_{13})B_3x_{11}x_{31}x_{32}$ and $1 < R < Q$.

7 Land: Achilles' Heel of ecology and economy

1 For a more comprehensive account of Marx's ecology, see an admirable book of J. B. Foster (2000).

8 Environment and North–South trade: another view

1 The Indian village is characterized by an access system, called 'nistar', different from the notion of a commons. In this system, the masses who controlled no land still had access to the residual – to road sides, to ditch banks, and to other areas too poor or too isolated for effective control and cultivation. For a case study of the 'nistar' system in this direction, see Bromley and Chapagain (1984).

Bibliography

Adams, R. (1992) 'Anthropological perspectives on ancient trade', *Current Anthropology* **33**: 141–60.

Alchian, A. (1953) 'The meaning of utility measurement', *American Economic Review* **42**: 26–50.

Allen, T. F. H. and Starr, T. B. (1982) *Hierarchy*, Chicago: The University of Chicago Press.

Altieri, M. A. and Masero, O. (1993) 'Sustainable rural development in Latin America: building from the bottom–up', *Ecological Economics* **7**: 93–121.

Andronov, A. A., Leontovich, E. A., Gordon, I. I. and Maier, A. G. (1973) *Qualitative Theory of Second-Order Dynamic Systems*, Jerusalem: Israel Program for Scientific Translations.

Armstrong, W. E. (1958) 'Utility and the "ordinalist fallacy" ', *Review of Economic Studies* **25**: 172–81.

Armytage, W. H. G. (1961) *A Social History of Engineering*, Cambridge, Mass.: MIT Press.

Arrow, K. (1997) 'Invaluable goods', *Journal of Economic Literature* **35**: 757–65.

Arrow, K. J. and Debreu, G. (1954) 'Existence of an equilibrium for a competitive economy', *Econometrica* **22**: 265–90.

Ayres, R. U. (1994) *Information, Entropy and Progress: A New Evolutionary Paradigm*, New York: American Institute of Physics Press.

Ayres, R. U. (1995) 'Economic growth: politically necessary but not environmentally friendly', *Ecological Economics* **15**: 97–9.

Bailey, K. D. (1990) *Social Entropy*, Albany: State University of New York Press.

Bar-Hillel, Y. (1955) 'An examination of information theory', *Philosophy of Science* **22**: 86–105.

Barbicr, E. and Markandya, A. (1990) 'The conditions for achieving environmentally sustainable development', *European Economic Review* **34**: 659–69.

Becker, G. S. (1996) *Accounting for the Tastes*, Cambridge: Harvard University Press.

Bettman, J. (1988) 'Processes of adaptivity in decision making', *Advances in Consumer Research* **15**: 1–4.

Boltzmann, L. (1964) *Lectures on Gas Theory*, Berkeley: University of California Press.

Boltzmann, L. (1974) 'The second law of thermodynamics', in B. McGuinness (ed.) *Theoretical Physics and Philosophical Problems*, Boston, Mass.: D. Reidel Publishing Company, 12–32.

Brillouin, L. (1950) 'Thermodynamics and information theory', *American Scientist* **38**: 594–9.

Brillouin, L. (1951*a*) 'Maxwell's demon cannot operate: information and entropy I', *Journal of Applied Physics* **22**: 334–7.

Brillouin, L. (1951*b*) 'Physical entropy and information theory II', *Journal of Applied Physics* **22**: 338–43.

Brillouin, L. (1953) 'The negentropy principle of information', *Journal of Applied Physics* **24**: 1152–63.

Brillouin, L. (1962) *Science and Information Theory*, 2nd edn. New York: Academic Press.

Bromley, D. W. (1989) 'Entitlements, missing markets, and environmental uncertainty', *Journal of Environmental Economics and Management* **17**: 181–94.

Bromley, D. W. and Chapagain, D. P. (1984) 'The village against the center: resource depletion in South Asia', *American Journal of Agricultural Economics* **66**: 868–73.

Brown, M. T. and Herendeen, R. A. (1996) 'Embodied energy analysis and EMERGY analysis: a comparative view', *Ecological Economics* **19**: 219–35.

Campbell, C. J. (1997) 'Depletion patterns show change due for production of conventional oil', *Oil and Gas Journal* December **29**: 33–9.

Carter, V. G. and Dale, T. (1974) *Topsoil and Civilization*, Norman, OK: University of Oklahoma Press.

Čebotarev, N. G. and Meĭman, N. N. (1949) *The Routh–Hurwitz Problem for Polynomials and Entire Functions* (in Russian), Moscow: Trudy Mat. Inst. Steklov.

Cherfas, J. (1991) 'Skeptics and visionaries examine energy saving', *Science* **251**: 154–6.

Chichilnisky, G. (1986) 'A general equilibrium theory of North–South trade', in W. P. Heller, R. M. Starr and D. A. Starrett (eds) *Equilibrium Analysis: Essays in Honor of Kenneth J. Arrow*, vol. 2, Cambridge University Press: 3–56.

Christensen, Paul P. (1987) 'Classical roots for a modern materials-energy analysis', *Ecological Modelling* **38**: 75–89.

Clausius, R. (1867) 'On the application of the theorem of the equivalence of transformations to interior work', in T. A. Hirst (ed.) *The Mechanical Theory of Heat with its Applications to the Steam-Engine and to the Physical Properties of Bodies*, London: John van Voorst, 215–50.

Colby, M. E. (1991) 'Environmental management in development: the evolution of paradigms', *Ecological Economics* **3**: 193–213.

Commoner, B. (1971) *The Closing Circle*, New York: Alfred A. Knopf.

Conrad, M. (1983) *Adaptability: The Significance of Variability from Molecule to Ecosystem*, New York: Plenum.

Costanza, R. (1980) 'Embodied energy and economic valuation', *Science* **210**: 1219–24.

Costanza, R., d'Arge, R., de Groot, R., Farber, S., Grasso, M., Hannon, B., Limburge, K., Naeem, S., O'Neill, R. V., Paruelo, J., Raskin, R. G., Sutton, P. and van den Belt, M. (1997) 'The value of the world's ecosystem services and natural capital', *Nature* **387**: 253–60.

Costanza, R. and Hannon, B. (1989) 'Dealing with the "mixed units" problem in ecosystem network analysis', in F. Wulft, J. G. Field and K.H. Mann (eds) *Network Analysis in Marine Biology: Methods and Applications*, Berlin: Springer-Verlag, 90–115.

Daly, H. (1992*a*) 'U.N. conferences on environment and development: retrospect on Stockholm and prospects for Rio', *Ecological Economics* **5**: 9–14.

Daly, H. (1992*b*) 'Allocation, distribution, and scale: toward an economics that is efficient, just, and sustainable', *Ecological Economics* **6**: 185–93.

Daly, H. (1993) 'The perils of free trade', *Scientific American* **269**: 24–9.

Daly, H. (1995) 'Consumption and welfare: two views of value added', *Review of Social Economy* LIII: 451–73.
Diamond, P. and Hausman, J. (1994) 'Contingent valuation: is some number better than no number?', *Journal of Economic Perspectives* **8**: 45–64.
Ehrlich, P. R., Ehrlich, A. H. and Daily, G. C. (1993) 'Food security, population, and environment', *Population and Development Review* 19, **1**: 1–32.
El-Hodiri, M. A., Loehman, E. and Whinston, A. (1972) 'An optimal growth model with time lags', *Econometrica* **40**: 1137–46.
England, R. W. (1986) 'Production, distribution, and environmental quality: Mr. Sraffa reinterpreted as an ecologist', *KYKLOS* **39**: 230–44.
Farber, S. (1995) 'Economic resilience and economic policy', *Ecological Economics* **15**: 105–7.
Fermi, E. (1956) *Thermodynamics*, New York: Dover.
Foster, J. B. (2000) *Marx's Ecology*, New York: Monthly Review Press.
Friedman, M. (1953) *Essays in Positive Economics*, Chicago: University of Chicago Press.
Frisch, R. (1926) 'Sur un problème d'économie pure', *Norsk Matematisk Forenings Skrifter* 1, **16**: 1–40.
Frisch, R. and Holmes, H. (1935) 'The characteristic solutions of a mixed difference and differential equation occurring in economic dynamics', *Econometrica* **3**: 225–39.
Funtowicz, S. O. and Ravets, J. R. (1990) 'Post normal science: a new sceice for new times', *Scientific European* **266**: 20–2.
Funtowicz, S. O. and Ravets, J. R. (1993) 'Science for the post-normal age', *Futures* **25**: 735–55.
Funtowicz, S. O., Ravets, J. R. and O'Connor, M. (1998) 'Challenges in the use of science for sustainable development', *International Journal of Sustainable Development* 1, **1**: 99–107.
Gale, D. (1960) *The Theory of Linear Economic Models*, Chicago: The University of Chicago Press.
Georgescu-Roegen, N. (1936) 'The pure theory of consumer's behavior', *Quarterly Journal of Economics* **50**: 545–93.
Georgescu-Roegen, N. (1954*a*) 'Choice and revealed preference', *Southern Economic Journal* **21**: 119–30.
Georgescu-Roegen, N. (1954*b*) 'Choice, expectations, and measurability', *Quarterly Journal of Economics* **68**: 503–34.
Georgescu-Roegen, N. (1958) 'Threshold in choice and the theory of demand', *Econometrica* **26**: 157 68.
Georgescu-Roegen, N. (1960) 'Economic theory and agrarian economics', *Oxford Economic Papers*, N.S., **XII**: 1–40.
Georgescu-Roegen, N. (1964) 'Measure, quality, and optimal scale', in C. R. Rao (ed.) *Essays on Econometrics and Planning Presented to Professor P. C. Mahalanobis*, Oxford: Pergamon, 231–56.
Georgescu-Roegen, N. (1966) *Analytical Economics: Issues and Problems*, Cambridge, Mass.: Harvard University Press.
Georgescu-Roegen, N. (1968) 'Revisiting Marshall's constancy of marginal utility of money', *Southern Economic Journal* **35**: 176–81.
Georgescu-Roegen, N. (1971) *The Entropy Law and the Economic Process*, Cambridge, Mass.: Harvard University Press.

Georgescu-Roegen, N. (1974) 'Dynamic models and economic growth', in *Energy and Economic Myths: Institutional and Analytical Economic Essays*, New York: Pergamon Press, 235–53.

Georgescu-Roegen, N. (1975) 'Energy and economic myths', *Southern Economic Journal* **XLI**: 347–81.

Georgescu-Roegen, N. (1976) *Energy and Economic Myths: Institutional and Analytical Economic Essays*, New York: Pergamon Press.

Georgescu-Roegen, N. (1977*a*) 'The measure of information: a critique', in J. Ross and C. Bilciu (eds) *Modern Trends in Cybernetics and Systems*, New York: Springer-Verlag, 187–217.

Georgescu-Roegen, N. (1977*b*) 'Matter matters, too', in K. D. Wilson (ed.) *Prospects for Growth: Expectations for the Future*, New York: Praeger, 293–313.

Georgescu-Roegen, N. (1977*c*) 'Inequality, limits and growth from a bioeconomic viewpoint', *Review of Social Economy* **XXXV**: 361–75.

Georgescu-Roegen, N. (1978) 'Technology assessment: the case of the direct use of solar energy', *Atlantic Economic Journal* **VI**: 15–21.

Georgescu-Roegen, N. (1979) 'Energy analysis and economic valuation', *Southern Economic Journal* **XLIV**: 1023–58.

Georgescu-Roegen, N. (1981) 'Energy, matter, and economic valuation: where do we stand?', in H. E. Daly and A. F. Umanã (eds) *Energy, Economics, and the Environment*, Colorado: Westview Press, 43–79.

Georgescu-Roegen, N. (1982) 'The energetic theory of economic value: a topical economic fallacy', *Working Paper* No. 82-W16, Vanderbilt University, Nashville, TN.

Georgescu-Roegen, N. (1984) 'Feasible recipes versus viable technologies', *Atlantic Economic Journal* **12**: 21–31.

Georgescu-Roegen, N. (1986) 'Man and production', in M. Baranzini and R. Scazzieri (eds) *Foundations of Economics*, Oxford: Basil Blackwell, 248–80.

Georgescu-Roegen, N. (1990) 'Thermodynamics, economics and information', in M. Alonso (ed.) *Organization and Change in Complex Systems*, New York: Paragon House, 225–34.

Georgescu-Roegen, N. (1992) 'Nicholas Georgescu-Roegen about himself', in M. Szenberg (ed.) *Eminent Economists*, New York: Cambridge University Press, 128–59.

Giampietro, M. (1994*a*) 'Sustainability and technological development in agriculture: a critical appraisal of genetic engineering', *BioScience* 44, **10**: 677–89.

Giampietro, M. (1994*b*) 'Using hierarchy theory to explore the concept of sustainable development', *Futures* 26, **6**: 616–25.

Giampietro, M. (1997) 'Linking technology, natural resources, and the socioeconomic structure of human society: A theoretical model', in L. Freese (ed.) *Advances in Human Ecology* 6, Greenwich, CT: JAI Press, 75–130.

Giampietro, M. and Bukkens, S. G. F. (1992) 'Sustainable development: scientific and ethical assessments', *Journal of Agriculture and Environmental Ethics* 5, **1**: 27–57.

Giampietro, M., Bukkens, S. G. F. and Pimentel, D. (1997) 'Linking technology, natural resources, and the socioeconomic structure of human society: examples and applications', in L. Freese (ed.) *Advances in Human Ecology* 6, Greenwich, CT: JAI Press, 131–200.

Gimapietro, M. and Mayumi, K. (1996) 'Carrying capacity and optimum population: theoretical analysis and simulations', in Fourth Biennial Meeting of the International Society for Ecological Economics, August 4–7, 1996, Boston University, Boston, MA.

Gimapietro, M. and Mayumi, K. (1998) 'Another view of development, ecological degradation, and North–South trade', *Review of Social Economy* LVI, **1**: 20–36.

Giampietro, M. and Mayumi, K. (eds) (2000) *Population and Environment*, Special Issue 22(2).

Giampietro, M. and Mayumi, K. (eds) (2001) *Population and Environment*, Special Issue 22(3).

Glansdorff, P. and Prigogine, I. (1971) *Thermodynamics Theory of Structure, Stability and Fluctuations*, New York: John Wiley & Sons.

Goldschmidt, R. (1930) 'Some aspects of evolution', *Science* **78**: 539–47.

Goldsmith, E. (1985) 'Is development the solution or the problem?', *The Ecologist* **15**: 210–19.

Gould, S. J. and Eldredge, N. (1979) 'Punctuated equilibria: the tempo and mode of evolution reconsidered', *Paleobiology* **3**: 115–51.

Gowdy, J. M. (1995) 'Trade and environmental sustainability: an evolutionary perspective', *Review of Social Economy* **LIII**: 493–510.

Gowdy, J. M. (1997) 'The value of biodiversity: markets, society, and ecosystems', *Land Economics* 73, **1**: 25–41.

Gribbin, J. (1980) *The Death of the Sun*, New York: Delacorte Press.

Haar, D. ter, (1954) *Elements of Statistical Mechanics*, New York: Rinehart.

Hanemann, M. (1994) 'Valuing the environment through contingent valuation', *Journal of Economic Perspectives* **8**: 19–43.

Hanna, S. (1997) 'The new frontier of American fisheries gvernance', *Ecological Economics* **20**: 221–33.

Hannon, B., Costanza, R. and Herendeen, R. (1986) 'Measures of energy cost and value in ecosystems', *Journal of Environmental Economics and Management* **13**: 391–401.

Hartley, R. V. L. (1928) 'Transmission of information', *Bell System Technical Journal* **7**: 535–63.

Hausman, J. A. (ed.) (1993) *Contingent Valuation: A Critical Assessment*, Amsterdam: North-Holland.

Hawkins, D. and Simon, H. (1949) 'Note: some conditions of macroeconomic stability', *Econometrica* **17**: 245–8.

Hicks, J. R. and Allen, R. G. D. (1934) 'A reconsideration of the theory of value', *Economica*, N.S., I: 52–76 and 196–219.

Homer-Dixon, T. A., Boutwell, J. H. and Rathjens, G. W. (1993) 'Environmental change and violent conflict', *Scientific American* **268**: 38–45.

Hopf, F. A. (1988) 'Entropy and evolution: sorting through confusion', in D. J. Weber and D. Smith (eds) *Entropy, Information and Evolution*, Cambridge, MA: The MIT Press, 263–74.

Huettner, David A. (1976) 'Net energy analysis: an economic assessment', *Science* **192**: 101–4.

Hughes, J. D. (1975) *Ecology in Ancient Civilizations*, Albuquerque: University of New Mexico Press.

Huntington, E. V. (1917) *The Continuum and Other Types of Serial Order*, Cambridge, MA: Harvard University Press.

Ising, G. (1926) 'A natural limit for the sensibility of galvanometers', *Philosophical Magazine* 1, **4**: 827–34.

Jaynes, E. T. (1957) 'Information theory and statistical mechanics', *Physical Review* **106**: 620–30.

Jehle, G. (1991) *Advanced Microeconomic Theory*, Englewood Cliffs, NJ: Prentice-Hall.

Jevons, F. (1990) 'Greenhouse – a paradox', *Search* **21**: 171–2.

Jevons, W. S. [1865] (1965) *The Coal Question: An Inquiry Concerning the Progress of the Nation, and the Probable Exhaustion of Our Coal-Mines*, 3rd ed. rev. by A. W. Flux, New York: Augustus M. Kelly.

Johnston, J. F. W. (1847) *Lectures on Agricultural Chemistry and Geology*, London: William Blackwood and Sons.

Johnston, J. F. W. (1851) *Notes on North America: Agricultural, Economical, and Social*, London: William Blackwood and Sons.

Judson, D. H. (1989) 'The convergence of neo-Ricardian and embodied energy theories of value and price', *Ecological Economics* **1**: 261–81.

Kaldor, N. (1980) 'The foundations of free trade theory and their implications for the current world recession', in E. Malinvaud and J. P. Fitoussi (eds) *Unemployment in Western Countries*, London: MacMillan Press, 85–100.

Kalecki, M. (1935) 'A macrodynamic theory of business cycles', *Econometrica* **3**: 327–44.

Kaplan, R. D. (1994) 'The coming anarchy', *Atlantic Monthly*, February: 44–76.

Kauffman, S. A. (1993) *The Origins of Order: Self-Organization and Selection in Evolution*, New York: Oxford University Press.

Kawamiya, N. (1983) *Entropii to Kougyoushakai no Sentaku* (in Japanese) (*Entropy and Future Choices for the Industrial Society*), Tokyo: Kaimei.

Kendall, H. and Pimentel, D. (1994) 'Constraints to the world food supply', *AMBIO* **23**: 198–205.

Khazzoom, J. D. (1987) 'Energy saving resulting from the adoption of more efficient appliances', *Energy Journal* 8, **4**: 85–9.

Khinchin, A. I. (1957) *Mathematical Foundations of Information Theory*, New York: Dover Publications.

Kleene, S. C. (1952) *Introduction to Metamathematics*, London: D. Van Nostrand.

Klein, M. J. (1969) 'Gibbs on Clausius', *Historical Studies in the Physical Sciences* **1**: 127–49.

Koestler, A. (1967) *The Ghost in the Machine*, New York: The MacMillan Co.

Koestler, A. (1969) 'Beyond atomism and holism – the concept of the holon', in A. Koestler and J. R. Smythies (eds) *Beyond reductionism*, London: Hutchinson, 192–232.

Koide, S. and Abiko, S. (1985) *Entoropii towa Nandarouka* (in Japanese) (*What is Entropy?*), Tokyo: Iwanami.

Kuhn, T. S. (1962) *The Structure of Scientific Revolutions*, Chicago: The University of Chicago Press.

Kurihara, Y. (1975) *Yugen no Seitaigaku* (in Japanese) (*Ecology in Bounded Systems*), Tokyo: Iwanami.

Landau, L. D. and Lifshitz, E. M. (1980) *Statistical Physics* 1, Oxford: Pergamon Press.

Leontief, W. (1961*a*) 'Lags and the stability of dynamic systems', *Econometrica* **29**: 659–69.

Leontief, W. (1961*b*) 'Lags and the stability of dynamic systems: a rejoinder', *Econometrica* **29**: 674–75.

Lewis, G. N. (1930) 'The symmetry of time in physics', *Science* **LXXI**: 569–77.

Liebig, J. von (1859) *Letters on Modern Agriculture*, New York: Wiley.

Liebig, J. von (1972) *Natural Laws of Husbandry*, New York: Arno Press.

Lotka, A. J. (1922) 'Contribution to the energetics of evolution', *Proceedings of the National Academy of Sciences* **8**: 37–48.

Lotka, A. J. (1956) *Elements of Mathematical Biology*, New York: Dover Publications.

Manara, Carlo F. (1980) 'Sraffa's model for the joint production of commodities by means of commodities', in L. Pasinetti (ed.) *Essays on the Theory of Joint Production*, London: Macmillan, 1–15.

Margalef, R. (1968) *Perspectives in Ecological Theory*, Chicago: The University of Chicago Press.

Markandya, A. and Pearce, D. (1988) 'Environmental considerations and the choice of the discount rate in developing countries', *Environment Department Working Paper* 3. Washington, D.C.: World Bank.

Martin, L. and Tesser, A. (eds) (1992) *The Construction of Social Judgements*. New Jersey: Lawrence Erlbaum Associates.

Martinez-Alier, J. (1991) 'Ecological perception, environmental policy and distributional conflicts: some lessons from history', in R. Costanza (ed.) *Ecological Economics: The Science and Management of Sustainability*, New York: Columbia University Press, 118–36.

Martinez-Alier, J. (1996) 'Merchandising biodiversity', *Capitalism, Nature, Socialism* **7**: 37–54.

Martinez-Alier, J., Munda, G. and O'Neill, J. (1998) 'Weak comparability of values as a foundation for ecological economics', *Ecological Economics* **26**: 277–86.

Marx, K. (1936) *Capital: A Critique of Political Economy, the Process of Capitalist Production*, New York: The Modern Library.

Marx, K. (1957) *Capital*, Vol. II, Moscow: Foreign Languages House.

Marx, K. (1959) *Capital*, Vol. III, Moscow: Foreign Languages House.

Marx, K. (1979) *The Letters of Karl Marx*, S. K. Padover (ed.) Englewood Cliffs, NJ: Prentice-Hall.

Marx, K. and Engels, F. (1982) *Collected Works*, vol. 38, New York: International Publishers.

Mas-Colell, A., Whinston, M. and Green, J. (1995) *Microeconomic Theory*. New York: Oxford University Press.

Mayumi, K. (1990) 'The law of diminishing returns radically reconstructed: its physico-chemical foundation and implication for the resources and environmental constraints in the future economy', in the First Biennial Meeting of the International Society for Ecological Economics, May 21–23, 1990, Washington, D.C: World Bank.

Mayumi, K. (1991) 'Temporary emancipation from land: from the industrial revolution to the present time', *Ecological Economics* **4**: 35–56.

Mayumi, K. (1993*a*) 'The exosomatic mode of human evolution, and a clarification of Nicholas Georgescu-Roegen's thoughts on entropy, the economic process, dialectics and evolution,' *Methodus: Bulletin of the International Network for Economic Method* 5, **1**: 88 92.

Mayumi, K. (1993*b*) 'Georgescu-Roegen's "fourth law of thermodynamics", the modern energetic dogma, and ecological salvation', in L. Bonati, U. Cosentino, M. Lasagni, G. Moro, D. Pitea and A. Schiraldi (eds) *Trends in Ecological Physical Chemistry*, Amsterdam: Elsevier, 351–64.

Mayumi, K. (1994) 'Farming versus manufacturing', *Capitalism, Nature, Socialism* 5, **1**: 115–20.

Mayumi, K. (1995) 'Nicholas Georgescu-Roegen (1906–1994): an admirable epistemologist', *Structural Change and Economic Dynamics* 6, **3**: 261–5.

Mayumi, K., Giampietro, M. and Gowdy, J. M. (1998) 'Georgescu-Roegen/Daly versus Solow/Stiglitz revisited', *Ecological Economics* **27**: 115–17.

Mayumi, K. and Gowdy, J. M. (eds) (1999) *Bioeconomics and Sustainability: Essays in Honor of Nicholas Georgescu-Roegen*, Cheltenham: Edward Elgar.

McMillan, B. (1953) 'The basic theorems of information theory', *Annals of Mathematical Statistics* **24**: 196–219.

Meadows, D. H., Meadows, D. L., Jøgen, R. and Behrens III, W. W. (1972) *The Limits to Growth*, New York: Universe Books.

Mierynyk, W. H. (1999) 'Economic growth theory and the Georgescu-Roegen paradigm', in K. Mayumi and J. Gowdy (eds) *Bioeconomics and Sustainability: Essays in Honor of Nicholas Georgescu-Roegen*, Cheltenham: Edward Elgar, 69–81.

Morroni, Mario (1992) *Production Process and Technical Change*, New York, US: Cambridge University Press.

Newman, P. (1991) 'Greenhouse, oil and cities', *Futures* May: 335–48.

Nicolis, G. and Prigogine, I. (1977) *Self-Organization in Nonequilibrium Systems*, New York: John Wiley & Sons.

Norgaard, R. B. (1981) 'Sociosystem and ecosystem coevolution in the Amazon', *Journal of Environmental Economics and Management* **8**: 238–54.

Norgaard, R. B. (1995) 'Beyond materialism: a coevolutionary reinterpretation of the environmental crisis', *Review of Social Economy* **LIII**: 475–92.

Nyquist, H. (1924) 'Certain factors affecting telegraph speed', *Bell System Technical Journal* **3**: 324–46.

Odum, E. P. (1971) *Fundamentals of Ecology*, Philadelphia: Saunders.

Odum, H. T. (1996) *Environmental Accounting: EMERGY and Environmental Decision Making*, New York: John Wiley & Sons.

Olshavsky, R. and Granbois, D. (1979) 'Consumer decision making – fact or fiction?', *Journal of Consumer Research* **6**: 93–100.

O' Neill, R. V. (1989) 'Perspectives in hierarchy and scale', in J. Roughgarden, R. M. May and S. Levin (eds) *Perspectives in Ecological Theory*, Princeton: Princeton University Press, 140–56.

O'Neill, R. V., DeAngelis, D. L., Waide, J. B. and Allen, T. F. H. (1986) *A Hierarchical Concept of Ecosystems*, Princeton, NJ: Princeton University Press.

Ostrom, E. (1990) *Governing the Commons: Institutions for Collective Action*, New York: Cambridge University Press.

Ozaki, M. (1983) 'Netsurikigaku dainihousoku kara sofuto enerugii pasu e (from the second law of thermodynamics to the soft energy path)' (in Japanese) *Gijutsu to Nigen (Technology and Man)* **12**: 15–22.

Parsons, H. L. (1977) *Marx and Engels on Ecology*, London: Greenwood Press.

Pasinetti, Luigi (1980) 'A note on basics, non-basics and joint productin', in L. Pasinetti (ed.) *Essays on the Theory of Joint Production*, London: Macmillan, 51–4.

Pastore, G., Giampietro, M. and Mayumi, K. (1996) 'Bioeconomic pressure as indicator of material standard of living', in Fourth Biennial Meeting of the International Society for Ecological Economics, August 4–7, 1996, Boston University, Boston, MA.

Patterson, Murray (1996) 'Commensuration and theories of value in ecological economics', a paper presented at the Ecological Summit '96, Copenhagen, Denmark, 19–23 August, 1996.

Peet, J. (1998) '. . . But what *is* the question . . . ?', in S. Ulgiati (chief ed.) *Advances in Energy Studies*, Rome: Museum of Science and Scientific Information, 129–42.

Pimentel, D., Harvey, C., Resosudarmo, P., Sinclair, K., Kurz, D., McNair, M., Crist, S., Shpritz, L., Fitton, L., Saffouri, R. and Blair, R. (1995) 'Environmental and economic costs of soil erosion and conservation benefits', *Science* **267**: 1117–23.

Pimentel, D., Hurd, L. E., Belloti, A. C., Foster, M. J., Oka, I. N. and Sholes, O. D. (1973) 'Food production and the energy crisis', *Science* **182**: 443–9.

Pimm, S. L. (1997) 'The value of everything', *Nature* **387**: 231–2.

Planck, M. (1945) *Treatise on Thermodynamics*, 7th edn. New York: Dover.

Planck, M. (1959) *The Theory of Heat Radiation*, New York: Dover Publications.

Plato (1977) *Timaeus and Critias*, New York: Penguin Books.

Ponting, C. (1991) *A Green History of the World*, New York: Penguin Books.

Pontryagin, L. S. [1942] (1955) 'On the zeros of some elementary transcendental functions', *American Mathematical Society Translations, Series 2*, **1**: 95–110.

Prigogine, I. (1978) *From Being to Becoming*, San Francisco: W.H. Freeman and company.

Radin, M. J. (1996) *Contested Commodities*, Cambridge, MA: Harvard University Press.

Randall, A. (1988) 'What mainstream economists have to say about the value of biodiversity', in E. O. Wilson (ed.) *Biodiversity*, Washington, D.C.: National Academy Press, 217–23.

Rockafellar, R. T. (1970) *Convex Analysis*, Princeton, NJ: Princeton University Press.

Rényi, A. (1970) *Probability Theory*, Amsterdam: North-Holland.

Røpke, I. (1994) 'Trade, development and sustainability – a critical assessment of the free trade dogma', *Ecological Economics* **9**: 13–22.

Rosen, R. (1977) 'Complexity as a system property', *International Journal of General Systems* **3**: 227–32.

Rosen, R. (1985) *Anticipatory Systems: Philosophical, Mathematical and Methodological Foundations*, New York: Pergamon Press.

Rosen, R. (1991) *Life Itself: A Comprehensive Inquiry into the Nature, Origin and Fabrication of Life*, New York: Columbia University Press.

Sahlins, M. (1996) 'The sadness of sweetness', *Current Anthropology* **37**: 395–428.

Sahlins, M. [1972] (1998) 'The original affluent society', in J. M. Gowdy (ed.) *Limited Wants, Unlimited Means: A Hunter-Gatherer Reader on Economics and the Environment*, Washington, D.C.: Island Press, 5–41.

Salthe, S. N. (1985) *Evolving Hierarchical Systems*, New York: Columbia University Press.

Samuelson, P. (1952) 'Probability, utility and the independence axiom', *Econometrica* **20**: 670–8.

Sargan, J. D. (1958) 'The instability of the Leontief dynamic model', *Econometrica* **26**: 381–92.

Sargan, J. D. (1961) 'Lags and the stability of dynamic systems: a reply', *Econometrica* **29**: 670–3.

Schneider, E. D. and Kay, J. J. 'Life as a manifestation of the second law of thermodynamics', *Mathematical and Computer Modelling* **19**: 25–48.

Schrödinger, E. (1957) *Statistical Thermodynamics*, Cambridge: The University Press.

Schrödinger, E. (1967) *What is Life & Mind and Matter*, London: Cambridge University Press.

Schumpeter, J. A. (1954) *History of Economic Analysis*, London: George Allen & Unwin Ltd.

Shackle, G. L. S. (1955) *Uncertainty in Economics and Other Reflections*, Cambridge: The University Press.

Shannon, C. E. (1951) 'Prediction and entropy of printed English', *The Bell System Technical Journal* **XXX**: 50–64.

Shannon, C. E. (1956) 'The bandwagon', *IRE Transactions-Information Theory* IT-2: 3.

Shannon, C. E. and Weaver, W. (1964) *The Mathematical Theory of Communication*, Urbana: University of Illinois Press.

Shingu, H. (1998) *Pursuit of Happiness: Beate Certe Omnes Vivere Volumus* (in Japanese) (Koufuku to iukoto), Tokyo: NHK Books.
Simon, H. A. (1962) 'The architecture of complexity', *Proceedings of the American Philosophical Society* **106**: 467–82.
Slesser, M. (1980) 'Can solar energy replace fossil-fissile energy sources?', *Solar Energy* **25**: 425–8.
Smith, A. (1937) *The Wealth of Nations*, E. Cannon (ed.) New York: The Modern Library.
Spash, C. and Hanley, N. (1995) 'Preferences, information and biodiversity preservation', *Ecological Economics* 12, **3**: 191–208.
Sraffa, Piero (1960) *Productions of Commodities by Means of Commodities*, Cambridge, London, UK: Cambridge University Press.
Steedman, Ian (1980) 'Basics, non-basics and joint production', in L. Pasinetti (ed.) *Essays on the Theory of Joint Production*, London: Macmillan, 44–50.
Stevens, T., Echeverria, J., Glass, R., Hager, T. and More, T. (1991) 'Measuring the existence value of wildlife: what do CVM estimates really show?', *Land Economics* **67**: 390–400.
Stigler, G. and Becker, G. S. (1977) 'De gustibus non est disputandum', *American Economic Review* **67**: 76–90.
Szilard, L. (1929) 'Über die Entropieverminderung in einem thermodynamischen System bei Eingriffen intelligenter Wesen', *Zeitschrift für Physik* **LIII**: 840–56.
Szilard, L. (1964) 'On the decrease of entropy in a thermodynamic system by the intervention of intelligent beings', *Behavioral Science* **9**: 301–10.
Tainter, J. A. (1988) *The Collapse of Complex Societies*, New York: Cambridge University Press.
Takamatsu, T. (1983) 'Kakudaikaishaku ni hisomu kikensei (Potential danger of stretching the meaning of thermodynamic entropy)' *Gijutsu to Nigen* (in Japanese) (*Technology and Man*) **12**: 23–30.
Tillman, F. A. and Russell, B. R. (1965) 'Language, information, and entropy', *Logique et Analyse* **8**: 126–40.
Toman, M. (1998) 'Why not to calculate the value of the world's ecosystems and natural capital', *Ecological Economics* **25**: 57–60.
Tribus, M. and McIrvine, E. C. (1971) 'Energy and information', *Scientific American* **225**: 179–88.
Tsuchida, A. (1982) *Shigen Butsurigaku Nyumon* (in Japanese) (*An Introduction to Physics of Natural Resources*), Tokyo: NHK Books.
Tsuchida, A. (1985) 'Seime o fukumu kei no netsurikigaku' (in Japanese) (Thermodynamics for living systems), in S. Ono (ed.) *Entoropii* (*Entropy*), Tokyo: Asakura, 38–58.
Tsuchida, A. (1992) *Netsugaku Gairon* (in Japanese) (*Thermodynamic Theory for Open Systems*), Tokyo: Asakura.
Tsuchida, A. and Murota, T. (1985) 'Fundamentals in the entropy theory of watercycle, ecocycle, and human economy', in The Conference on Man's Coevolution with the Biosphere in the Age of Advanced Technology, York University, Toronto, Canda, January 21–25, 1985.
Ulanowicz, R. E. (1986) *Growth and Development: Ecosystem Phenomenology*, New York: Springer-Verlag.
U. S. Department of Commerce (1987) *Statistical Abstract of the United States*, 107th edn.
Vatn, A. and Bromley, D. W. (1994) 'Choices without prices without apologies', *Journal of Environmental Economics and Management* 26, **2**: 129–48.
Watkins, K. (1992) *Fixing the Rules: North–South Issues in International Trade and the GATT Uruguay Round*, London: Catholic Institute for International Relations.

Weiskel, T. C. (1989) 'The ecological lessons from the past: an anthropology of environmental decline', *The Ecologist* **19**: 98–103.
White, L. Jr. (1967) 'The historical roots of our ecological crisis', *Science* **155**: 1203–7.
Whyte, L. L., Wilson, A. G. and Wilson, D. (eds) (1969) *Hierarchical Structures*, New York: American Elsevier Publishing Company, Inc..
Wiener, N. (1961) *Cybernetics*, Cambridge, Mass: M.I.T. Press.
Wilder, R. L. (1952) *Introduction to the Foundations of Mathematics*, New York: John Wiley & Sons.
Wilkinson, R. G. (1973) *Poverty and Progress: An Ecological Perspective on Economic Development*, New York: Praeger.
Wilson, E. O. (1998) *Consilience*, New York: Alfred A. Knopf.
Wrigley, E. A. (1962) 'The suppy of raw materials in the industrial revolution', *The Economic History Review, Second Series* 2, **15**: 1–16.
Yamamoto, Y. (1987) *Netsugaku Shisou no Shiteki Tenkai* (in Japanese) (*Historical Development of Thermodynamic Thought*), Kyoto: Gendai Sugakusha.
Zipf, G. K. (1941) *National Unity and Disunity: The Nation as a Bio-social Organism*, Bloomington, IN: Principia Press.

Index

Adams, R. McC. 102
adaptability 100, 116, 121
Africa 104
agribusiness 89
agricultural economists 81
agriculture 5, 53, 81–4, 92
agriculturists 81
air 64; convection 50, 52, 59
algorithms 110
Allen, R. G. D. 11
'ambience' 109
American Indians 87
American Revolution 87
ammeters 43
anticipatory behaviour 28–30
anticipatory systems 28, 31, 112
Archimedean Axiom 37
Aristotle 112
Arrow, K. J. 11, 14, 18
autocatalytic loop 122–3
automobiles 100
autotrophs 121
axioms 110
Ayres, R. U. 103

balanced sustained growth 23
Bangladesh 102
Barbier, E. 107
basic commodities 69
Basic Equations 69
Becker, G. S. 20, 142
Bendixson's test 127–8
bio-geochemical cycles 101
biocycles 50
Bioeconomic Pressure 118, 124
bioeconomics 1
biological evolution 1, 98
biological organs 59
Black Death 84
blast furnaces 86
Boltzmann's function 38
Boltzmann, Ludwig 32, 47
Boltzmann–Planck constant 39, 42
bound information 42
Brillouin, L. 3, 42–4
Bromley, D. W. 14, 20
Brundtland Report 103
Building and Maintenance 117, 123
Bukkens, S. G. F. 107

capacity 34
capital equipment 73
carbon dioxide 9, 52, 114
carnivores 121
Carnot engine 54, 80
Carter, V. G. 80, 87
Čebotarev, N. G. 140
charcoal 85
charcoal pig iron 85
Chichilnisky, G. 102
chloro-fluoro-carbon 45
choice of codes 33
Christianity 106
Circulating Investment 117, 120
civilization 95, 101
classical perpetual motions 53
classical thermodynamics 40
Clausius, R. 57–60
closed curves 127
closed system 4, 46, 54, 59, 142
co-evolution 99
coal 4, 78, 85, 87, 92
cognition 12
coke 85; furnaces 86; pig iron 85
coldness 52
collectors 74, 143

commodities 10, 21, 66–7
Commoner, B. 89–90, 143
commonsense approach 19
communication channel 3, 34
communication engineering 33
complementarity 3, 9–11
complete decoding 111
'complexions' 42
complexity 106
compression 54–5
concrete 80
consilience 2
consumer(s) 8, 17, 121
consumer choice: axioms of 2, 8–14; theory 2, 12
consumption 121
contingent valuation method (CVM) 7, 12–14
continuous distributions 37
convexity 9
corn 90
Cort, H. 86
cost 70
cost–benefit analysis 6
Costanza, R. 14, 65
cotton 86
countries: developed 97, 103; developing 97, 103–4
Critias 95
critical environmental loading 119
crop rotation 84
'culture' 89
cyclic process 57

Dale, T. 80, 87
Daly, H. 119
Darby, A. 85
Dark Ages 84
Debreu, G. 14
decomposers 121
deforestation 14, 97, 107
degradation 56–7, 79, 120
delays 21, 24–8, 139
'demon' 43
desertification 97
detritus 53, 121
deviation 43
dialectics 111
Diamond, P. 12
diffusion 54
dimension 43, 67–8, 101
discount rate dilemma 105
discrete distributions 37
disgregation 57–60
dissipated energy 70
dissipated matter 70; *see also* disgregation
distributional equity 104
DNA 120
Doctrine of Minimum 91
droughts 97
dung 14, 107
Dupuit–Marshall principle 13
dynamic equilibrium 94, 106
dynamic models 30
dynamic systems 21, 119

ecological crisis 102–6
ecological economics 1
ecological succession 94
economic behaviour 2
economic man 18–20
economic process 69
economic valuation 8, 13
economists 112
efficiency 80, 99, 116, 121
efficient cause 112
EFT1 80, 98
EFT2 80–3, 98
'EFT2 fetishism' 106
elementary process 93
embedding 12
embodied energy analysis 4, 65–72
emergent properties 115
endosomatic energy 116
energetic dogma 60
energy 4, 42, 56, 90, 118; diffusion 54, 81; throughput 118
Energy and Mining 117, 123
England 84–7
entropy 3, 39, 45–64, 79; disposal 4, 47–8, 50–2
environment 109, 123
environmental degradation 5, 79, 89, 98–102
environmental loading 119, 124
environmental problems 45–64
Environmental Security 117, 123
environmental services 8
environmental valuation 8–18
epistemology 44
European settlers 87
evolution 30, 98, 143
evolutionary biology *see* biological evolution
evolutionary change 30
exosomatic devices 116, 123
exosomatic energy 116–17, 120, 123

exosomatic evolution 30, 98
exosomatic organs 1, 59
expansion 54
exports 88
extended utility function 142
extensive variables 101, 119
external references 109, 111

farming 91–5
fauna 95
fertilizer 14, 53, 95, 107
feudalism 85
final cause 112
fire 92
fissile fuels 4, 78
Fixed Investment 117, 120, 123
floods 97
flora 94
flow rate 22
flow–fund model 4, 60–3, 65–78, 93
flows 4, 69
focal level 115
Food Security 117, 123
forests 84, 87
formal cause 112
formal system 110
formalization 110
fossil fuels 4, 54, 62, 78, 80
Foster, J. B. 144
France 85
free energy 32, 120
free trade 102
Friedman, M. 20
fuel 14, 107
fuelwood 14, 107
functional transparency 15
Fundamental Proposition 63
funds 4, 22, 65, 69
Funtowicz, S. O. 108

General Agreement on Tariffs and Trade (GATT) 102
Germany 85
Giampietro, M. 107
global warming 103
glucose 49
gold 90
Goldschmidt, R. 2
Gowdy, J. 105
granulation 80
gravity 64
Green Revolution 100, 104
greenhouse effect 45

Hanemann, M. 12
Hanley, N. 11
Hanna, S. 20
'harmonious cycles' 52
Hartley, R. V. L. 33–4
Hausman, J. 12
Hawkins–Simon condition 26, 28
heat 54, 58
heat diffusion *see* energy diffusion
Heckscher–Ohlin theory 102
herbivora 95
herbivores 121
hesitation 14, 16
heterotrophs 121
Hicks, J. R. 11
hierarchical systems 114–16
high-entropy resources 86
holon 115
Homo oeconomicus (*HO*) 8
Hopf, F. A. 107
Household Sector 117, 123
humans 106, 116, 121, 123
humus 53
hypercycle 120

IFIAS 66
imbalanced sustained growth 25
incumbents 121
India 102
indicators 113, 124
indifference 8
Industrial Revolution 5, 79, 84–7
industry 83
information 3, 32–44
informational energy 37
input 48, 80, 99; flows 4, 70
integral curves 9, 15, 126–9
intelligence 33
intensive variables 101, 118–19
intransitivity 17
inverse Laplace transforms 26, 139
iron 80, 90
irreversibility 40, 59, 142
Ising, G. 43
Islam 106
isolated system 142

Japan 92, 103
Jaynes, E. T. 3, 40–2
Jevons' paradox 100
Jevons, W. S. 100
Johnston, J. F. W. 88

joint production 65–9
Judaism 106

Kaldor, N. 102
Kawamiya, N. 63
Keynes' *General Theory* 20
kinetic energy 43
Kleene, S. C. 110
Klein, M. J. 59
Koestler, A. 115
Krilium 80
Kuznets, Simon 111

labour 67, 117; cost 66; positions 121; productivity 124
lag systems 21
Lagrange multipliers 41
land 79–95; constraint 5, 79–95; saving 94
land-based resources 5
Landau, L. D. 142
landscape fitness analysis 19
Laplace transforms 26, 139
law of diminishing returns 90–1
leisure 122
Leontief dynamic model 2, 21–8, 130–41
Leontief system 3
Leontief, W. 21
Lewis, A. 102
Liebig, J. von 5, 81–3, 88, 91
limestone 80
liming 84
linear differential model 3
List, F. 102
Loamium 80
local non-satiation 9
local people 105
Lotka's maximum energy flux 99
Lotka, A. J. 143
low-entropy resources 80, 86, 102

machines 123
maintenance capital 77
Manara, C. F. 143
manufacturing 83, 91–5, 116
manuring 84, 89
marginal rate of substitution 10
marginal utility of money 3, 13
Markandya, A. 107
Maron, H. 89
Marshall 13
Martinez-Alier, J. 13
Marx, K. 5, 81–4, 87
material cause 112
material entropy 4, 56–7; *see also* entropy
mathematical decoding 110
matter 4, 53–64
matter diffusion 54, 81
Maxwell's demon 39
measurement systems 109–10
Meĭman, N. N. 140
messages 33
metabolism 120
meteorite 54
methane 52
methodological individualism 2, 18–20
mineral resources 5, 65
Minimum Entropy Production Principle 99
mining 85
mixing entropy 61, 90
models 111
modern agriculture *see* agriculture
modern farming *see* farming
molecular weight 52
monocultured lands 97, 103
monotonicity *see* non-satiation
motive power 92

NAFTA issues 103
natural gas 90
'Natural Law' 109
natural system 109
natural-resources depletion 97
nature 1, 82, 93, 106
negative entropy 3, 32, 39–44, 47; *see also* entropy
negentropy 32, 42; *see also* negative entropy
neoclassical synthesis 7
neoclassical utility theory 7
net consumption 23
net products 22
New Homo oeconomicus (*NHO*) 15
Newcomen's engine 85
NGOs 105
'nistar' 144
nitrogen 9, 91, 121
non-basic commodities 69
non-preference 8
non-satiation 2, 8–9
North–South trade 102–6
nuclear energy 4, 78
numerical assessments 6
Nyquist, H. 33

Odum, H. T. 119
Oedipus effect 113
oil 4, 78, 87, 90, 92

Onicescu, Octav 37
Onsager relations 143
open systems 4, 49–53, 142
ophelimity index 11
Ostrom, E. 20
output 80; flows 4, 70
oxygen 9, 121
ozone depletion 103

Palaeozoic era 80
partial processes 93
Pasinetti, L. 143
Pearson, Karl 44
Peet, J. 113
petroleum products 53
phenomena 109
phenomenological coefficients 142
photosynthesis 80
photovoltaic cells 78
pig iron 86
Planck, Max 42, 59
plastics 90
Plato 95
Polanyi, K. 102
polarization 102
policies 20
pollution 48, 53, 90, 97
polythenes 90
Pontryagin, L. S. 140
'Post-Normal Science' 108, 113
postulate: Dedekind 11; density 11; indifference 8, 15; linearity 11
predictions 110
preferences 8, 12; invariance of 3, 12–13; lexicographic 3, 11
preferential set 8
prices 71, 75
Prigogine, I. 99, 116, 119
primary producers 121
primary sectors 116
principle of: decreasing marginal utility 12; growth of wants 13; irreducibility of wants 13; subordination of wants 12
probabilistic binary choice 3, 14–18
probability 15, 34
processes 21, 71, 119
production 121
production rules 110
Promethean technique 92
protest bids 12
Prussian East Asian Expedition 89
pseudo-measures 37
pseudo-transitivity 15
psychological threshold 3, 14
puddling process 86

qualitative change 2, 30
quantum mechanics 142
quasi-explosive feature 24, 30
quasi-polynomial 140

Randall, A. 18
Ravets, J. R. 108
reactive models 28
recipes 119
recycling 53–64
reflexive systems 112
refrigerators 101
refuse 70
resource(s) 45–64, 105; substitution 86, 90
risk 11
roles 121
Romans 84
Rosen, R. 5, 29, 108–10, 120

Sargan, J. D. 21
saturation point 9, 126–9
scaling 19
Schrödinger: formulation 41; inequality 48; theory 46–9
Schumpeter, J. A. 2, 44
science 109
scientists 113
sea 53
'self' 109
self-organization 115–16, 120
self-sufficiency 105
semantic scheme 109
Service Sector 117, 123
Shackle, G. L. S. 36
Shannon, C. E. 3, 33–6, 44
Siemens–Martin process 86
signal elements 33
signal shaping 33
simile 111
Simon, H. A. 119
sizes 28, 101
Smith, A. 94
Smoluchowsky 43
social equity 105
social evolution 30
social welfare 18
society 120–2
socioeconomic systems 104
soil 53, 81, 91; erosion 97
solar radiation/energy 54, 62, 76
solar technology 4, 72–8

'sorting' 52, 64
Spash, C. 11
special fuels 92
speed of throughput 99
spoliation system 81
Sraffa's analysis 4, 65–72
stability 106, 116
Standard Commodity 66
standard of living 104, 118, 124
Standard System 67
statistical entropy 32
statistical thermodynamics 40
steady-state systems 49–53, 120–2
steam engine 92
Steedman, I. 143
Stevens, T. 11
Stigler, G. 20
Stirling's asymptotic formula 35
stochastic event 36
Stolper–Samuelson theorem 102
Strength of the Exosomatic Energy Hypercycle 117, 125
strong viability 74
'struggle for entropy' 52
sub-natural system 109–10, 113
Sugita, M. 47
'survival of the first' 107
sustainability 2, 5, 104–6, 108–16
Szilard, L. 3, 39–40

tastes 7, 20
technical idleness 93
technological development 124
technological efficiency 124
technological improvement 101
technology 73, 86
theoretical decoding 110
thermodynamic(s): flows 142; forces 142; Fourth Law 4, 60, 64; linear 142; Third Law 47
Third World countries 97, 104, 107
tillage 89
time interval 25
time saving 94
total human time 116, 122
trade 5, 102–6
transmission 33
transparency 112
transportation 86, 92
Triadic Structure 114, 122
Tsuchida, A. 4, 39, 50

Ulanowicz, R. E. 120
uncertainty 3, 14, 36
United States 87–91
unmixing 56
unsustainability 98–102
utility: function 10; index 9

valuation methods 11
van't Hoff Box 61
Vatn, A. 14
viability 91–3

wages 67
Walrasian system 14
wants 3, 12–13
'warm glow' effects 12
waste 45, 52, 59, 82
water 64, 85, 92; cycle 4, 50, 52, 59
water mills 85
Watkins, K. 103
Watt's steam engine 86
weak viability 74
Weaver, W. 34
West Africa 107
Western hedonism 106
wheat 85, 88
White, L. 106
Wiener, N. 3, 36–8
Wilkinson, R. G. 85
Wilson, E. O. 2
wood 87
wool 86
work 55, 58
Wrigley, E. A. 86

For Product Safety Concerns and Information please contact our EU
representative GPSR@taylorandfrancis.com
Taylor & Francis Verlag GmbH, Kaufingerstraße 24, 80331 München, Germany

www.ingramcontent.com/pod-product-compliance
Ingram Content Group UK Ltd.
Pitfield, Milton Keynes, MK11 3LW, UK
UKHW022124190926
475702UK00013B/1622
9780415638111